Teaching Human Development for Educators

A volume in
Theory to Practice: Educational Psychology for Teachers and Teaching
Mike Yough, Jane S. Vogler, and Eric M. Anderman, *Series Editors*

**Theory to Practice: Educational Psychology
for Teachers and Teaching**

Mike Yough, Jane S. Vogler, and Eric M. Anderman, *Series Editors*

Teaching Learning for Effective Instruction (2023)
    Michelle M. Buehl and Jane S. Vogler

Teaching to Prepare Advocates (2022)
    Mike Yough and Lynley Anderman

Teaching Motivation for Student Engagement (2021)
    Debra K. Meyer and Alyssa Emery

Teaching on Assessment (2021)
    Sharon L. Nichols and Divya Varier

Teaching Human Development for Educators

edited by

M Cecil Smith
Southern Illinois University Carbondale

Carlton J. Fong
Texas State University

Russell N. Carney
Missouri State University

INFORMATION AGE PUBLISHING, INC.
Charlotte, NC • www.infoagepub.com

Library of Congress Cataloging-in-Publication Data

A CIP record for this book is available from the Library of Congress
http://www.loc.gov

ISBN: 979-8-88730-487-8 (Paperback)
 979-8-88730-488-5 (Hardcover)
 979-8-88730-489-2 (E-Book)

Copyright © 2024 Information Age Publishing Inc.

All rights reserved. No part of this publication may be reproduced, stored in a retrieval system, or transmitted, in any form or by any means, electronic, mechanical, photocopying, microfilming, recording or otherwise, without written permission from the publisher.

Printed in the United States of America

CONTENTS

1 Editors' Introduction: Teaching Human Development for Educators 1
   M Cecil Smith, Carlton J. Fong, and Russell N. Carney

2 Teaching Human Development Using Human Development: The Science of Learning as a Guide for Future Educators 11
   Elias Blinkoff, Hailey Gibbs, Roberta Michnick Golinkoff, and Kathy Hirsh-Pasek

3 The Student as a Developing Person in Context: Socio-Ecological Theory, Intersectionality, and Social Justice 47
   Gabriel Velez, Keshia Harris, and Carly Offidani-Bertrand

4 Intentionally Integrating Developmental Theory and Research Into Teacher Education: Examples From the Field 71
   Sarah M. Kiefer, Raven Robinson, Rebecca West Burns, and Kerrijo Ellis

5 The Why and How of What We Do: Using Case Studies to Understand Adolescent Development for Teacher Education 95
   Dana L. Haraway and Ann Allred

6 Strategies for Centering Inclusion and Equity in Human Development Courses for Preservice Educators 115
   Alison C. Koenka, Korinthia D. Nicolai, and Richard Garries

7   Creating Clarity Through Understanding Complexity:
    Building a Case for Development as a Critical Component
    of Educator Preparation 137
    Lisa Looney, Andréa C. Minkoff, and Gabriela Wilson

8   Considerations and Importance of Generational Changes
    for Teaching 165
    *Elizabeth J. Pope, Katrina A. Dotzler, Heidi Legg Burross,
    and Paul A. Schutz*

9   It Doesn't End at 18: Insight Into Adult Human Development
    as an Instrumental Area for Preservice Teachers to
    Understand, Apply, and Teach 183
    Abbie M. Bordewyk, Allison Fowler, and Kate E. Snyder

    About the Contributors 195
    Subject Index 205

CHAPTER 1

EDITORS' INTRODUCTION

Teaching Human Development for Educators

M Cecil Smith
Southern Illinois University Carbondale

Carlton J. Fong
Texas State University

Russell N. Carney
Missouri State University

The central idea of this volume is that teaching about how children, youth, and adults develop and change over time is critical to the preparation of well-prepared classroom teachers. Simply put, teachers need to understand human development in the same way that they need to understand their subject matter, classroom management strategies, or methods of assessing student learning. Unlike Athena, who was said to have emerged completely grown from the forehead of Zeus, students do not come into the classroom fully formed. Rather, students—even preschool age children—have a rich and varied developmental history of growth and change. And, they continue to grow and change over the course of any given academic year. As they mature physically, so do their cognitive abilities, providing them with improved thinking and problem-solving skills and greater awareness of self and others. Their social and emotional skills, too, continue to grow through their relationships and interactions with peers, teachers, family members, and others—both within and outside of school. These developmental changes have many and varied influences on how students learn.

This book, *Teaching Human Development for Educators*, is a volume in the series Theory to Practice: Educational Psychology for Teachers and Teaching. It is intended for instructors who teach human development content in teacher preparation programs, either within the context of educational psychology courses or as distinct child, adolescent, or even adult development courses. Teachers are guides and coaches and confidantes who nurture and support their students' developing skills and interests. They hear their students' wishes, fantasies, and expressions of their personal and academic goals. They soothe students' anxieties and fears and help them navigate friendships, and to imagine and plan their future. All these interactions take place within the messy variability of individuals' growth and change and, certainly, no two students are alike. Teacher candidates who lack strong knowledge of human development are, thus, ill-prepared to perform these roles as they begin their teaching careers.

Educators who are well-versed in the study of human development are better able to create age-appropriate, equitable, and safe classroom spaces with developmentally appropriate learning tasks. Such teachers can set realistic expectations for their students' behaviors because they understand what children and youth can do at different ages and stages of development. Knowledge of human development gives teachers insights into setting appropriate learning and behavioral goals for students and a leg up in developing and interpreting assessments of their students' learning and behavior.

Knowledge about human development holds many advantages for teachers. They have greater appreciation for their students' diversity, for example, recognizing that individual as well as group differences among students lends vitality and interest to teaching. Such understandings may lead teachers to adopt more culturally responsive pedagogical practices when teaching students from diverse social, economic class, racial, and cultural backgrounds. Teachers benefit from awareness that they, too, will continue to grow and change in many ways over the course of their teaching careers. It is not simply awareness of aging, though that is important knowledge. Understanding that one's own growth may be impeded by, for example, unresolved psychosocial tasks in childhood and youth yields insights into one's adult behaviors and life choices. Knowing how stress affects health and well-being, and how to cope with the everyday stressors that are a part of teaching is a helpful byproduct of understanding human growth and development.

In an age where the quality of teacher education programs has never been more important, the authors of these chapters argue that educators need a fundamental understanding of human growth, development, and change at different ages and stages across the lifespan. The present volume's authors draw upon the latest research, including their own, as well as their classroom experiences and teaching innovations to help college instructors select and convey essential content on human development to prepare education professionals to work with infants, children, adolescents, and adults across diverse educational settings.

Educational psychologists, who typically have preparation in the psychology of human development, are well-suited to provide instruction to teacher candidates about the theories, principles, methods, and research findings in the field of human development (Anderson et al., 1995). Alongside courses in learning theories, human motivation, assessment methods, and classroom management strategies, educational psychology faculty typically teach human development courses in schools and colleges of education.

Unfortunately, over recent decades, teacher preparation programs have removed or otherwise weakened educational psychology coursework as an emphasis in teacher training—largely in response to shifting program accreditation standards (Patrick et al., 2011). Often, teacher candidates are required to take only a single educational psychology course prior to student teaching and graduation. Such a course might, of necessity, address a variety of topics (e.g., learning theories, behavior management, assessment, and motivation) as well as content regarding human development, leaving little time to examine these topics in necessary depth. University administrators and faculty are not entirely at fault. National teacher preparation accreditation standards tend to be broad and generic. While these standards do not specify the number or types of courses that teacher candidates must take (e.g., Council for the Accreditation of Educator Preparation, 2022), teacher preparation programs typically include coursework in specific content areas (e.g., math, science, social studies), and may require little more than a single course in human development. State boards of education that oversee teacher education programs also often fail to recognize the value of deep preparation in human development for teachers-in-training, instead devoting attention to specifics regarding clinical practice and supervision

Despite these lacks and omissions, the editors are firm in their belief that educational psychology faculty members can prepare teacher candidates with a strong grounding in human development—even when programmatic opportunities to do so are constrained. The chapters that follow in this book provide a variety of perspectives and ideas for instruction in human development that will be of great benefit to instructors and students alike. ■

AN ORGANIZATIONAL OVERVIEW OF THE VOLUME

Broadly speaking, the chapters in this volume include: (a) brief summaries of the empirical research that supports the teaching of human development as it applies to PreK–12, and postsecondary education; (b) descriptions of instructional practices used in college courses that are deemed effective in teaching about human development; and (c) discussions of issues that influence the teaching of human development theories, research, and classroom applications having clear connections between the empirical literature and the instructional practices.

In their chapter, "Teaching Human Development Using Human Development: The Science of Learning as a Guide for Future Educators," Elias Blinkoff, Hailey Gibbs, Roberta Golinkoff, and Kathy Hirsh-Pasek argue that teacher training programs across the country should put more emphasis on the science of learning—not only in terms of the content knowledge presented, but also in terms of the ways in which preservice teachers are taught. A science of learning model draws upon current research from a variety of fields, including education, psychology, cognitive science, and so forth (as well-documented via their lengthy list of references), and has deep intersection with the study of human development.

In particular, citing Golinkoff, Hirsh-Pasek and others, the chapter authors make the case that students learn best from lessons that contain six evidence-based features. That is, lessons should be: *active, engaging, meaningful, socially interactive, iterative,* and *joyful.* Blinkoff et al. go on to describe each of those six important features, and their benefits, in some detail, arguing that lessons characterized by these six features help students to develop important 21st century skills. Termed the "six-Cs," these skills are: *collaboration, communication, content, critical thinking, creative innovation,* and *confidence.*

Blinkoff et al. suggest that applying their pedagogical approach to teacher preparation demonstrates effective instructional practices that teacher candidates may adopt and eventually utilize in their own classrooms. The approach is culturally responsive in that students' lived experiences are valued and built upon. Finally, as the authors conclude, teacher candidates "deserve to learn in ways that reflect the best science so that they can teach in the ways that humans best learn."

Gabriel Velez, Keshia Harris, and Carly Offidani-Bertrand contributed a chapter, "The Student as a Development Person in Context: Socio-ecological Theory, Intersectionality, and Social Justice." Their chapter adopts a social justice approach for teaching human development with a focus on a socio-ecological framework. Learners from marginalized backgrounds, including women, LGBTQ youth, and minoritized students face significant structural barriers to education which ultimately shape their identities and life outcomes. The authors explain Spencer's (1999) phenomenological variant of ecological systems theory (PVEST) as a useful framework for educators, underscoring how dynamic and multifaceted ecosystems form the contexts in which students develop. Understanding and use of PVEST theory can help educators to support youth from marginalized backgrounds, according to the authors. One of the systems the authors emphasize is the interlocking systems of oppression that marginalized young people face, especially considering students' intersectional (i.e., race, gender, social class) identities.

The authors also discuss equitable teaching strategies that reimagine what academic success means according to student interpretations within their cultural context and that critically examine students' educational ecosystems and behaviors. They suggest that educators need to know about the different "capacities and supports" that students from different cultural backgrounds bring with them to school and the classroom. Finally, Velez et al. offer several suggestions for educators to apply PVEST. The applications can help teachers to think more critically about the complex mechanisms that underlie students' behavior, to consider how socio-ecological contexts are interpreted and responded to by students, and how they, as teachers of youth, can build supportive learning environments that promote positive identity-based outcomes for their students.

Sarah Kiefer, Raven Robinson, Rebecca Burns, and Kerrijo Ellis contributed a chapter titled "Intentionally Integrating Developmental Theory and Research Into Teacher Education: Examples From the Field." As the title suggests, the authors make the case that educational psychology (e.g., human development, teacher education research) should be incorporated into teacher education programs. They describe concrete ways to go about doing this, as well as detailing the benefits to teacher candidates that should ensue. Indeed, "through building sustainable collaborations and by integrating human development and teacher education across the curriculum, educational psychology instructors and teacher educators can prepare teacher candidates and practicing educators to be responsive to the diverse developmental and learning needs of PK–12 learners" (Kiefer et al. (this volume, p. 73). Incorporating such content should result in several benefits, according to the authors. Next, the authors provide examples of how they facilitate the integration of educational psychology content into teacher preparation through the use of "signature assignments" (a reflective blog, a case study paper, and a lesson plan) and "collaborative teacher inquiry." Kiefer et al. conclude by advocating for the integration of developmental theory and research into teacher education.

Building upon the practice of assigning teacher candidates to conduct case studies of young learners, Dana Haraway and Ann Allred describe how they incorporate educational psychology content into a teacher preparation course by assigning case studies for teacher learning. Their chapter,

"The Why and How of What We Do: Using Case Studies to Understand Adolescent Development for Teacher Educators," focuses specifically on using educational psychology's most prominent developmental, learning, and motivation theories to prepare teachers to teach young adolescents in middle schools. In a novel approach, teacher candidates' learning is also situated within the context of their understanding of various school "structures"—in particular, how middle schools are typically organized to deliver curriculum and instruction and promote student learning and development.

Writing from their complementary perspectives as course instructor (Haraway) and a student in the course (Allred), they describe an educational psychology course in which Master of Arts in Teaching (MAT) students enroll for their final semester, post-student teaching. Students are required to complete a comprehensive case study assignment in which they demonstrate understanding of (a) young adolescents' development, (b) knowledge of middle level philosophy and organization, and (c) middle school teachers' professional roles and responsibilities. Here, students create fictitious characters—teachers and middle grades adolescents—rather than observing or interviewing actual "live" adolescent subjects. Candidates also learn about the characteristics of effective middle schools and participate in a "mock" site visit to a middle school and evaluate the degree to which the school's environment and practices align with the AMLE criteria for an "exemplary" school. The authors' report was that candidates expressed greater confidence in their ability to make the transition from teacher candidate to professional educator as a result of the mock case study project.

The chapter by Alison Koenka, Korinthia Nicolai, and Richard Garries, "Strategies for Centering Inclusion and Equity in Human Development Courses for Preservice Educators," centers the matters of inclusion and equity squarely in the context of teaching human development courses. Inclusion and equity are, in the view of these authors, topics that educational psychologists have not paid adequate attention to in the context of teacher preparation. An important idea from their chapter is how the literature on educational psychology and human development has mostly neglected the racialized and culturalized perspectives of students of color. Addressing this lack, Koenka et al. describe nine instructional strategies that educational psychology faculty can employ to promote equity and inclusion in the human development courses that they teach. These strategies address curriculum, assessment methods, and classroom discussions.

The authors situate the recommended strategies within the literature on critical race theory, stereotype threat, and motivation. They encourage human development instructors to center the development of youth from diverse populations throughout the curriculum. Turning to student work, the authors suggest that examinations and course assignments should emphasize content mastery, must enable student choice, and address the relevance of the course materials to students' lives. Koenka et al. further encourage educational psychology instructors to get to know their students to facilitate a sense of belonging in the classroom. Finally, the authors recommend that guest scholars who vary across racial and/or gender identity, and career paths be invited to participate in class discussions.

Lisa Looney, Andréa Minkoff, and Gabriela Wilson title their chapter "Creating Clarity Through Understanding Complexity: Building a Case for Development as a Critical Component of Educator Preparation." Briefly, they make the case that developmental (and educational) psychology content should be a fundamental part of teacher education programs, and not take a back seat to the traditional focus on content related to curriculum and instruction—especially for those planning to work with middle and high school students.

They describe *complexity* via ecological systems theory (e.g., Bronfenbrenner, 1976). Systems theories suggest that developing children exist in "multiple, interrelated, complex environments," and these environments influence their "developmental trajectories." In addition, Looney et al. propose that the notion of *intersectionality* helps us to further understand the complexity of children (and teachers) in terms of their various social identifications, for example, race, class, gender, sexuality, and so forth. In their words, having training in developmental and educational psychology is important because it helps teachers understand "the complexity of the intersectionality present in the educational environment" and helps to "decenter dominate norms and to create spaces that are inclusive of the lived experiences of marginalized youth."

The focus of the Looney et al. chapter is on bringing developmental and educational psychology to secondary level educators. Key points throughout the chapter are (a) the uniqueness of developmental paths and (b) that there is no single "best practice" in teaching students from different backgrounds. Looney et al. believe that teachers need to understand the complexity of the education milieu (e.g., students' and teachers' lived experiences), and devise methods that allow for students' various identities and assets and "maintain a social justice approach to their teaching." Along these lines, Looney et al. recommend that preservice teachers become "developmental systems experts" instead of "content matter and instructional experts." The authors call for teacher preparation programs to emphasize developmental and educational psychology. The result of this emphasis will be that adolescent students will have teachers who understand their developmental needs.

In their chapter titled "Considerations and Importance of Generational Changes for Teaching," Elizabeth Pope, Katrina Dotzler, Heidi Burross, and Paul Schutz do a masterful job of explaining how familiar developmental theories help us to better understand the importance of generational changes for teachers and students. They begin by calling upon Bronfenbrenner's (1976) ecological system's (ES) approach, describing the increasingly complex and ever-changing social historical contexts in which students and teachers find themselves. As the reader likely knows, Bronfenbrenner's theory is characterized by a series of concentric circles, with the individual located within the center, and then encircled, consecutively, by a microsystem, mesosystem, exosystem, macrosystem, and chronosystem. Each system is increasingly distant from the self, though each exerts influence on the developing individual. Pope et al. place today's social media influences within the individual's microsystem and, hence, they emphasize social media's prominent role in this innermost circle.

Next, the authors introduce self-determination theory (SDT; e.g., Deci & Ryan, 2000). SDT describes three basic and important student needs: autonomy, competence, and relatedness. Autonomy has to do with students having some control in their learning—as opposed to the classroom being totally teacher-directed. Competence should result when students "are provided with developmentally appropriate, challenging tasks that align with their own internal values and beliefs" (Pope et al., this volume, p. 175.). Such tasks are ones with which they can be successful. In this regard, they refer to Vygotsky's (1934/1987) zone of proximal development (ZPD) where the student can accomplish tasks with the assistance of a more accomplished peer or a teacher. Finally, relatedness has to do with the students' connections with others (e.g., the student feeling they belong to a social group). Teachers play an important role in meeting these needs in the school setting.

A central point made by Pope et al. is that teachers must keep on top of trends to adjust their pedagogical approach to better support current students' basic needs, rather than view them as changes that have resulted in individual or groups of students who are "lacking" in values, skills, abilities, and so forth—things that may not be a part of their cultural contexts. Rather than interpreting differences as deficits, they argue for asset-based pedagogies (ABP) approaches that build on the diverse personal and cultural knowledge students bring to the classroom. The authors close by listing seven suggestions for bridging generations.

Adults' developmental tasks and growth processes are often overlooked in teacher preparation. This oversight is ironic because teachers-in-training are largely young adults who are experiencing dramatic changes in their lives—everything from development in the prefrontal cortex (which is involved in judgment and decision-making) to separating themselves from parents and family and developing a stronger sense of personal identity. Further, as young teachers enter the profession, they will be teaching not only young students, but also working with adult colleagues and interacting with the parents of their students. As Abbie Bordewyck, Allison Fowler, and Kate Snyder point out in their chapter, "It Doesn't End at 18: Insight into Adult Human Development," teacher candidates need to acquire an understanding of not only child and youth development, but also adult development. They need to better understand their own developmental changes as well as the growth and change that their older colleagues and parents of their children confront. Such knowledge can assist young teachers to develop empathy for parents, appreciate and learn from senior colleagues' perspectives, and prepare their own students for lives of growth and change.

Bordewyck et al. cite Arnett's (2000) controversial theory of emerging adulthood—a developmental period between the late teens to late 20s—to suggest that important developmental changes occur during these years that significantly impact individuals who are preparing to become teachers. Certainly, for teacher candidates in their late teens and early 20s, the ability to make decisions independent of parents, to accept personal responsibility for one's decisions and actions, and to achieve financial independence may not be fully realized. Given these conditions, it may be important for teacher educators to provide support and scaffolding for teacher candidates to ease their strain and help them gain confidence in their abilities to teach and manage a classroom. Further, Bordewyck et al. suggest that teacher educators should help teacher candidates to develop mature epistemic beliefs (i.e., that knowledge is context dependent rather than certain) through exposure to and critical analysis of multiple viewpoints. Finally, teacher educators, too, must examine their own beliefs and biases regarding adult development and seek to avoid conveying negative "age-ist" views about adult learners.

FINAL THOUGHTS

Collectively, the chapters in this volume offer powerful ideas and evidence-based strategies for effective instruction of human development theories, concepts, principles, and research findings for teacher candidates. While educational psychology has frequently been marginalized as a disciplinary contributor to the preparation of PreK–12 educators, it is a foundational field that provides essential knowledge about how students learn and also, critically, how children and youth develop and change over time. The chapters contained here explain *why* teachers need to understand human development and *how* they can incorporate such knowledge into their teaching. Teachers' understanding of the complex systems that act and interact to influence students' growth, change, and behaviors guides the actions they take to enhance students' learning and achievement. We are particularly pleased that several chapters address issues of equity and inclusivity and the necessity of engaging in culturally responsive, social justice-oriented practices in classrooms given the great diversity among learners in schools today. Finally, we are confident that many teacher educators can benefit (as can their teacher candidates) from adopting the various instructional strategies and assignments that the contributing authors have described in these chapters.

REFERENCES

Anderson, L. M., Blumenfeld, P., Pintrich, P. R., Clark, C. M., Marx, R. W., & Peterson, P. (1995). Educational psychology for teachers: Reforming our courses, rethinking our roles. *Educational Psychologist, 30*(3), 143–157. https://doi.org/10.1207/s15326985ep3003_5

Arnett, J. J. (2000). Emerging adulthood: A theory of development from the late teens through the twenties. *American Psychologist, 55*, 469–480. https://doi.org/10.1037/0003-066X.55.5.469

Bronfenbrenner, U. (1976). *The ecology of human development.* Harvard University Press.

Council for the Accreditation of Educator Preparation. (2022). *Standard 1: Content and pedagogical knowledge.* https://caepnet.org/standards/2022-itp/standard-1

Deci, R. M., & Ryan, E. L. (2000). Self-determination theory and facilitation of intrinsic motivation, social development, and well-being. *American Psychologist, 55*, 68–78. https://doi.org/10.1037/0003-066X.55.1.68

Patrick, P., Anderman, L. H., Bruening, P. S., & Duffin, L. C. (2011). The role of educational psychology in teacher education: Three challenges for educational psychologists. *Educational Psychologist, 46*(2), 71–83. https://doi.org/10.1080/00461520.2011.538648

Vygotsky, L. S. (1987). Thinking and speech. In R. W. Rieber & A. S. Carton (Eds.), *The collected works of L. S. Vygotsky, Volume 1: Problems of general psychology* (pp. 39–285). Plenum Press. (Original work published 1934)

CHAPTER 2

TEACHING HUMAN DEVELOPMENT USING HUMAN DEVELOPMENT

The Science of Learning as a Guide for Future Educators

Elias Blinkoff
Temple University

Hailey Gibbs
Center for American Progress

Roberta Michnick Golinkoff
University of Delaware

Kathy Hirsh-Pasek
*Temple University
and The Brookings Institution*

> Imagine you are a Kindergarten teacher giving your students a vocabulary test. Each student is presented with an image of a lion and expected to identify it by filling in a label underneath the picture. When one student hands in her test, you see that she wrote "cat," instead. You mark an "X" on the student's paper.
>
> Now you are in a third grade math class in an underserved urban elementary school. Your students frequently face opportunity gaps and struggle to master fundamental math content. Each week, you administer a timed multiplication quiz. Today's covers the seven times tables. A student hands in their quiz with just two questions answered, even though they accurately and effortlessly stated all their times tables from 0 to 12 when you began yesterday's class with an activity that required the students to practice their times tables with each other in small groups.
>
> One last example: You are an English for speakers of other languages (ESOL) teacher working with a class of ninth grade students. You supplement their core English course with in-class time to work on their reading assignments. Several students continue to struggle with grade-level reading. Only after the second failed assignment do you realize that your students are still overcoming a significant language barrier that impedes their ability to decode the high school-level text.

These vignettes describe what happens when teachers are not trained to recognize the principles of learning and human cognition that undergird how children, and even adults, think. The kindergarten teacher who marked her student's "cat" response as incorrect reacted to that answer just as she would have if the student said, "bathtub." Even though both answers are technically wrong, the student clearly recognized that cats and lions share four legs, claws, a tail, and sharp teeth, reflecting a level of conceptual understanding that should have been recognized and celebrated as meaningful and relevant prior knowledge. That is—the answer "cat," while technically wrong, is a better answer than "bathtub."

In the third grade math class, the student who struggled to complete the written multiplication quiz mastered the math content based on their verbal responses. What might be going on here? A teacher equipped with the lens of human development might recognize that some students lack confidence during timed tests, or perhaps that they are slow writers and cannot show their knowledge as readily in written form as they can orally.

Now to the ESOL classroom: Teachers may fail to recognize that students cannot analyze complicated texts if they do not have the language skills in their home language to do so. A student's language ability predicts their later reading ability (Pace et al., 2019). And more pointedly, even if a student has superb letter-to-sound decoding skills, if they are unable to map those sounds to meaningful words in an unknown language, they cannot delve as deeply into the content, and potentially recognize how their prior knowledge from their native language supports second-language comprehension.

Once teachers are equipped with knowledge of human development, they bring new insights into the classroom, understanding how students' answers reflect the ways in which they learn best. Teacher preparation is about a mindset and a pedagogical approach that will heighten classroom practice and allow for deep learning that is generalizable and "sticky." Achieving this goal requires that all teachers build an understanding of human development, rooted in the science of learning, beginning in their preservice training programs.

This chapter presents a model of teacher training that prioritizes this emphasis on human development. Principles of human learning and development are not meant to be merely memorized by teachers during their preservice courses as isolated facts. Rather, instructors of human development in teacher education programs must provide future teachers with the knowledge and expertise to understand how human development can be facilitated in the classroom by using these principles in their own instruction. Only then will future teachers respond to their students based on their knowledge of *how* children learn, and better understand *what* children need to learn to achieve their goals and to meet educational standards of success.

CURRENT TEACHER EDUCATION PEDAGOGY: *HOW* DO STUDENTS LEARN? HOW CAN THIS CREATE A NEW PEDAGOGICAL FRAMEWORK?

Teacher education programs face structural and instructional challenges that may be resolved through a common curricular focus on human development and the study of how students learn. Darling-Hammond and colleagues (2005) indicate that most educational programs have historically taught "teaching" through highly theoretical, disconnected courses with limited alignment between theory and practice. This disconnect has consequences: It leads to the kinds of practices and misunderstandings that are noted in our examples above. As a start, teaching human development and using pedagogical frameworks that are rooted in the science of learning, and even providing firsthand experience learning through these frameworks in teacher training programs, would prepare future teachers to implement the methods that they learned and experienced in their own classrooms.

Darling-Hammond and colleagues (2005) highlight how many effective teacher education programs are based on a foundation of how students learn. These programs

> begin their course of study in teaching with work on learning and development—hoping to start new teachers with a focus upon students and student learning from the beginning. Such courses require students very early on in their programs to observe children and to collect detailed information about their development and learning. (p. 400)

This requires teacher candidates to practice seeing the world through the eyes of the students they will teach. However, this intensive focus on student learning and development is not typical in teacher education programs, even today.

More than a decade later, Darling-Hammond and Oakes (2019) warned that teacher preparation, as a whole, has not changed much. Through an extensive evaluation process, their research identified just seven teacher education programs in the United States that organize around principles from the science of learning as a core pedagogical focus. Given that there are approximately 26,000 state-approved teacher education programs across the country, this is concerning (Kuenzi, 2018). A study of nearly 600 U.S. educators found that they continued to endorse myths about learning, despite their training. For example, 71% of educators believed the myth that children have a dominant learning style related to their senses (Macdonald et al., 2017). This underscores just how critical it is for teachers to have a comprehensive knowledge of how their students learn. This context leads Darling-Hammond and Oakes (2019) to declare

> if teachers are able to teach in ways that reflect the outcomes we desire for students, which are informed by historical and current understandings of the workings of learning and are consistent with practices that can support deeper learning, then teacher preparation has a high bar to meet. (p. 11)

In other words, teaching the way that students learn is essential in our schools now. If this objective is to be achieved, teacher education programs are vital partners in this effort.

This movement to prioritize the science of how students learn and develop in teacher education includes two main components, an introduction to underlying evidence from the science of learning, and opportunities for teacher candidates to connect theory and practice. A third element, which we suggest is not used frequently enough in most teacher education, is active participation along the lines of the science of learning principles presented here. Only when teacher candidates use these for their *own* learning can they come to understand how best to help their *students* learn. The science of learning is a relatively new, interdisciplinary field that combines research from psychology, neuroscience, education, machine learning, cognitive science, and sociocultural studies to understand how humans learn (Meltzoff et al., 2009; Sawyer, 2014). Several research teams that intersect developmental psychology and education inform how the science of learning stands to benefit teacher trainees. These novel frameworks use the science of learning and can guide educators in the development and implementation of equitable education systems, so that all students, from the K–12 level through those in teacher education programs, as we argue here, can gain key 21st-century skills (Darling-Hammond et al., 2020; Golinkoff & Hirsh-Pasek, 2016; Hirsh-Pasek et al., 2022; Hirsh-Pasek et al., 2020; Learning Policy Institute & Turnaround for Children, 2021; Nasir et al., 2021). Our question concerns how best to prepare teachers so that they can utilize the latest learning techniques.

EQUIPPING TOMORROW'S TEACHERS WITH EVIDENCE: HOW AND WHAT STUDENTS NEED TO LEARN

The science of *how* students learn offers a pedagogical roadmap—a kind of mindset and a suite of instructional features that teachers can infuse into their lessons to promote deep, generalizable, and "sticky" learning. *What* students need to know to thrive in a fast-paced, global world offers the flip side of this educational coin. We can ask what a graduate of our classroom or school would need to know to thrive and maximize their future success. Teachers need to be thinking broadly about what an educated person is and how they can foster that individual's development.. Using the science of learning as a foundation, Golinkoff and Hirsh-Pasek (2016) and Hirsh-Pasek et al. (Hirsh-Pasek et al., 2022; Hirsh-Pasek et al., 2020) offer a consensus view on 21st-century skills that are evidence-based, malleable (they can be changed with the right experience), and measurable in the classroom.

The science of learning model that Golinkoff and Hirsh-Pasek (2016) and Hirsh-Pasek et al. (Hirsh-Pasek et al., 2022; Hirsh-Pasek et al., 2020) propose suggests that students learn best when lessons are: *active* with emphasis on inquiry and reflection; *engaging* rather than distracting; *meaningful* with connections between new and prior knowledge; *socially interactive* through teacher-facilitated student collaboration; an *iterative* process with opportunities for hypothesis generation and testing; and *joyful* instead of dull (Hirsh-Pasek et al., 2022; Hirsh-Pasek et al., 2020; Hirsh-Pasek et al., 2015; Zosh et al., 2022; Zosh et al., 2018). These principles of how students learn (Figure 2.1) naturally appear in guided play (Zosh et al., 2022; Zosh et al., 2018)—a pedagogical approach that combines a clear learning goal identified by the teacher with student agency to engage in their own learning process (Weisberg et al., 2016). Further, they promote a set of 21st-century skills identified by Golinkoff and Hirsh-Pasek (2016) as the 6 Cs:

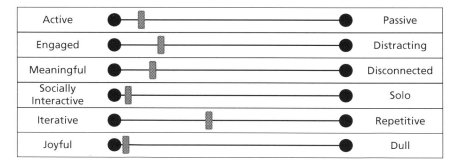

Figure 2.1 The playful learning principles demonstrating the "how" of learning. *Note:* The playful learning principles can be represented on a spectrum. A learning activity is rated on its alignment with the principles through observation (Hirsh-Pasek et al., 2015, Hirsh-Pasek et al., 2020; Hirsh-Pasek et al., 2022; Zosh et al., 2018; Zosh et al., 2022).

Collaboration, communication, content, critical thinking, creative innovation, and confidence.

Principles of *How* Students Learn

Insights from the science of learning have directly informed a synthesis of principles to explain how students learn (Hirsh-Pasek et al., 2022 Hirsh-Pasek et al., 2020; Hirsh-Pasek et al., 2015; Zosh et al., 2022; Zosh et al., 2018). Students gain academic and social benefits from active playful learning. In an active playful learning episode, specifically using guided play—a subtype of playful learning situated between the extremes of entirely child-led free play and entirely adult-led direct instruction (Zosh et al., 2022; Zosh et al., 2018)—an adult facilitates a learner's acquisition of a targeted learning goal by either curating the learning environment (e.g., a high-quality children's museum exhibit), or furthering exploration and engagement in a playful activity (e.g., promotion of inquiry through an open-ended question, such as, "What could you use that piece to make?"; Weisberg et al., 2016; Zosh et al., 2022; Zosh et al., 2018). As reviewed by Zosh and colleagues (Zosh et al., 2022; Zosh et al., 2018), these features of guided play may explain why it supports student's academic skills across the disciplines and why, when we have a learning goal in mind, it offers a more successful pedagogical tool. In sum, guided play borrows the best of direct instruction by focusing on a targeted learning goal, but in a context that maintains student agency and supports learners' abilities to deeply encode, retain, and reason critically about their new knowledge.

While it is easy to think of these principles governing how students learn as exclusive to the K–12 classroom, or to early childhood education, they apply across development and even into higher education. Knowledge of these principles will not only benefit the students of future teachers, but teacher candidates themselves. When students at all levels are active, engaged, socially interactive, and have opportunities to recognize meaning in their learning, iterate, and experience joy, they are more likely to internalize their learning, and build the deep, enduring knowledge structures that support future growth. In what follows, we consider the case of preservice teachers and how teaching human development means curating educational experiences that make each of these learning principles come alive.

Active Learning

Lecturing is a very efficient way to present information. However, as reflected in student evaluations, it may induce an "illusion" of learning (Deslauriers et al., 2019). Pedagogical models in which learners are simply passive recipients of information, taking notes without having an opportunity to question, probe further, or use their learning, result in more superficial, shorter-term learning outcomes and students have difficulty answering deeper, conceptual questions or engaging in near transfer to similar learning tasks (e.g., Hake, 1998; Freeman et al., 2014; Mazur, 2009; Schell & Mazur, 2015; Sokoloff & Thornton, 1997; Versteeg et al., 2019). The importance of active learning was suggested both by Piaget, a developmental researcher who recognized that children learn through engaging with their environment, especially with other people (Webb, 1980), and Vygotsky, who described learning as a socially facilitated process (Vygotsky, 1987). Active learning can occur at the college level when professors give students in-class activities to work on together. Working with others to derive a joint answer to questions that require application of new knowledge makes the learning concrete for students and goes beyond abstract principles. Take, for example, the following scenario in early math: Teacher candidates are asked to work on this multifaceted problem in small groups of no more than four students and to derive a joint answer to the questions posed. They are invited to use their textbook and their collateral readings.

> Johnny is five years old and counting the number of M&Ms scattered on the table in front of him. He starts by counting the brown M&Ms—one, two, three—and then counts the blue M&Ms—three, four, five—and finally the orange M&Ms, eight, nine, ten, eleven. His mother asks him how many M&Ms there are and he says proudly, "Eleven!" Johnny's mother then asks him to count again, but to start with the blue ones this time. He does and gets the same answer after counting using the same number sequence he used before.

Students are asked to use this scenario to decide which mathematical principles are exemplified and to define them. They are then asked to decide which ones Johnny has mastered and to be prepared to defend their position with the other members of the class.

Surely, the learning principles underlying early math (Gelman & Gallistell, 1986) could be taught directly to teacher candidates through lectures, but even if the professor offers rich examples to illustrate the principles, students will still only have a narrow view of how these principles apply. Given a scenario in which they are invited to uncover which principles are operating and how they are exemplified, students' learning will be deepened to the point they can use what they have learned in an actual classroom. Requiring students to construct their knowledge together is using active, rather than passive, learning.

Studies in child development and education offer further support for active learning and illustrate how being told information may limit the depth of learning that a student can experience, whether they are in preschool, K–12 education, or teacher training. Bonawitz and colleagues (2011) found that preschoolers who received direct instruction from an adult about a toy's function, or even overheard direct instruction to another child, limited their exploration of the toy and discovery of its other functions compared to peers who explored the toy without an initial instructional demonstration. Active learning also promotes early literacy (Zosh et al., 2013) and math skills (Fisher et al., 2013).

Moreno and colleagues (2001) found that seventh graders showed more enjoyment in their learning and more effectively transferred their biological knowledge of how plants adapt to different environments to new situations when they gained that content through an active, virtual simulation, rather than more passive instruction. Similarly, Wolf and Fraser (2008) identified greater cohesiveness among middle school science students when engaged in active, inquiry-based instruction versus passive instruction. Lazonder and Harmsen's (2016) meta-analysis of active, inquiry-based learning broadly supported its effectiveness across development from childhood through adolescence when adult guidance is provided.

In higher education, flipped classrooms, peer instruction, and other innovative overhauls to the traditional lecture create opportunities for students to actively engage with their learning, with measurable positive impacts to their subsequent understanding and content mastery (e.g., Passeri & Mazur, 2019; Schell & Mazur, 2015). For example, college students asked to retain information for the purpose of teaching a peer, rather than just performing on a test, showed greater retention of learned material (Benware & Deci, 1984). In a meta-analysis of active learning in undergraduate science, technology, engineering, and math (STEM) courses, Freeman et al. (2014) found that students' exam scores increased and failure rates decreased with the approach, compared to lecture-based instruction. Adults who received feedback after providing an incorrect response to a prompt retained new information better than those who simply received a report of their performance (Potts & Shanks, 2014).

However, some prerequisites (e.g., cognitive and metacognitive abilities like analogical reasoning, beliefs about agency, prior knowledge about a subject, and/or the ability to provide students with sufficient guidance through the approach, especially if it is novel) may be necessary for students to maximally benefit from active learning (Brod, 2021). Cognitive and metacognitive behaviors respectively involve students employing strategies to support their learning and then monitoring the effectiveness of those strategies (Artz & Armour-Thomas, 1992). These abilities are not static and can be developed through active learning (Grabinger & Dunlap, 1995), but even in higher education, it is important for educators to recognize their students' relative familiarity with active learning (Zinski et al., 2017) and provide adequate instructional scaffolding (Brod, 2021).

There are considerable benefits to investing in active learning for teacher candidates, given that lecture-based instruction remains dominant in higher education. Recognizing the fact that taking notes on a computer can lead to mindless engagement with the material (Mueller & Oppenheimer, 2014), students who will shortly become teachers will have experienced years of mostly passive learning. But this is not how children (or adults) learn best. Anytime we can engage in problem-based learning and promote joint problem-solving, we increase the likelihood that students will come to realize how much more they learn when they are active, but educators' facilitation of active learning will be necessary.

Engaged Learning

Fredricks, Blumenfeld, and Paris (2004) offer a three-part definition of engagement in learning involving behavioral engagement (e.g., effort, persistence, participation), emotional engagement (e.g., reactions to course material), and cognitive engagement (e.g., investment in learning, problem-solving skills). All three are critical for learning because they support the learners' ability to stay on-task. For students to benefit from active learning, they must remain undistracted and focused on the educational activity at hand. This is challenging for younger children, who are more susceptible to diversion (Wetzel et al., 2019). In the classroom, even subtle distractions from decorations impede learning learning (Fisher et al., 2014). For educators who work with young children, providing opportunities for their students to exercise a greater degree of choice and to interact with their peers generates more positive peer engagement. Teacher-structured activities that promote warm, supportive interactions enable positive teacher–student engagement. Young learners with more positive teacher relationships have been found to have higher achievement, decreased levels of internalizing behaviors, and higher social competence (Vitiello et al., 2012). Even limiting the comings and goings of visitors in the classroom, creating opportunities for students to work together on targeted learning activities, and scaffolding students' organization of learning materials helps reduce distractions and encourage on-task, focused engagement (Zosh et al., 2022).

The benefits of consistent, focused engagement go beyond early education: College students who multitask on their laptop during class show poorer performance on subject tests than those who remain engaged with the course material—as do other students with a view of their screen (Sana et al., 2013). Deslauriers and colleagues (2019) found that college students *felt* that they had learned less in introductory physics classes that incorporated active learning strategies to support engagement due to increased cognitive demand on their part. Yet they showed greater learning gains. For college students learning online, they found the courses easier to focus on when they offered opportunities for engagement through thought-provoking discussions that fostered changes in beliefs or understanding about the course material, considerations of broader societal problems, and links between course material and their own prior experiences (Buelow et al., 2018).

Engagement happens, too, when students work in small groups to develop solutions to scenarios. Given that the research on mind-wandering shows that more than a third of a lecture is lost to mind wandering or responding to emails or other tasks unrelated to the learning episode (Lindquist & McLean, 2011; Risko et al., 2013; Schooler et al., 2014), working together with peers to derive answers from the materials likely keeps students far more engaged than listening solitarily to a lecture.

Meaningful Learning

Students practice meaningful, or deep, learning when they recognize the relevance of the knowledge or skills gained. They connect new content with broader ideas, prior knowledge, and/or experiences that occurred inside, or outside, the classroom. This connection to the past facilitates transfer of new knowledge to future situations (Darling-Hammond, Barron, et al., 2008; Darling-Hammond, Flook, et al., 2020; Mayer, 2002; Zosh et al., 2022; Zosh et al., 2018).

Facilitation of meaningful learning may occur at the level of an individual lesson's structure, or at the level of the learning environment with respect to how that lesson is connected to prior knowledge and experiences from in- and out-of-school. An example of meaningful lesson structure is the "World of Words (WOW)" vocabulary intervention for early childhood and elementary education. In WOW, students learn scientific vocabulary within conceptual categories (e.g., stem, leaf, and roots associated with plant; Neuman et al., 2021). This intervention is based on research demonstrating how students' comprehension depends on prior knowledge. In a study of fourth graders' reading skills, Ouellette (2006) found that the students' depth of vocabulary knowledge (i.e., their ability to define a word with connections to relevant features, and offer synonyms)—but not their breadth of expressive vocabulary (i.e., their ability to name words from pictures)—predicted reading comprehension. O'Reilly et al. (2019) similarly found a positive relation between high school students' relevant background knowledge and vocabulary. Thus, reading comprehension across grade levels benefits from learning in a meaningful context with established connections between terms and concepts.

A meaningful learning environment can be fostered through culturally responsive, or relevant teaching (Gay, 2000, 2002; Ladson-Billings, 1995a, 1995b, 2021). In this context, educators are encouraged to recognize students' "funds of knowledge" gained at home or in their community as instructional resources to leverage when teaching (Moll et al., 1992). These "funds" are intentionally inclusive, as demonstrated by the movement to bring Hip Hop into the classroom to introduce students to the richness of language and promote social development and creativity (Love, 2015).

Meaningful learning is important for the youngest learners up through higher education, including in teacher training. Glisczinski (2007) surveyed 153 teacher education students in their final year of training. Nearly 75% of the respondents reported experiencing an event that led them to question their beliefs, values, attitudes, feelings, concepts, or actions while enrolled in higher education, but just 43% then engaged in critical thinking about the event in an effort to understand its impact and recognize its connection to prior knowledge or beliefs. This reflection and contextualization of new knowledge enables meaningful learning. In a study with 30 university students in a science teacher training program, Yalçin and colleagues (2017) found significant increases in learners' knowledge of physical concepts they would need to teach by encouraging them to consider instances of the concepts in their own lives, and to reflect on the degree to which the concepts would be relatable to their future students' experiences. This method enhanced the preservice teachers' awareness of the course concepts in context.

A problem-based approach to teacher training is a compelling method for making teacher education meaningful through connections between theory and practice (Filipenko & Naslund, 2016). For example, in a problem-based project used by an author of this chapter, students are presented with a description of a fictitious high schooler named Arielle who has suddenly changed her behavior. She begins to fail her classes—a departure from her previously flawless academic record—changes her appearance, and quits some of the activities she enjoyed most (e.g., basketball). Students work together in regularly reshuffled peer groups (depending on the task) to first probe various possibilities (e.g., depression, pregnancy), to teach each other about what Arielle might be experiencing, and how to address it. The problem continues for several days with various requirements that encourage the students to become very invested in understanding the nature of Arielle's problem. It takes on great meaning for them as they reflect on the students they knew in high school who developed similar issues. It prompts them to examine and learn about the range of challenges adolescents might experience. For the teacher candidate, this exercise is both personally meaningful, and can be leveraged as an experiential learning tool later in their own classrooms.

Socially Interactive Learning

Decades of research demonstrate that learning occurs within a sociocultural context in which learners gain knowledge and skills from others (Rogoff, 2003; Vygotsky, 1987). This social interaction may occur in dialogic reading when young children answer adults' questions about a book while reading together, which supports language development (e.g., Hargrave & Sénéchal, 2000; Whitehurst et al., 1994). However, this approach is not universally beneficial for all children (Manz et al., 2010; Melzi et al., 2019), leading researchers to suggest interventions that may remain socially interactive, but are socioculturally aligned with how caregivers and their children typically share books (Manz et al., 2010; Melzi et al., 2019).

The value of social interaction extends beyond adults and children to peers. Ramani (2012) found that 4- and 5-year-olds built more complex block structures and engaged in more positive communication with each other during the task when it was presented in a student-led, adult-facilitated playful context, not directed by an adult. In the classroom, students across subjects, and grade levels as far as higher education, demonstrate greater learning outcomes from socially interactive, group instruction compared to independent, or whole-class instruction (Lou et al., 1996).

As Lou et al. (1996) suggests, college-aged students likewise benefit from socially interactive course design. In a study with three literacy teacher preparation classes, Hurst and colleagues (2013) found that preservice teachers perceived that social interaction, which was used to support the course aims and took on a variety of formats, ranging from discussions between pairs of students to whole-class activities, improved the students' learning and supported critical thinking and problem-solving. Cabrera and colleagues (2002) found that second-year undergraduates from 23 higher education institutions both preferred and benefited academically and socially from collaborative learning practices. Learning through socially enriched activities helps learners to recall prior knowledge, make connections, and consolidate new ideas (Hurst et al., 2013, p. 390). Furthermore, it appears to keep students on task and requires them to contribute to the discussion. Attending class without having read the material becomes more difficult when all group members are expected to help answer the applied questions the professor has raised.

Iterative Learning

The process of learning about the world through exploration, observation, and hypothesis testing begins when 3.5- to 5-month infants are surprised by a screen unexpectedly rotating through a solid object (Baillargeon, 1987; Baillargeon et al., 1985). This surprised reaction facilitates learning later in childhood. For example, Stahl and Feigenson (2017) taught 3- to 6-year-old children novel words following an event that either violated or failed to violate their expectations. Children were significantly better at learning verbs and nouns related to the event when the event itself was inconsistent with their expectations. During naturalistic play, Schulz and Bonawitz (2007) found that preschoolers engaged in self-directed free play preferred to explore a familiar toy over a novel one, but only if an adult demonstrated ambiguity in the familiar toy's function. This observation prompted further investigation. Research across the disciplines indicates that students learn from repeated experiences. For example, adolescent English learners learned more vocabulary words from reading and listening to the same text over four consecutive days, rather than on a weekly basis over four weeks (Serrano & Huang, 2023).

Iteration goes beyond mere repetition, however. Iterative thinking involves experimentation, hypothesis-testing, and the repeated engagement with material that can help the learner build on previous knowledge (Zosh et al., 2022; Zosh et al., 2018). It builds on the notion of learning as a scientific process involving the use of existing knowledge to generate new hypotheses, test those hypotheses, and update understanding based on the results of those tests. In a classroom, this could involve the use of activities or assignments that can be completed in more than one way, or that encourage group activity so that students can collaborate and think critically about how to solve problems, communicating their unique strategies and testing them to find out what works. Rote memorization helps learners to encode a specific set of facts, but iterative thinking helps learners build connections, see a more complex picture, and generate deep conceptual understanding that supports the development of new knowledge.

Iterative thinking can also take place in a situation where students are placed in the field early during their educational training—as is the case at the University of Delaware. In their first experience, teacher candidates are asked to mentor students in after-school programs in under-resourced communities. They then write a paper about their experiences and are asked to connect the concepts they learned in the course to experiences they shared with their mentee. Thus, reading and learning their course material in the university classroom is only the first step. True mastery of the educational concepts in those courses comes when students iteratively advance their learning by recognizing when those same concepts apply in the world.

Joyful Learning

The relation between emotion and cognition is well-established (Isen, 1984), and positive affect also relates to students' academic outcomes. Specifically, students' executive function (EF) skills (e.g., self-control, attention, working memory, inhibition) and problem-solving are associated with school readiness and long-term academic achievement. Since EF can improve with training and mood, students should engage in joyful activities (e.g., the arts or sports) to support gains in EF and academic achievement (Diamond, 2014). Joyful learning helps to bolster intrinsic motivation, potentially through increases in dopamine levels that are implicated in the brain's reward pathways (Cools, 2011; Dang et al., 2012). Making learning opportunities joyful often occurs within minds-on, active learning experiences. Similarly, students will likely appreciate when they make meaningful connections between their learning and prior knowledge or lived experience. Joyfulness helps to reduce distraction and supports student persistence in the face of challenges.

Adult learners likewise benefit from joyful education. In a study with 129 adult English as a second language students, Moskowitz and Dewaele (2021) found that students' perceptions of their teachers' happiness and involvement predicted their own attitude and motivation, illustrating what the authors referred to as "the process of positive emotional contagion between teachers and students" (p. 1). Pleasurable experiences with learning can also encourage learners to embrace more cognitively challenging tasks and entertain connections between prior knowledge and new information. Medical students using a video game to simulate a home visit with a patient showed significant growth in their medical knowledge from pre- to posttest. They also recognized the game as an enjoyable, but still educationally valuable resource (Duque et al., 2008). Lucardie (2014) found that adult learners participating in a general education certification program experienced greater engagement and deeper understanding of course content when the learning experience was fun. When learners enjoy what they are doing, they are more apt to feel intrinsically engaged, and to enjoy the deep processing and long-term memory activation they gain from focused participation in an educational experience (Willis, 2007).

Developing a teacher education program in which teacher candidates are both taught *through* these principles and have opportunities to practice them can encourage their transfer into their later instruction (e.g., Novak & Wisdom, 2018). When these instructional characteristics—active, engaging, meaningful, socially interactive, iterative, and joyful—are present, they create a nexus of conditions that best support student learning and engagement across elementary, secondary, and higher education. When learners see value and generalizability in their learning, they create the habits of mind that both support lifelong learning and create the ideal conditions that foster the development of key skills researchers agree are critical for 21st-century success.

WHAT STUDENTS NEED TO LEARN AT ALL LEVELS OF EDUCATION

A consensus is emerging among science of learning and development researchers (e.g., Hirsh-Pasek et al., 2022; Hirsh-Pasek et al., 2020; Learning Policy Institute & Turnaround for Children, 2021), educators (Ferlazzo, 2012; Schwartz, 2020), and employers (Davis, 2020; Wagner, 2008) that it is necessary to transition away from traditional methods of education narrowly focused on academic achievement in reading and math. While these subjects remain important, these stakeholders all advocate for a whole-child approach to instruction that provides students with a breadth of skills for the 21st century. Golinkoff and Hirsh-Pasek (2016) proposed their 6 Cs model to reach this goal, informed by the science of learning and child development. The 6 Cs scaffold each other from collaboration to confidence but acknowledge students' individual differences. Each C includes four levels (Figure 2.2), through which students may progress at their own pace across different learning environments. For example, a student may be a skilled and confident communicator while directing the school play but lack confidence in Spanish class. The flexibility of the 6 Cs approach even extends to its classroom implementation. When designing lessons aligned with the 6 Cs, teachers can promote these skills in their students while meeting required standards or content objectives. They are also encouraged to design lessons that account for their students' interests and backgrounds (Golinkoff & Hirsh-Pasek, 2016; Hirsh-Pasek et al., 2022; Hirsh-Pasek et al., 2020).

As with the learning principles described in the previous section, the 6 Cs are relevant even at the college level. Two authors of this chapter—Drs. Kathy Hirsh-Pasek and Roberta Golinkoff—who jointly developed the model we describe, use these principles to foster the Cs in their own classes at Temple University and the University of Delaware. The suite of skills we offer here represents a broad spectrum of abilities that underlie the capacity to learn specific content, but moreover to adopt the mindset that enables learning at any level, in any discipline. Students in Drs. Hirsh-Pasek and Golinkoff's classes achieve success in psychology and their education more broadly. This is attributable to the fact that they develop the capacity

	Collaboration	Communication	Content	Critical Thinking	Creative Innovation	Confidence
LEVEL 4	Building it together	Tell a joint story	Expertise	Evidence	Vision	Dare to fail
LEVEL 3	Back and forth	Dialogue	Making connections	Opinions	Voice	Calculated risks
LEVEL 2	Side by side	Show and tell	Wide breadth/ Shallow understanding	Truths differ	Means-end	Where do I stand?
LEVEL 1	On my own	Raw emotion	Early learning/ Situation specific	Seeing is believing	Experimentation	Barrel on

Figure 2.2 Overview of the "6 Cs" as a dynamic skill set from collaboration to confidence. *Note:* The "6 Cs" are scaffolded from collaboration through confidence with four levels of student growth associated with each skill. Student progress through the "6 Cs" may vary. *Source:* Golinkoff & Hirsh-Pasek, 2016; Hirsh-Pasek et al., 2020; Hirsh-Pasek et al., 2022.

to collaborate, communicate, demonstrate content mastery, think critically and creatively, and have confidence in their ability to do so. The students establish a foundation for success. Instruction in teacher education that both introduces and consistently targets these 6 Cs will enable teacher candidates and their future students to respectively facilitate and experience high-quality, evidence-based classroom instruction.

Collaboration

Collaboration is the foremost skill of the 6 Cs and central to human nature. It involves learning how to appropriately interact with others and control impulses. Effective collaboration is a prerequisite for community-building, including in the classroom (Hirsh-Pasek et al., 2022; Hirsh-Pasek et al., 2020). Our biological predisposition to collaborate was was shown by Piazza and colleagues (2020), who found that 9- to 15-month infants demonstrated similar patterns of brain activity with adults when communicating and playing together. Foundational social skills even predict students' later academic achievement. For example, Cooper et al. (2014) determined that students who demonstrated low or average reading skills, but higher social skills, in kindergarten later outperformed their peers with similar reading skills, yet lower social skills, when they reached 5th grade. Slavin (2014) broadly described the effectiveness of cooperative, or collaborative, learning in K–12 education, provided that five strategies are incorporated: (a) the construction of student groups with mutually supportive members, (b) the establishment of group goals, (c) individual accountability for group members, (d) the introduction of communication and problem-solving strategies, and (e) integration of group activities with other pedagogical methods as a replacement for individual classwork. Personal engagement in collaborative learning even bolstered third graders' understanding of democratic values (Erbil & Kocabas, 2018), demonstrating the scope of the practice's impact.

As mentioned in the context of active, engaged, and socially interactive learning, students, including teacher candidates, enhance their collaboration anytime they have the freedom to work with their peers through, for example, jointly developing solutions to problems, brainstorming possible causes for a given scenario, or even giving one another feedback on material they produce for a class or a lesson.

Communication

Communication, which both follows from collaboration and enables its growth, includes speaking, listening, reading, and writing (Golinkoff &

Hirsh-Pasek, 2016; Hirsh-Pasek et al., 2022; Hirsh-Pasek et al., 2020). This skill likewise emerges in infancy and builds across development. When caregivers respond to their infants in a timely manner and with contingent recognition of their infants' original vocalization or intention, the infants' later language skills are supported (Tamis-LeMonda et al., 2014). This linguistic foundation fosters students' later academic achievement and social skills. As Pace and colleagues (2019) revealed, students' language skills at kindergarten entry predicted their academic performance in reading and math, as well as social skills, in later elementary grades. In the process of teaching and learning, effective communication is critical (Wahyuni, 2017). First-graders whose teachers read texts out loud with a focus on the type of text, instructions on how to understand the text, and an emphasis on retelling the narrative, showed higher outcomes in vocabulary, listening comprehension, and language proficiency (Baker et al., 2020). Among older students, the role of communication in reading also impacts later academic success. In a study with high-schoolers, Whitten and colleagues (2016) found that students who read for pleasure demonstrated higher competency in tests of English, math, science, and history (also see Attiyat, 2019).

Communication is a complex and challenging skill. To truly develop the ability, teacher candidates are urged to, for example, argue their point of view rather than succumb to the view of students in their group who volunteer the most or dominate the conversation. Learning to persuade others, make one's case based on evidence and sound rationale, and articulate one's perspective in a meaningful and engaging way is the foundation to good communication.

Content

Content in this model is considered broadly, both with respect to its relation to other 6 Cs skills and the material students are expected to master. Deeper content learning rests on the foundation of collaborating and communicating with others. It recognizes the importance of reading and math, but counters recent shifts to exclusively focus on those subjects (Berliner, 2009, 2011) by acknowledging the educational value of science, social studies, and the arts. Further, this model's definition of content is not aligned with a specific curriculum, permitting any curricular standards to be met as students develop the full breadth of 6 Cs skills (Golinkoff & Hirsh-Pasek, 2016; Hirsh-Pasek et al., 2022; Hirsh-Pasek et al., 2020). Content also includes EF skills such as working memory, attention, and cognitive flexibility (Diamond, 2014; Golinkoff & Hirsh-Pasek, 2016; Hirsh-Pasek et al., 2022; Hirsh-Pasek et al., 2020). These skills foster learning. For example, Duncan and colleagues'

(2007) meta-analysis of six longitudinal studies examining school readiness and academic achievement indicated that students' early attention skills predicted their later achievement, with initial achievement levels and cognitive abilities controlled. Ahmed and colleagues (2018) similarly found that children's working memory skills at just 54 months significantly predicted their reading comprehension at Age 15. EF also predicts kindergarten readiness and subsequent learning (Kalstabakken et al., 2021). Improved behavior regulation, a subcomponent of EF, corresponds to growth in emerging literacy, vocabulary, and math skills throughout prekindergarten (McClelland et al., 2007). Recent research suggests that encouraging reflection, intentional exploration, and opportunities for self-regulated learning through playful environments designed to promote developing EF supports later learning (Distefano et al., 2020).

When teacher candidates apply their learning, they are deepening their understanding of content. It is important for their instruction to offer opportunities to recognize the concepts they are learning in practice, iterate on newly learned materials and deepen their understanding, and embrace practices in the classroom that embody the principles we have described here, which all enable learners to develop content knowledge.

Critical Thinking

As students gather content knowledge inside and outside the classroom, they must engage in critical thinking to process it and evaluate its quality (Golinkoff & Hirsh-Pasek, 2016; Hirsh-Pasek et al., 2022; Hirsh-Pasek et al., 2020). Unfortunately, students struggle with this task, particularly when analyzing online resources (Walraven et al., 2009), a key skill for the 21st-century. However, critical thinking can be taught through a variety of strategies and transferred to new situations (see Halpern, 2014 for review). Halpern and Dunn (2021) point to teaching critical thinking skills as a lynchpin for all individuals to generate solutions to complex real-world problems. Effective critical thinking depends on effortful cognition, even when it is very challenging, and exercising analytic abilities with open-mindedness to entertain creative solutions to problems (Halpern & Sternberg, 2020). One potential way to encourage students to engage in this challenging task is to couch critical thinking in a broaderactive playful learning context. Huang and colleagues (2017) administered a collaborative, concept-mapping task related to basketball in an elementary school physical education class and found significant improvements in critical thinking skills. The ability to teach and learn critical thinking even extends to adulthood. In an intervention study, Motz and colleagues (2021) found that by training adult participants to categorize types of logical fallacies and allowing them to practice, they could enhance the participants' critical thinking skills over-and-above control (no training) and no critical thinking practice comparison groups.

In teacher training, students must question and recognize the limits of existing knowledge, but also understand how to find valid answers to their questions. They benefit from challenging their beliefs—perhaps by revising misconceptions about student learning, such as the effectiveness of lecture instruction—and from engaging with others to do so. Given that teacher candidates need to consider how information, such as evidence from the science of learning, may contribute to practice during coursework and once established in the classroom, it is beneficial for teacher education programs to foster robust critical thinking skills in their trainees.

Creative Innovation

The practice of creative innovation rests on content knowledge and critical thinking. Students must reflect on what they learned and apply it through problem-solving (Hirsh-Pasek et al., 2022; Hirsh-Pasek et al., 2020). Garaigordobil and Berrueco (2011) demonstrated that weekly game play supported preschoolers' creative innovation. After 24 weeks of play sessions, intervention students outperformed control students in measures of verbal and artistic creativity. Adults can broadly support creative thinking through modeling exploratory behaviors motivated by curiosity (e.g., asking questions, hypothesis-testing; Jirout, 2020). Children's exploratory behaviors may also promote their own curiosity. In a study with preschoolers, Evans and colleagues (2021) found that children who explored more while trying to remove a ball from a jar using a collection of everyday objects were more likely to generate creative solutions to the problem. This finding points to the importance of purposeful, iterative exploration in children's creative thinking, an increasingly valued capacity in the 21st-century (Lucas, 2016). The recent development of a tool to measure creativity in K–12 classrooms suggests that creative innovation emerges when the learning environment is one of openness to new ideas with trust between students and their teacher, as well as among classmates. Classroom tasks to promote creativity should be active and collaborative (Richardson & Mishra, 2018).

When teacher candidates enter the field, they must begin to see how creativity operates each time they work with a student. What can they offer to keep the child's attention and engagement going and continue to deepen their student's learning? How can they take an existing course lesson and turn it into an opportunity to foster not only content knowledge through collaboration and communication, but an enduring love of learning? Engaging teacher candidates in creative problem-solving creates a learning environment wherein teacher and student alike can iterate successfully, take joy in an activity together, and build the foundation of intellectual confidence that shapes further engagement in other learning opportunities. This approach prepares teacher candidates to facilitate similar experiences in their own classrooms.

Confidence

The final skill in the 6 Cs model encourages students to take reasonable risks in the classroom, then persist, even if faced with failure (Golinkoff & Hirsh-Pasek, 2016; Hirsh-Pasek et al., 2022; Hirsh-Pasek et al., 2020). This reflects "grit," defined as "perseverance and passion for long-term goals" (Duckworth et al., 2007, p. 1087). Confidence is also related to a "growth mindset," the belief that abilities can be improved through effort and appropriate strategies and instruction over time because they are not fixed (Haimovitz & Dweck, 2017).

Taken together, the 6 Cs framework is a set of developmental competencies that build on one another and offer a tool for educators to promote content mastery within a suite of skills that students will need to achieve their goals inside and outside the classroom. The principles of how students learn provide the fertile ground that supports the development of these skills, and a breadth of research from child psychology through higher education reveals that the principles and skills all have relevance throughout development in supporting students' learning. Teacher candidates often report feeling very unsure about their abilities (Clark & Newberry, 2019), particularly when they first enter the classroom, and not surprisingly, it takes time and multiple experiences working with students in the classroom to determine what works and what does not. Using the model we have described above in the course of teacher preparation can help boost self-efficacy by educating teacher candidates in the ways they will subsequently teach in their own professional experiences.

PUTTING THE *HOW* AND *WHAT* TOGETHER TO ALIGN THEORY AND PRACTICE IN SCHOOLS

Hirsh-Pasek and colleagues (Hirsh-Pasek et al., 2022; Hirsh-Pasek et al., 2020) suggest that the educational approach they propose can be thought of as two complementary checklists (Figure 2.3) that can guide future teachers towards a healthy and vibrant classroom in which both teachers and students are empowered to support best learning practices. By way of

Directions: Make a checkmark in the box next to each playful learning or 6 Cs element if it is present in the activity you are facilitating or observing

Part I: Principles of How Kids Learn	Part II: The 6 Cs
Active ☐	Collaboration ☐
Engaged ☐	Communication ☐
Meaningful ☐	Content ☐
Socially Interactive ☐	Critical Thinking ☐
Iterative ☐	Creative Innovation ☐
Joyful ☐	Confidence ☐

Figure 2.3 Playful learning and the "6 Cs" checklist. *Source:* Hirsh-Pasek et al., 2020.

example, seventh graders at Radnor Middle School in suburban Philadelphia have completed long-term, interdisciplinary projects related to their local watershed each year since 1987 (Springer, 1994). These projects maximize student agency. They are active, engaging, meaningful, socially, interactive, iterative, and joyful with potential connections to all 6 Cs (Hirsh-Pasek et al., 2020). Yet Radnor Township's median household income was over $139,000 in 2021 dollars between 2017 and 2021 (U.S. Census Bureau, 2022), potentially raising questions about the implementation of the model in underserved communities. However, a recent mixed methods study documented its effectiveness in a school district in the Midwestern United States where 78% of the students identified as Hispanic or Latino and 95% qualified for free or reduced-price lunch based on federal guidelines. The district's educators implemented the playful learning principles and fostered the 6 Cs through interdisciplinary thematic instruction (Lonning et al., 2010; Shanahan et al., 1995). For example, one theme was "The Farmer's Market," and students completed many projects related to it, including the production of a musical about vegetables (Blinkoff et al., 2023).

Importantly, the principles can be flexibly applied to enhance any curriculum by offering a pedagogical approach that shifts mindsets and sparks deeper learning that is more fulfilling for future teachers and students alike. These frameworks also enable the implementation of strengths-based pedagogies that value students' experiences outside of the classroom within a larger instructional system. These pedagogies include culturally responsive teaching, or "using the cultural characteristics, experiences, and perspectives of ethnically diverse students as conduits for teaching them more effectively" (Gay, 2002, p. 106), and Gloria Ladson-Billings' (1995a, 1995b, 2021) similar concept of culturally relevant pedagogy, "a theoretical model that not only addresses student achievement but also helps students to accept and affirm their cultural identity while developing critical perspectives that challenge inequities that schools (and other institutions) perpetuate" (Ladson-Billings, 1995b, p. 469).

Incorporating the science of learning into educational theory and practice stands to promote more equitable education. It is through these principles that we may reduce the instructional disparities between what Anyon (1980) called the "executive elite" classrooms, in which children of affluent professionals routinely honed their critical thinking and communication skills through active inquiry, and the "working class" classrooms, where students from underserved communities were subjected to rote, procedural lessons led by the teacher with limited student agency. Rather, the experiences that all students bring into the classroom are taken as valuable "funds of knowledge" (Moll, 1992) to inform instruction. Yet a recent review by Duke and colleagues (2021) emphasizes the magnitude of this challenge, and indicates that these concerning inequities persist today, as demonstrated by the limited inquiry-based learning and student agency offered during social studies and literacy instruction in underserved schools. An example of a school using the checklist in a culturally responsive way makes these educational values come alive. Returning to the Midwest, a teacher organized a replica of a Spanish market, in which students produced small goods to sell. The students enjoyed learning to make the goods and the experience of the market itself (Blinkoff et al., 2023). Given the large number of Latine students in the district, this experience represented one way in which their culture was validated in the classroom. Even beyond the culturally responsive component of meaningful learning, this activity represented a synthesis of many other principles of how children learn. It was active, engaging, and joyfully festive with the potential for social interaction among students and their teacher, as well as iterative attempts at making items through trial and error. The experience likely supported all the students' 6 Cs. Now, our challenge is to introduce teacher candidates to this method of planning and instructing around the science of learning principles we present, so these deep learning experiences are routine.

PUTTING THE HOW AND WHAT TOGETHER TO ALIGN THEORY AND PRACTICE IN TEACHER EDUCATION

The model presented here asks teachers to design lessons that reflect the playful learning principles of how students learn (Zosh et al., 2022; Zosh et al., 2018) to promote the 6 Cs outcomes—what students need to know for the 21st-century (Golinkoff & Hirsh-Pasek, 2016). It also offers an evidence-based way to think about educating teachers for optimal learning (Hirsh-Pasek et al., 2022; Hirsh-Pasek et al., 2020). In fact, we suggest that teacher candidates will more effectively and easily implement Hirsh-Pasek and colleagues' (Hirsh-Pasek et al., 2022; Hirsh-Pasek et al., 2020) model in their future classrooms if they are introduced to its principles, and even provided with opportunities to learn through the model themselves, during their teacher education training. Despite the power of this approach, few college classrooms are using discovery-based inquiry to teach teachers how to teach. Consider the following example: In an introductory teacher preparation course taught at Texas A&M University, the instructor requires both lecture attendance and a midterm and final examination (Shaw, 2012). But they also require a philosophy of teaching project that is parceled out into sequential assignment submissions throughout the semester, an interdisciplinary group project, and regular chapter reflections that scaffold the students' engagement with the material. The instructor incorporated some degree of active learning, engagement, meaningfulness, and social interaction into the course. By teaching using these principles, this instructor employs the tools in human development that help to adapt course material to the students' strengths, pulling from their lived experiences through their reflections on the course material, and creating a forum for shared understanding that allows for iterative engagement with key course concepts.

The syllabus for this course is not entirely constructed in accordance with principles from the science of learning, however. It articulates that regular lecture attendance is still required, a more passive pedagogical approach that does not enable deep understanding of concepts (Mazur, 2009). Although a class observation may reveal some socially interactive learning among students in the lecture, another format focused exclusively on active learning might be more effective. Ultimately, this example serves to illustrate how many educator preparation courses model passive learning. This pedagogical approach yields learning in students that is more easily forgotten and less widely applicable even when attempting to teach about the power of interactive, discovery-based education. There is irony in this approach.

The long history of federal educational intervention might well be the culprit. This intervention came to shape how preservice teacher education programs have been designed and taught (Drummond & Andrews, 1980). By 2010, the Common Core State Standards initiative, a state-level standards movement developed in collaboration between state governors and education officials, was adopted by 41 states, four territories, and the District of Columbia in the United States (Common Core State Standards Initiative, 2021; Kaufman et al., 2018). One intended advantage of this initiative was that states might adopt a more centralized rather than a fractionated education system. Yet, instruction narrowly focused on English language arts and math outcomes in the context of a broader, standards-based accountability movement (Berliner, 2009, 2011; Common Core State Standards Initiative, 2021; Loveless, 2021). Even instruction in these subjects was limited to more superficial memorization and procedural learning (Berliner, 2009, 2011). Moreover, since their implementation, teacher education programs have struggled to equip preservice educators with the tools needed to teach the standards, let alone go beyond them (Walsh, 2013). Even more troubling, as noted previously, teacher education traditionally separates "foundations" courses, involving the development of expertise in specific content areas (curricula), and "methods" courses (pedagogy), involving the development of expertise in instructional practice (Darling-Hammond, Hammerness, et al., 2005; Darling-Hammond & Oakes, 2019; Grossman et al., 2009).

This divide between theoretical coursework and practical experience led many educators to feel inadequately prepared for the classroom (Grossman et al., 2009). It also forced teachers to be confined to scripted programs that delivered only what was prescribed by the educational standards. Teachers were conduits, not guides, in their students' learning. In a post-pandemic environment, education desperately needs a course correction. It is time to practice what we teach in teacher preparation classrooms—active playful learning that nourishes a suite of skills. It is time to redefine what counts as successful teacher training. Here, we argue that part of the solution will come from redesigning our programs so that they incorporate lessons from the science of learning. We know a tremendous amount about how children learn, about what they need to learn, and about how to educate teachers and students in culturally responsive and inclusive ways.

CONCLUSION

The winds of change are here. The global pandemic is forcing us to reimagine what education can and should be. Our systems were largely designed when people, rather than robots, worked on assembly lines and long before anyone knew about the internet. As new tools became available, we merely patched new professional developments into our preK–12 classrooms, without much consideration for how those innovations were being implemented. As *Time* magazine once quipped, if Rip van Winkle were to return today after his 100-year nap, only the education system would look the same (Wallis & Steptoe, 2006).

This system will not change if teachers are not trained with the best evidence on *how* and *what* children must learn—if they cannot see the complexity in a child's answer, assuming that it is wrong because it does not match a prescribed response, and if they cannot spark development across the breadth of skills required in a global economy. If we continue to lecture at teachers as they passively take notes on active, engaged learning, we are simply not doing our job. We are promoting the "sage on the stage" model

(King, 1993) that no longer reflects best practices in education. If we portray students as empty vessels to be filled, then our classrooms will remain paragons of the past. We know how to teach and model human development for aspiring teachers. They deserve to learn in ways that reflect the best science so that they can teach in the ways that humans best learn.

KEY CHAPTER TAKEAWAYS

- Recent research on teacher education indicates limited emphasis on human development and the science of learning.
- A growing consensus in developmental and educational research emphasizes the importance of designing instruction that aligns with the science of learning.
- The model of how students learn (playful learning principles) and what they need to learn for the 21st-century (6 Cs) presented here is broadly applicable to classrooms from preschool through higher education, is designed to be flexible across course content, and can be implemented at scale in teacher education programs.
- Evaluate human development courses against the checklists offered by Hirsh-Pasek and colleagues (2020) and Hirsh-Pasek and colleagues (2022) to determine if principles based on the science of learning have been implemented.
- Reflect on the accessibility of the principles for teacher candidates to advance their own learning and apply the principles in their future classrooms.
- Adapt current instruction on the science of learning guided by the model presented in this chapter to ensure that it is accessible to teacher candidates and maximizes the inherent flexibility of the principles.

KEY WORDS

Active learning
Creative innovation
Critical thinking
Engaged learning
Iterative learning
Joyful learning
Meaningful learning
Science of learning
Socially interactive learning

REFERENCES

Ahmed, S. F., Tang, S., Waters, N. E., & Davis-Kean, P. (2018). Executive function and academic achievement: Longitudinal relations from early childhood to adolescence. *Journal of Educational Psychology, 111*(3), 446–458. https://psycnet.apa.org/doi/10.1037/edu0000296

Anyon, J. (1980). Social class and the hidden curriculum of work. *Journal of Education, 162*(1), 67–92. https://doi.org/10.1177/002205748016200106

Artz, A. F., & Armour-Thomas, E. (1992). Development of a cognitive-metacognitive framework for protocol analysis of mathematical problem solving in small groups. *Cognition and Instruction, 9*(2), 137–175. https://doi.org/10.1207/s1532690xci0902_3

Attiyat, N. M. A. (2019). The impact of pleasure reading on enhancing writing achievement and reading comprehension. *Arab World English Journal, 10*(1), 155–165. https://dx.doi.org/10.24093/awej/vol10no1.14

Baillargeon, R. (1987). Object permanence in 3.5- and 4.5-month-old infants. *Developmental Psychology, 23*(5), 655–664. https://doi.org/10.1037/0012-1649.23.5.655

Baillargeon, R., Spelke, E. S., & Wasserman, S. (1985). Object permanence in five-month-old infants. *Cognition, 20*(3), 191–208. https://doi.org/10.1016/0010-0277(85)90008-3

Baker, D. L., Santoro, L., Biancarosa, G., Baker, S. K., Fien, H., & Otterstedt, J. (2020). Effects of a read aloud intervention on first grade student vocabulary, listening comprehension, and language proficiency. *Reading and Writing, 33*, 2697–2724. https://doi.org/10.1007/s11145-020-10060-2

Benware, C. A., & Deci, E. L. (1984). Quality of learning with an active versus passive motivational set. *American Educational Research Journal, 21*(4), 755–765. https://doi.org/10.3102/00028312021004755

Berliner, D. C. (2009). MCLB (much curriculum left behind): A U.S. calamity in the making. *The Educational Forum, 73*(4), 284–296. https://doi.org/10.1080/00131720903166788

Berliner, D. C. (2011). Rational responses to high stakes testing: The case of curriculum narrowing and the harm that follows. *Cambridge Journal of Education, 41*(3), 287–302. https://doi.org/10.1080/0305764X.2011.607151

Blinkoff, E., Bustamante, A. S., Burchinal, M., Gunersel, A. B., Golinkoff, R. M., & Hirsh Pasek, K. (2023). *Implementing district-level thematic instruction to support students' 21st-century skills.* Manuscript in preparation.

Bonawitz, E., Shafto, P., Gweon, H., Goodman, N. D., Spelke, E., & Schulz, L. (2011). The double-edged sword of pedagogy: Instruction limits spontaneous exploration and discovery. *Cognition, 120*(3), 322–330. https://doi.org/10.1016/j.cognition.2010.10.001

Brod, G. (2021). How can we make active learning work in K–12 education? Considering prerequisites for a successful construction of understanding. *Psychological Science in the Public Interest, 22*(1), 1–7. https://doi.org/10.1177/1529100621997376

Buelow, J. R., Barry, T. A., & Rich, L. E. (2018). Supporting learning engagement with online students. *Online Learning, 22*(4), 313–340. https://doi.org/10.24059/olj.v22i4.1384

Cabrera, A. F., Crissman, J. L., Bernal, E. M., Nora, A., Terenzini, P. T., & Pascarella, E. T. (2002). Collaborative learning: Its impact on college students' development and diversity. *Journal of College Student Development, 43*(1), 20–34.

Clark, S., & Newberry, M. (2019). Are we building preservice teacher self-efficacy? A large-scale study examining teacher education experiences. *Asia-Pacific Journal of Teacher Education, 47*(1), 32–47. https://doi.org/10.1080/1359866X.2018.1497772

Common Core State Standards Initiative. (2021). *About the standards.* https://www.thecorestandards.org/about-the-standards/#:~:text=The%20standards%20define%20the%20knowledge,courses%2C%20and%20workforce%20training%20programs

Cools, R. (2011). Dopaminergic control of the striatum for high-level cognition. *Current Opinion in Neurobiology, 21*(3), 402–407. https://doi.org/10.1016/j.conb.2011.04.002

Cooper, B. R., Moore, J. E., Powers, C. J., Cleveland, M., & Greenberg, M. T. (2014). Patterns of early reading and social skills associated with academic success in elementary school. *Early Education and Development, 25*(8), 1248–1264. https://doi.org/10.1080/10409289.2014.932236

Dang, L. C., Donde, A., Madison, C., O'Neill, J. P., & Jagust, W. J. (2012). Striatal dopamine influences the default mode network to affect shifting between object features. *Journal of Cognitive Neuroscience, 24*(9), 1960–1970. https://doi.org/10.1162/jocn_a_00252

Darling-Hammond, L., Barron, B., Pearson, P. D., Schoenfeld, A. H., Stage, E. K., Zimmerman, T. D., Cervetti, G. N., & Tilson, J. L. (2008). *Powerful learning: What we know about teaching for understanding.* Jossey-Bass.

Darling-Hammond, L., Flook, L., Cook-Harvey, C., Barron, B., & Osher, D. (2020). Implications for educational practice of the science of learning and development. *Applied Developmental Science, 24*(2), 97–140. https://doi.org/10.1080/10888691.2018.1537791

Darling-Hammond, L., Hammerness, K., Grossman, P., Rust, F., & Shulman, L. (2005). The design of teacher education programs. In L. Darling-Hammond, J. Bransford, P. LePage, K. Hammerness, & H. Duffy (Eds.), *Preparing teachers for a changing world: What teachers should learn and be able to do* (pp. 390–441). Jossey-Bass.

Darling-Hammond, L., & Oakes, J. (2019). *Preparing teachers for deeper learning.* Harvard Education Press.

Davis, M. R. (2020). Microsoft, Verizon, and other big U.S. companies design their ideal high school courses. *Education Week.* https://www.edweek.org/ew/articles/2020/02/05/if-you-could-design-a-high-school.html

Deslauriers, L., McCarty, L. S., Miller, K., Callaghan, K., & Kestin, G. (2019). Measuring actual learning versus feeling of learning in response to being actively engaged in the classroom. *Proceedings of the National Academy of Science, 116*(39), 19251–19257. https://doi.org/10.1073/pnas.1821936116

Diamond, A. (2014). Want to optimize executive functions and academic outcomes? Simple, just nourish the human spirit. In P. D. Zelazo & M. D. Sera (Eds.), *Minnesota symposia in child psychology: Developing cognitive control processes: Mechanisms, implications, and interventions* (pp. 205–230). John Wiley & Sons. https://doi.org/10.1002/9781118732373.ch7

Distefano, R., Galinsky, E., & Zelazo, P. D. (2020). The influence of neuroscience on early childhood education. In D. F. Gullo & M. E. Graue (Eds.), *Scientific influences on early childhood education: From diverse perspectives to common practices* (1st ed.). Routledge. https://doi.org/10.4324/9780429468285

Drummond, W. H., & Andrews, T. E. (1980). The influence of federal and state governments on teacher education. *The Phi Delta Kappan, 62*(2), 97–100. http://www.jstor.org/stable/20385767

Duckworth, A. L., Peterson, C., Matthews, M. D., & Kelly, D. R. (2007). Grit: Perseverance and passion for long-term goals. *Journal of Personality and Social Psychology, 92*(6), 1087–1101. https://psycnet.apa.org/doi/10.1037/0022-3514.92.6.1087

Duke, N. K., Halvorsen, A. L., Strachan, S. L., Kim, J., & Konstantopoulos, S. (2021). Putting PjBL to the test: The impact of project-based learning on second graders' social studies and literacy learning and motivation in low-SES school settings. *American Educational Research Journal, 58*(1), 160–200. https://doi.org/10.3102/0002831220929638

Duncan, G. J., Dowsett, C. J., Claessens, A., Magnuson, K., Huston, A. C., Klebanov, P., Pagani, L. S., Feinstein, L., Engel, M., Brooks-Gunn, J., Sexton, H., Duckworth, K., & Japel, C. (2007). School readiness and later achievement. *Developmental Psychology, 43*(6), 1428–1446. https://doi.org/10.1037/0012-1649.43.6.1428

Duque, G., Fung, S., Mallet, L., Posel, N., & Fleiszer, D. (2008). Learning while having fun: The use of video gaming to teach geriatric house calls to medical students. *Journal of the American Geriatrics Society, 56*(7), 1328–1332. https://doi.org/10.1111/j.1532-5415.2008.01759.x

Erbil, D. G., & Kocabaş, A. (2018). Cooperative learning as a democratic learning method. *Journal of Research in Childhood Education, 32*(1), 81–93. https://doi.org/10.1080/02568543.2017.1385548

Evans, N. S., Todaro, R. D., Schlesinger, M. A., Golinkoff, R. M., & Hirsh-Pasek, K. (2021). Examining the impact of children's exploration behaviors on creativity. *Journal of Experimental Child Psychology, 207,* 1–17. https://doi.org/10.1016/j.jecp.2021.105091

Ferlazzo, L. (2012, October 27). *Response: Working smarter, not harder, with neuroscience in the classroom.* Education Week. https://www.edweek.org/teaching-learning/opinion-response-working-smarter-not-harder-with-neuroscience-in-the-classroom/2012/10

Filipenko, M., & Naslund, J.-A. (Eds.). (2016). *Problem-based learning in teacher education.* Springer. https://doi.org/10.1007/978-3-319-02003-7

Fisher, A. V., Goodwin, K. E., & Seltman, H. (2014). Visual environment, attention allocation, and learning in young children: When too much of a good thing may be bad. *Psychological Science, 25*(7), 1362–1370. https://doi.org/10.1177/0956797614533801

Fisher, K. R., Hirsh-Pasek, K., Newcombe, N., & Golinkoff, R. M. (2013). Taking shape: Supporting preschoolers' acquisition of geometric knowledge through guided play. *Child Development, 84*(6), 1872–1878. https://doi.org/10.1111/cdev.12091

Fredricks, J. A., Blumenfeld, P. C., & Paris, A. H. (2004). School engagement: Potential of the concept, state of the evidence. *Review of Educational Research, 74*(1), 59–109. https://doi.org/10.3102/00346543074001059

Freeman, S., Eddy, S. L., McDonough, M., Smith, M. K., Okoroafor, N., Jordt, H., & Wenderoth, M. P. (2014). Active learning increases student performance in science, engineering, and mathematics. *Proceedings of the National Academy of Science, 111*(23), 8410–8415. https://doi.org/10.1073/pnas.1319030111

Garaigordobil, M., & Berrueco, L. (2011). Effects of a play program on creative thinking of preschool children. *The Spanish Journal of Psychology, 14*(2), 608–618. https://doi.org/10.5209/rev_SJOP.2011.v14.n2.9

Gay, G. (2000). *Culturally responsive teaching: Theory, research, and practice.* Teachers College Press.

Gay, G. (2002). Preparing for culturally responsive teaching. *Journal of Teacher Education, 53*(2), 106–116. https://doi.org/10.1177/0022487102053002003

Gelman, R., & Gallistel, C. R. (1986). *The child's understanding of number.* Harvard University Press.

Glisczinski, D. J. (2007). Transformative higher education: A meaningful degree of understanding. *Journal of Transformative Education, 5*(4), 317–328. https://doi.org/10.1177/1541344607312838

Golinkoff, R. M., & Hirsh-Pasek, K. (2016). *Becoming brilliant: What science tells us about raising successful children.* American Psychological Association. https://doi.org/10.1037/14917-000

Grabinger, R. S., & Dunlap, J. C. (1995). Rich environments for active learning: A definition. *Research in Learning Technology, 3*(2), 5–34. https://doi.org/10.1080/0968776950030202

Grossman, P., Hammerness, K., & McDonald, M. (2009). Redefining teaching, re-imagining teacher education. *Teachers and Teaching: Theory and Practice, 15*(2), 273–289. https://doi.org/10.1080/13540600902875340

Haimovitz, K., & Dweck, C. S. (2017). The origins of children's growth and fixed mindsets: New research and a new proposal. *Child Development, 88*(6), 1849–1859. https://doi.org/10.1111/cdev.12955

Hake, R. R. (1998). Interactive-engagement versus traditional methods: A six-thousand-student survey of mechanics test data for introductory physics courses. *American Journal of Physics, 66*(1), 64–74. https://doi.org/10.1119/1.18809

Halpern, D. F. (2014). *Thought and knowledge: An introduction to critical thinking* (5th ed.). Psychology Press.

Halpern, D. F., & Dunn, D. S. (2021). Critical thinking: A model of intelligence for solving real-world problems. *Journal of Intelligence, 9*(2), 1–7. https://doi.org/10.3390/jintelligence9020022

Halpern, D., & Sternberg, R. (Eds.). (2020). *Critical thinking in psychology* (2nd ed.). Cambridge University Press. https://doi.org/10.1017/9781108684354

Hargrave, A. C., & Sénéchal, M. (2000). A book reading intervention with preschool children who have limited vocabularies: The benefits of regular reading and dialogic reading. *Early Childhood Research Quarterly, 15*(1), 75–90. https://doi.org/10.1016/S0885-2006(99)00038-1

Hirsh-Pasek, K., Golinkoff, R. M., Nesbitt, K., Lautenbach, C., Blinkoff, E., & Fifer, G. (2022). *Making schools work: Bringing the science of learning to joyful classroom practice.* Teachers College Press.

Hirsh-Pasek, K., Hadani, H. S., Blinkoff, E., & Golinkoff, R. M. (2020). *A new path to education reform: Playful learning promotes 21st-century skills in schools and beyond.* The Brookings Institution. https://www.brookings.edu/wp-content/uploads/2020/10/Big-Ideas_Hirsh-Pasek_PlayfulLearning.pdf

Hirsh-Pasek, K., Zosh, J. M., Golinkoff, R. M., Gray, J. H., Robb, M. B., & Kaufman, J. (2015). Putting education in "educational" apps: Lessons from the science of learning. *Psychological Science in the Public Interest, 16*(1), 3–34. https://doi.org/10.1177/1529100615569721

Huang, M.-Y., Tu, H-Y., Wang, W.-Y., Chen, J.-F., Yu, Y.-T., & Chou, C.-C. (2017). Effects of cooperative learning and concept mapping intervention on critical thinking and basketball skills in elementary school. *Thinking Skills and Creativity, 23,* 207–216. http://dx.doi.org/10.1016/j.tsc.2017.01.002

Hurst, B., Wallace, R., & Nixon, S. B. (2013). The impact of social interaction on student learning. *Reading Horizons: A Journal of Literacy and Language Arts, 52*(4). https://scholarworks.wmich.edu/reading_horizons/vol52/iss4/5

Isen, A. M. (1984). Toward understanding the role of affect in cognition. In R. S. Wyer, Jr., & T. K. Srull (Eds.), *Handbook of social cognition* (pp. 179–236). Lawrence Erlbaum Associates.

Jirout, J. (2020). Supporting early scientific thinking through curiosity. *Frontiers in Psychology, 11,* 1717. https://doi.org/10.3389/fpsyg.2020.01717

Kalstabakken, A. W., Desjardins, C. D., Anderson, J. E., Berghuis, K. J., Hillyer, C. K., Seiwert, M. J., Carlson, S. M., Zelazo, P. D., & Masten, A. S. (2021). Executive function measures in early childhood screening: Concurrent and predictive validity. *Early Childhood Research Quarterly, 57,* 144–155. https://doi.org/10.1016/j.ecresq.2021.05.009

Kaufman, J. H., Opfer, V., Bongard, M., & Pane, J. D. (2018). *Changes in what teachers know and do in the Common Core era: American teacher panel findings from 2015 to 2017.* RAND Corporation. https://www.rand.org/pubs/research_reports/RR2658.html

King, A. (1993). From sage on the stage to guide on the side. *College Teaching, 41*(1), 30–35. https://doi.org/10.1080/87567555.1993.9926781

Kuenzi, J. J. (2018). *Teacher preparation policies and issues in the Higher Education Act.* Congressional Research Service. https://files.eric.ed.gov/fulltext/ED593607.pdf

Ladson-Billings, G. (1995a). But that's just good teaching! The case for culturally relevant pedagogy. *Theory Into Practice, 34*(3), 159–165. https://doi.org/10.1080/00405849509543675

Ladson-Billings, G. (1995b). Toward a theory of culturally relevant pedagogy. *American Educational Research Journal, 32*(3), 465–491. https://doi.org/10.3102/00028312032003465

Ladson-Billings, G. (2021). *Culturally relevant pedagogy: Asking a different question.* Teachers College Press.

Lazonder, A. W., & Harmsen, R. (2016). Meta-analysis of inquiry-based learning: Effects of guidance. *Review of Educational Research, 86*(3), 681–718. https://doi.org/10.3102/0034654315627366

Learning Policy Institute & Turnaround for Children. (2021). *Design principles for schools: Putting the science of learning and development into action.* https://k12.designprinciples.org/sites/default/files/SoLD_Design_Principles_REPORT.pdf

Lindquist, S. I., & McLean, J. P. (2011). Daydreaming and its correlates in an educational environment. *Learning and Individual Differences, 21*(2), 158–167. https://doi.org/10.1016/j.lindif.2010.12.006

Lonning, R. A., DeFranco, C. T., & Weinland, T. P. (2010). Development of theme-based, interdisciplinary, integrated curriculum: A theoretical model. *School Science and Mathematics, 98*(6), 312–319. https://doi.org/10.1111/j.1949-8594.1998.tb17426.x

Lou, Y., Abrami, P. C., Spence, J. C., Poulsen, C., Chambers, B., & d'Apollonia, S. (1996). Within-class grouping: A meta-analysis. *Review of Educational Research, 66*(4), 423–458. https://doi.org/10.2307/1170650

Love, B. L. (2015). What is hip-hop-based education doing in *nice* fields such as early childhood and elementary education? *Urban Education, 50*(1), 106–131. https://doi.org/10.1177/0042085914563182

Loveless, T. (2021). *Between the state and the schoolhouse: Understanding the failure of Common Core.* Harvard Education Press.

Lucardie, D. (2014). The impact of fun and enjoyment on adult's learning. *Procedia–Social and Behavioral Sciences, 142*, 439–466. https://doi.org/10.1016/j.sbspro.2014.07.696

Lucas, B. (2016). A five-dimensional model of creativity and its assessment in schools. *Applied Measurement in Education, 29*(4), 278–290. https://doi.org/10.1080/08957347.2016.1209206

Macdonald, K., Germine, L., Anderson, A., Christodoulou, J., & McGrath, L. M. (2017). Dispelling the myth: Training in education or neuroscience decreases but does not eliminate beliefs in neuromyths. *Frontiers in Psychology, 8*, 1314, 1–16. https://doi.org/10.3389/fpsyg.2017.01314

Manz, P. H., Hughes, C., Barnabas, E., Bracaliello, C., & Ginsburg-Block, M. (2010). A descriptive review and meta-analysis of family-based emergent literacy interventions: To what extent is the research applicable to low-income, ethnic-minority or linguistically-diverse young children? *Early Childhood Research Quarterly, 25*(4), 409–431. https://doi.org/10.1016/j.ecresq.2010.03.002

Mayer, R. E. (2002). Rote versus meaningful learning. *Theory Into Practice, 41*(4), 226–232. https://doi.org/10.1207/s15430421tip4104_4

Mazur, E. (2009). Farewell, lecture? *Science, 323*(5910), 50–51. https://doi.org/10.1126/science.1168927

McClelland, M. M., Cameron, C. E., Connor, C. M., Farris, C. L., Jewkes, A. M., & Morrison, F. J. (2007). Links between behavioral regulation and preschoolers' literacy, vocabulary, and math skills. *Developmental Psychology, 43*(4), 947–959. https://doi.org/10.1037/0012-1649.43.4.947

Meltzoff, A. N., Kuhl, P. K., Movellan, J., & Sejnowski, T. J. (2009). Foundations for a new science of learning. *Science, 325*(5938), 284–288. https://doi.org/10.1126/science.1175626

Melzi, G., Schick, A. R., & Scarola, L. (2019). Literacy interventions that promote home-to-school links for ethnoculturally diverse families of young children. In C. M. McWayne, F. Doucet, & S. M. Sheridan (Eds.), *Ethnocultural diversity and the home-to-school link* (pp. 123–143). Springer. https://doi.org/10.1007/978-3-030-14957-4_8

Moll, L. C., Amanti, C., Neff, D., & Gonzalez, N. (1992). Funds of knowledge for teaching: Using a qualitative approach to connect homes and classrooms. *Theory Into Practice, 31*(12), 132–141. https://doi.org/10.1080/00405849209543534

Moreno, R., Mayer, R. E., Spires, H. A., & Lester, J. C. (2001). The case for social agency in computer-based teaching: Do students learn more deeply when they interact with animated pedagogical agents? *Cognition and Instruction, 19*(2), 177–213. https://doi.org/10.1207/S1532690XCI1902_02

Moskowitz, S., & Dewaele, J.-M. (2021). Is teacher happiness contagious? A study of the link between perceptions of language teacher happiness and student attitudes. *Innovation in Language Learning and Teaching, 15*(2), 117–130. https://doi.org/10.1080/17501229.2019.1707205

Motz, B., Fyfe, E. R., & Guba, T. P. (2021). *Learning to call bullsh*t via induction: Categorization training improves critical thinking performance.* https://doi.org/10.31234/osf.io/65qfj

Mueller, P. A., & Oppenheimer, D. M. (2014). The pen is mightier than the keyboard: Advantages of longhand over laptop note taking. *Psychological Science, 25*(6), 1159–1168. https://doi.org/10.1177/0956797614524581

Nasir, N. S., Lee, C. D., Pea, R., & McKinney deRoyston, M. (2021). Rethinking learning: What the interdisciplinary science tells us. *Educational Researcher, 50*(8), 557–565. https://doi.org/10.3102/0013189X211047251

Neuman, S. B., Samudra, P., & Danielson, K. (2021). Effectiveness of scaling up a vocabulary intervention for low-income children, pre-K through first grade. *The Elementary School Journal, 121*(3), 385–409. https://doi.org/10.1086/712492

Novak, E., & Wisdom, S. (2018). Effects of 3D printing project-based learning on preservice elementary teachers' science attitudes, science content knowledge, and anxiety about teaching science. *Journal of Science Education and Technology, 27*, 412–432. https://doi.org/10.1007/s10956-018-9733-5

O'Reilly, T., Wang, Z., & Sabatini, J. (2019). How much knowledge is too little? When a lack of knowledge becomes a barrier to comprehension. *Psychological Science, 30*(9), 1344–1351. https://doi.org/10.1177/0956797619862276

Ouellette, G. P. (2006). What's meaning got to do with it: The role of vocabulary in word reading and reading comprehension. *Journal of Educational Psychology, 98*(3), 554–566. https://doi.org/10.1037/0022-0663.98.3.554

Pace, A., Alper, R., Burchinal, M. R., Golinkoff, R. M., & Hirsh-Pasek, K. (2019). Measuring success: Within and cross-domain predictors of academic and social trajectories in elementary school. *Early Childhood Research Quarterly, 46*, 112–125. https://doi.org/10.1016/j.ecresq.2018.04.001

Passeri, S. M. R. R., & Mazur, E. (2019). Peer instruction-based feedback sessions improve the retention of knowledge in medical students. *Revista Brasileira de Educação Médica, 43*(3), 155–162. https://doi.org/10.1590/1981-527120 15v43n2RB20180230

Piazza, E. A., Hasenfratz, L., Hasson, U., & Lew-Williams, C. (2020). Infant and adult brains are coupled to the dynamics of natural communication. *Psychological Science, 31*(1), 6–17. https://doi.org/10.1177/0956797619878698

Potts, R., & Shanks, D. R. (2014). The benefit of generating errors during learning. *Journal of Experimental Psychology: General, 143*(2), 644–667. https://doi.org/10.1037/a0033194

Ramani, G. B. (2012). Influence of a playful, child-directed context on preschool children's peer cooperation. *Merrill-Palmer Quarterly, 58*(2), 159–190. http://www.jstor.org/stable/23098461

Richardson, C., & Mishra, P. (2018). Learning environments that support student creativity: Developing SCALE. *Thinking Skills and Creativity, 27,* 45–54. https://doi.org/10.1016/j.tsc.2017.11.004

Risko, E. F., Buchanan, D., Medimorec, S., & Kingstone, A. (2013). Everyday attention: Mind wandering and computer use during lectures. *Computers & Education, 68,* 275–283. https://doi.org/10.1016/j.compedu.2013.05.001

Rogoff, B. (2003). *The cultural nature of human development.* Oxford University Press.

Sana, F., Weston, T., & Cepeda, N. J. (2013). Laptop multitasking hinders classroom learning for both users and nearby peers. *Computers & Education, 62,* 24–31. https://doi.org/10.1016/j.compedu.2012.10.003

Sawyer, R. K. (2014). Introduction: The new science of learning. In R. K. Sawyer (Ed.), *The Cambridge handbook of the learning sciences* (2nd ed., pp. 1–18). Cambridge University Press.

Schell, J., & Mazur, E. (2015). Flipped the chemistry classroom with peer instruction. In J. Garcia-Martinez & E. Serrano-Torregrosa (Eds.), *Chemistry education: Best practices, opportunities, and trends* (pp. 319–334). Wiley-VCH.

Schooler, J. W., Mrazek, M. D., Franklin, M. S., Baird, B., Mooneyham, B. W., Zedelius, C., & Broadway, J. M. (2014). The middle way: Finding the balance between mindfulness and mind-wandering. In B. H. Ross (Ed.), *The psychology of learning and motivation* (pp. 1–33). Burlington Academic Press.

Schulz, L. E., & Bonawitz, E. B. (2007). Serious fun: Preschoolers engage in more exploratory play when evidence is confounded. *Developmental Psychology, 43*(4), 1045–1050. https://doi.org/10.1037/0012-1649.43.4.1045

Schwartz, S. (2020). *How top teachers make student voice a high priority.* Education Week. https://www.edweek.org/teaching-learning/how-top-teachers-make-student-voice-a-high-priority/2020/03

Serrano, R., & Huang, H.-Y. (2023). Time distribution and intentional vocabulary learning through repeated reading: A partial replication and extension. *Language Awareness, 32*(1), 1–18. https://doi.org/10.1080/09658416.2021.1894162

Shanahan, T., Robinson, B., & Schneider, M. (1995). Integrating Curriculum: Avoiding some of the pitfalls of thematic units. *The Reading Teacher, 48*(8), 718–719. https://www.jstor.org/stable/20201542

Shaw, N. (2012). *The teaching profession* [Syllabus]. Texas A&M University Commerce.

Slavin, R. E. (2014). Making cooperative learning powerful. *Educational Leadership, 72*(2), 22–26.

Sokoloff, D. R., & Thornton, R. K. (1997). Using interactive lecture demonstrations to create an active learning environment. *The Physics Teacher, 35*(6), 340–347. https://doi.org/10.1119/1.2344715

Springer, M. (1994). *Watershed: A successful voyage into integrative learning*. National Middle School Association.

Stahl, A. E., & Feigenson, L. (2017). Expectancy violations promote learning in young children. *Cognition, 163*, 1–14. https://doi.org/10.1016/j.cognition.2017.02.008

Tamis-LeMonda, C. S., Kuchirko, Y., & Song, L. (2014). Why is infant language learning facilitated by parental responsiveness? *Current Directions in Psychological Science, 23*(2), 121–126. https://doi.org/10.1177%2F0963721414522813

U.S. Census Bureau. (2022). *QuickFacts: Radnor Township, Delaware County, Pennsylvania*. U.S. Census Bureau. https://www.census.gov/quickfacts/radnortownshipdelawarecountypennsylvania

Versteeg, M., van Blankenstein, F. M., Putter, H., & Steendijk, P. (2019). Peer instruction improves comprehension and transfer of physiological concepts: A randomized comparison with self-explanation. *Advances in Health Sciences Education, 24*, 151–165. https://doi.org/10.1007/s10459-018-9858-6

Vitiello, V. E., Booren, L. M., Downer, J. T., & Williford, A. (2012). Variation in children's classroom engagement throughout a day in preschool: Relations to classroom and child factors. *Early Childhood Research Quarterly, 27*(2), 210–220. https://doi.org/10.1016/j.ecresq.2011.08.005

Vygotsky, L. S. (1987). *Mind in society: The development of higher psychological processes*. Harvard University Press.

Wagner, T. (2008). Rigor redefined. *Educational Leadership, 66*(2), 20–25. https://www.ascd.org/el/articles/rigor-redefined

Wahyuni, A. (2017). The power of verbal and nonverbal communication in learning. In *Proceedings of the 1st International Conference on Intellectuals' Global Responsibility (ICIGR 2017)* (pp. 80–83). https://doi.org/10.2991/icigr-17.2018.19

Wallis, C., & Steptoe, S. (2006). How to bring our schools out of the 20th century. *Time*. http://content.time.com/time/subscriber/article/0,33009,1568480,00.html

Walraven, A., Brand-Gruwel, S., & Boshuizen, H. P. A. (2009). How students evaluate information and sources when searching the World Wide Web for information. *Computers & Education, 52*(1), 234–246. https://doi.org/10.1016/j.compedu.2008.08.003

Walsh, K. (2013). 21st-century teacher education. *Education Next, 13*(3). https://www.educationnext.org/21st-century-teacher-education/

Webb, P. K. (1980). Piaget: Implications for teaching. *Theory Into Practice, 19*(2), 93–97. https://doi.org/10.1080/00405848009542880

Weisberg, D. S., Hirsh-Pasek, K., Golinkoff, R. M., Kittredge, A. K., & Klahr, D. (2016). Guided play: Principles and practices. *Current Directions in Psychological Science, 25*(3), 177–182. https://doi.org/10.1177/0963721416645512

Wetzel, N., Scharf, F., & Widmann, A. (2019). Can't ignore—Distraction by task-irrelevant sounds in early and middle childhood. *Child Development, 90*(6), e819–e830. https://doi.org/10.1111/cdev.13109

Whitehurst, G. J., Arnold, D. S., Epstein, J. N., Angell, A. L., Smith, M., & Fischel, J. E. (1994). A picture book reading intervention in daycare and home for children from low-income families. *Developmental Psychology, 30*(5), 679–689. https://doi.org/10.1037/0012-1649.30.5.679

Whitten, C., Labby, S., & Sullivan, S. L. (2016). The impact of pleasure reading on academic success. *The Journal of Multidisciplinary Graduate Research, 2,* 48–64. https://jmgr-ojs-shsu.tdl.org/jmgr/index.php/jmgr/article/view/11/10

Willis, J. (2007). The neuroscience of joyful education. *Educational Leadership, 64*(9). https://www.ascd.org/el/articles/the-neuroscience-of-joyful-education

Wolf, S. J., & Fraser, B. J. (2008). Learning environment, attitudes, and achievement among middle-school science students using inquiry-based laboratory activities. *Research in Science Education, 38,* 321–341. https://doi.org/10.1007/s11165-007-9052-y

Yalçin, S. A., Yalçin, P., Akar, M. S., & Sağirli, M. Ö. (2017). The effect of teaching practices with real life content in light and sound learning areas. *Universal Journal of Educational Research, 5*(9), 1621–1631. https://doi.org/10.13189/ujer.2017.050920

Zinski, A., Blackwell, K. T. C. P. W., Belue, F. M., & Brooks, W. S. (2017). Is lecture dead? A preliminary study of medical students' evaluation of teaching methods in the preclinical curriculum. *International Journal of Medical Education, 8,* 326–333. https://doi.org/10.5116/ijme.59b9.5f40

Zosh, J. M., Brinster, M., & Halberda, J. (2013). Optimal contrast: Competition between two referents improves word learning. *Applied Developmental Science, 17*(1), 20–28. https://doi.org/10.1080/10888691.2013.748420

Zosh, J. M., Gaudreau, C., Golinkoff, R. M., & Hirsh-Pasek, K. (2022). The power of playful learning in the early childhood setting. In S. Friedman, S. Bredekamp, M. Masterson, B. Willer, & B. L. Wright (Eds.), *Developmentally appropriate practice in early childhood programs serving children from birth through age 8* (4th ed., pp. 81–107). NAEYC.

Zosh, J. M., Hirsh-Pasek, K., Hopkins, E. J., Jensen, H., Liu, C., Neale, D., Solis, S. L., & Whitebread, D. (2018). Accessing the inaccessible: Redefining play as a spectrum. *Frontiers in Psychology, 9,* 1124. https://doi.org/10.3389/fpsyg.2018.01124

CHAPTER 3

THE STUDENT AS A DEVELOPING PERSON IN CONTEXT

Socio-Ecological Theory, Intersectionality, and Social Justice

Gabriel Velez
Marquette University

Keshia Harris
University of Colorado Boulder

Carly Offidani-Bertrand
California State University San Marcos

Understanding the role of human development in education is important. Social, environmental, and interpersonal factors interact to influence developmental processes, learning opportunities, and outcomes from childhood through adulthood. Unfortunately, every student's capacity to learn is not valued equally in the current U.S. education system. Learners from marginalized backgrounds (e.g., women, students with disabilities, LGBTQ youth, minoritized students) often encounter long-standing structural barriers that lead to roadblocks in their educational experiences and shape their identities and life trajectories (Chaney, 2014; Kuhfeld et al., 2018). Course tracking and socioeconomic status undermine intelligence and academic performance of Black and Latinx students and drive racial–ethnic achievement gaps (Bowman et al., 2018; Chambers, 2009; Kotok, 2017). This stratification in K–12 schooling persists into higher education and the U.S. labor market (Sullivan et al., 2016). Inequities in educational experiences and outcomes operate at multiple levels; stemming from broader inequalities tied to societal norms and values and influencing intimate experiences and socialization within classrooms. For example, structural inequalities create persistent experiences of marginalization and oppression for students of color and shape interpersonal relationships between educators and students (Okonofua & Eberhardt, 2015).

As scholars trained to account for ecological systems, we propose that in order to address the ways racial inequality manifests itself within different levels of society (institutionally, interpersonally, and individually) educators must understand their students as developing agents who respond to and understand racial inequality in dynamic interaction within systems of their socio-ecological context. Our chapter aims to provide a theoretical rationale, building from Bronfenbrenner's (1976) ecological systems theory, for why it is essential for instructors of educational psychology to teach human development theory to preservice and in-service teachers. Understanding the developmental processes and challenges that students face is critical to fostering orientations and strategies in educators that are attuned to how young people experience, interpret, and respond to injustice and inequity.

Given the vulnerability of racially marginalized groups in educational settings, bringing developmental perspectives to education is imperative. In this chapter, we argue teaching human development to future educators through socio-ecological theory—specifically Spencer's phenomenological variant of ecological systems theory (PVEST; Spencer et al., 1997)—can provide effective tools to pursue social justice and equity within the classroom. PVEST can help educators understand variance in diverse students' needs and be sensitive to the complexities of how dynamic, multifaceted ecosystems shape students' development. Furthermore, it is increasingly critical for 21st century pedagogical practices to incorporate understandings of cultural variance in learning and communication given the needs of students of a variety of racial and ethnic backgrounds (Spencer et al., 2020). PVEST offers a framework to untangle these complexities: centering the student, drawing attention to unique intersectionalities and how they are experienced by these young people, and providing a clear way to approach individual students as agents responding to context (Velez & Spencer, 2018). Using PVEST in training future educators can foster a richer understanding of their students as holistic, dynamic, and contextually-situated developing individuals in order to better serve their educational needs.

In the first section, we offer evidence for the usefulness of conceptualizing student learning in the context of human development. We address how socio-ecological frameworks can help contextualize individuals within broader social systems and understand the unique developmental processes of a given student. Second, we describe how to use PVEST to better prepare educators to support youth from marginalized backgrounds. We provide empirical examples of how a shift to this more nuanced understanding can reframe thinking about Black, Brown, and other marginalized young people (including those with identities situated at interlocking systems of oppression). Finally, building on this theoretical and empirical basis, we address what applicable and necessary tools PVEST can offer future educators to address inequity, promote social justice, and implement anti-racist teaching in classrooms.

SOCIO-ECOLOGICAL FRAMEWORKS ON HUMAN DEVELOPMENT

Education research has worked to untangle and delineate the many pathways through which broader social environments impact individuals, and particularly to understand how educational contexts shape the unique learning and developmental processes of students. This body of research largely attests to the fact that learning, and teaching, is a relational process embedded in multilayered social contexts (Gergen, 2009; Gross & Lo, 2018). It shows how social relationships between educators and students, and the feelings these relationships generate, matter for the ways individuals focus, persist, and ultimately learn (Fish & Syed, 2018; Spencer et al., 2020). Understanding the complexity of these relationships and contexts requires a robust theoretical model to connect these dynamics, learning, and human development. We propose that incorporating Bronfenbrenner's and Spencer's theoretical models of socio-ecological and recursive developmental processes can help educators respond to the diverse needs of their students and address sources of educational inequality.

Educators would benefit from approaching their relationships with students with a more explicit understanding of the ways that inequality shapes students' lives at multiple levels of their social world, as well as the ways they can play a role in supporting diverse students who navigate these challenges. One of the most important theoretical models in the fields of education and developmental science is Bronfenbrenner's ecological systems theory, which pushed these fields to move beyond the individualist focus that characterizes psychology to account for the interplay between the environment and individuals in children's development and learning (Anderson et al., 2014; Bronfenbrenner, 1973, 1976; Fish & Syed, 2018). The ecological systems model presented a structure through which developmental scientists could identify and organize social and environmental factors impacting children, such as relationships and interconnections across contexts. Bronfenbrenner's model can thus help educators move from thinking just about an individual student and their success or struggle in learning in the classroom to seeing a holistic, developing person responding adaptively to experiences within educational institutions, as well as within their broader environment. It also brings into the learning context diverse identities, community and family dynamics, and relationships with peers and teachers.

Bronfenbrenner (1976) characterized an individual's environment as an ecological system containing a "nested arrangement of structures" (p. 5). This system starts at the innermost level with individuals and their core psychological phenomena and progresses towards more external levels of social context (Bronfenbrenner, 1973, 1976). The microsystem, the second level of the model, consists of the developing individual's experiences with those who have direct contact and relationships with them such as parents, siblings, teachers, and peers. The mesosystem, the third level, refers to the interrelations between the actors and settings in the microsystem, for example relationships between the individual's teachers and parents. The fourth level, the exosystem, contains formal and informal structures pervading microsystems and mesosystems, including schools, community organizations, and neighborhoods. The outermost level in terms of structure is the macrosystem, which describes broader social and cultural elements that shape and influence relationships in the lower levels of the system, such as cultural ideologies, socioeconomic status, or racial hierarchies. Finally, the chrono-system adds a third dimension to the model and refers to the ways that interrelationships between the various levels within the system develop over time to impact developmental processes and outcomes.

Though it originated with a focus on integrating the influence of social contexts into developmental science, Bronfenbrenner's model has taken hold in education because of its applied utility for understanding young people's learning and maturation. When it was developed in the 1960s and 1970s, the model was revolutionary as a theoretical framework that did not attempt to eliminate or reduce the complexity of social environments and their impact on the individual, but instead provided a structure through which the many elements and levels could be organized and understood (Fish & Syed, 2018). This social ecological theory has since been adapted to the field of education to study the way characteristics of the learner and educational environments interact to shape student learning (Anderson et al., 2014). Educators and researchers use this model as a "conceptual and operational framework" (De Wet, 2010; Daro & Dodge, 2009, p. 39) to better understand the role of various direct and indirect contextual factors on child development, as well as the way individual experiences and social relationships influence learning over time. Particularly, the ecological systems model has been employed to better conceptualize the experiences of different racial-ethnic groups within diverse educational contexts, and the way cultural norms and institutional expectations interact with implications for diverse students' experiences (Anderson et al., 2014; Spencer et al., 2020).

One of the defining features of Bronfenbrenner's model is the conceptualization of the environment from the developing person's perspective. Others have expanded on this model to further emphasize the role of perception and phenomenological experience. Margaret Beale Spencer observed that though individuals may experience the same or similar environmental contexts and factors, their developmental trajectories are shaped by how they perceive and experience the context (Spencer, 2007). Her model—PVEST, the phenomenological variant of ecological systems theory (see Figure 3.1; Spencer et al., 1997)—can help scholars and educators make sense of the ways an individual's unique experiences inform

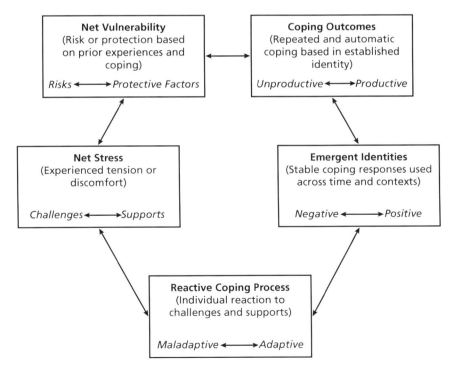

Figure 3.1 Spencer's PVEST (based on Spencer & Tinsley, 2008).

their interpretation and understanding of their socio-ecological environment, with implications for developmental processes and outcomes. PVEST outlines recursive meaning making processes that impact how net vulnerability—a balance of risk and protective factors—shapes young people's responses to stressors and interpretation of social and cultural context. These developmental processes consist of recursively testing various coping strategies—drawing on supports while engaging with challenges—that become internalized over time as underlying individual identities.

The PVEST model has been shown to be particularly useful in terms of examining the variable pathways through which young people who hold intersectional racial, ethnic, gender and cultural identities negotiate the complex implications of their particular social positions, including learning how they fit into their culturally specific social groups (e.g., Thompson et al., 2013; Velez & Spencer, 2018). Young people make sense of themselves and come to situate their identities relationally, in response to social information from their environment. Developing youth learn to adapt to the demands of their sociocultural environment and these coping processes shape their daily experiences and long-term processes of identity formation. The PVEST model helps researchers and educators understand how maladaptive behavioral outcomes can emerge as adaptive responses to a social context that poses many challenges and lacks opportunities for support. Young people perceive and respond to stereotypes and prejudices they encounter within their environment, and this shapes their understanding of their role in their society, and consequently impacts their identities. Accordingly, it also can help educators understand the importance of proactive educational strategies that can help young people not only learn educational content but also receive the support they need to construct positive identities as learners. For young people to be successful within institutions of learning, they must learn how to feel confident navigating these institutions and to interpret challenges as opportunities for growth as opposed to evidence of their lack of capacity. Researchers and educators can also use PVEST to consider their own positionality and the implications of their identities in interaction with those of students, in order to reflect on social dynamics that shape how students perceive and interpret their actions.

Bronfenbrenner and Spencer's models are foundational theories that have informed many initiatives to develop inclusive educational supports that are attentive to diverse student needs and perspectives, particularly for historically marginalized students. Still, within educational literature there tends to be an emphasis on examining the impacts of particular "objective" risk factors (such as SES or race) in the socio-ecological context (e.g., Condly, 2006; Velez & Spencer, 2018), without a corresponding understanding of the ways that unique variations within an individual's personal and social characteristics will differentially shape how these risk factors are perceived, understood, and ultimately managed. Alternatively, there is a considerable amount of literature dedicated to identifying "objective" supports that can facilitate student success, though we know that not all educational interventions are perceived as positive or supportive despite their intentions (Fish & Syed, 2018; Spencer, 1999). Bringing phenomenological experience to the fore via PVEST can elucidate the developmental coping and identity processes that young people go through in the process of learning and adapting to educational institutions.

PVEST AS A CONCEPTUAL TOOL FOR EDUCATING EDUCATORS

Educators must understand the variability in perception and needs of their diverse students to be reflexive and responsive in these relationships. Educators must also be aware of the different capacities and supports students from different cultural backgrounds bring to the table, rather than simply holding all students to standards and expectations that are dictated by a primarily White cultural environment. Educators must move past stereotypes to truly value the strengths and resilience of historically marginalized groups and the individuals that come from them. PVEST can facilitate personal reflection among educators on their own identities in ways that can allow them to be more compassionate in their relationships with students. Ultimately, learning is best supported in an environment in which students feel confident enough to make mistakes without fearing judgment or punishment, and this can only occur when educators and students have positive and mutually supportive relationships (Gross & Lo, 2018).

In this section, we elaborate on this applied utility of PVEST. We first discuss the value for student educators to learn about psychosocial development, and then detail how PVEST can serve as a framework for understanding and working with students. We provide examples drawn from empirical studies that specifically employ PVEST to demonstrate these connections.

Understanding Development as an Educator

Educators in K–12 schools in the United States face many demands. Interactions with students at the interpersonal level are shaped by a multitude of pressures across ecosystems (such as standardized testing, time limitations, students' family expectations, and social dynamics outside the classroom). These are real challenges with roots in structural conditions beyond educators' control. Still, it is important for educators to have the frameworks and tools to understand how central goals of education—that is, students' development as individuals and learners—link to events, trends, norms, and expectations at individual, interpersonal, and structural levels.

In reference to institutions and educational systems, a rich understanding of human development is powerful in deconstructing problematic traditional models of education. Many systems of education prioritize "banking models," wherein students are conceptualized (often implicitly) as empty receptacles into which knowledge must be transferred. Educators' main task is to transmit knowledge, with relational and contextual factors only mattering as they affect this process (Freire, 1970/1993). Ecosystem theories, however, are fundamentally in opposition to this framework for students' maturation and intellectual growth. Learning is a developmental process shaped by relationships and interactions, embedded within different levels of sociocultural context, and driven by the individual's agentic action. The process of a student learning effectively and developing a sense of educational self-efficacy as a part of their identity is inherently informed by what is going on around them, social dynamics, their understandings of themselves, and their relations and interactions with others in educational settings.

A second problematic element that pervades many modern educational systems is bias and stereotyping, whether conscious or implicit. Even if educators share identities with their students, socialized presuppositions of class, gender, socioeconomic status, and race/ethnicity can inform how educators treat students (e.g., Jussim & Harber, 2005). Socially salient ideas—for example, about who an Asian-American, female, wealthy, urban student is like—can influence how an educator might approach and interact with an individual—for example, the Asian-American, female, wealthy, urban high school freshman in their class. Nuanced understandings of development push educators to eschew generalized ways of thinking about students, reflect on and deconstruct their positionality, and appreciate the impact biases and stereotypes have on young students. Knowledge of developmental theory alone may not address issues of bias and stereotypes (especially implicit expressions) but can be an important foundation for recognizing the influence of socialized stereotypes and categories on the individual identities of educators and students (i.e., individually) and in relationships between the two (i.e., interpersonally).

PVEST: A Framework for Educators

Beginning at the individual level, a core element of PVEST is that all humans are vulnerable. Privilege, challenges, cultural upbringing, family dynamics, and classroom interventions are not inherently helpful or harmful. Rather, young people experience these events and processes as part of a dynamic system in which they are embedded. A second element is that developing individuals have agency within overlapping socio-ecological systems. Attitudes, behaviors, and outcomes are not essentialized as results of an individual's intellectual ability, personality, or race/ethnicity—to name just a few possibilities—but rather as active coping strategies that emerge in response to environmental challenges and supports. These processes and responses are shaped by developing identities, which are formed in relation to interpersonal and systems dynamics: norms and expectations about who they are or should be. For example, stereotypes about Black male youth inform how a Black male high school student makes sense of future opportunities, who they are, their potential as a learner (i.e., at an individual level), and what others expect of them (i.e., at an interpersonal level). A focus on vulnerability and adaptive coping is beneficial to educators in development as a guide to move beyond the surface level of what they see from students. It can draw attention away from a sole focus on behaviors and outcomes in the classroom to reveal the more complex meaning-making processes that underlie them, as students make sense of and cope with the world around them (i.e., at an institutional level), including stereotypes and biases.

Overall, PVEST can contribute to the training of future educators by guiding nuanced thinking about students to move beyond traditional passive banking models of teaching and learning, as well as problematic cycles of bias and stereotypes. It draws attention to how students may be entering, experiencing, and coping with classrooms, schools, and other institutionalized educational settings. For example, a teacher's efforts to provide extra guidance or academic support to a student may be perceived as intrusive or embarrassing. On the other hand, a disciplinary infraction may be intended to serve as a necessary limit to maintain class order in a learning environment, but may be interpreted as a reputation threat that requires response.

The focus on interpretation and agency also challenges educators to eschew deterministic frameworks. Students' backgrounds—for example, racial/ethnic, cultural identities, experiences of trauma—may present risk or protective factors, but these alone do not determine students' experience of challenge and support or coping responses. PVEST draws attention to how students perceive and cope with individual (e.g., struggling to understand concepts), interpersonal (e.g., interactions with teachers), and structural and systemic (e.g., biases and stereotypes) challenges. Based on these understandings, educators can form ecologically valid, effective supports in tune with students' psychosocial development.

Empirical Examples of Value to Educators

Beyond this broad value of PVEST, its application offers concrete pathways to reconceptualize thinking about students and deconstruct problematically racialized frameworks. Empirical research employing PVEST serves as a bridge from theory to applied utility within classrooms and schools. As a first example, Tinsley and Spencer (2010) investigated educational expectations of a sample of primarily African American adolescents in relation to various protective or risk factors related to schools (e.g., school climate, relationships with teachers), perceptions of ecological contexts (e.g., perception of opportunities, stereotypes about gender and racial/ethnic groups), and coping resources. Younger adolescents' thinking about future schooling was connected to school climate, while interpretations about broader socio-ecological context (i.e., feeling there were fair opportunities in the United States) mattered for educational expectations across ages. Framed developmentally, as adolescents age, they may think less about belonging in school as affecting their educational trajectory and focus more on issues of opportunity in the broader society. This finding offers concrete pathways for addressing the achievement gap and inequality in higher education access, moving beyond framing these issues as rooted solely in educational resources (i.e., access to technology, curriculum) to turn our focus to students' psychosocial experiences and processing of external challenges to their growth.

A second example is Harris and colleagues' study (2019) on racial identity, prosocial behavior, and aggression in African American male adolescents. The researchers were motivated by the pervasive framing of this group as violent, dangerous, and aggressive. They found older adolescents believed others in society held Black people in low regard, and these feelings were related to increased verbal aggression. Interpreted through PVEST, negative, hostile stereotypes are created by implicit and explicit messages across socio-ecological systems (e.g., treatment in schools, policing, and incarceration). In turn, young African American males cope with discrimination via verbal aggression. This study contextualizes what is labeled as problematic behavior and often leads to disciplinary action in schools. The findings challenge educators to examine their own role and positionality in this process—that is, how they convey or reinforce such messages—as well as how momentary behaviors (such as a verbally aggressive response to a teacher) may be the result of psychosocial coping with negative messaging and racism.

Teaching PVEST to Educators

These empirical examples draw specifically on PVEST and demonstrate its utility in deconstructing thinking about students, particularly those with marginalized identities. The first (Tinsley & Spencer, 2010) addresses motivation and educational achievement, and the second (Harris et al., 2019) focuses on behavior and discipline. Generally, PVEST can help educators reframe challenges with students as linked to psychosocial processes of interpretation and response. One question, however, is how to make this nuanced, complex theory offer concrete benefits for a specific educator. In other words, "What are effective guidelines for teaching PVEST in the context of the lived reality educators face in their daily work?"

One strength of PVEST is a focus on context and perception. We suggest a similar approach to teaching the framework to educators in development. Teaching and learning contexts vary considerably, such as by student demographics, the communities they are embedded within, the material resources available to students and educators, and the goals and missions of the educational institutions. An effective starting point can be the specific circumstances of educators in training: mapping out the ecological systems of their placements or future teaching settings. These educators in training can be led in deconstructing what each level of the ecosystem might look like for one of their particular students or classrooms, detailing important influences in the microsystem, mesosystem, exosystem, and macrosystem. For example, an educator could explore how experiences of authority and discipline in the classroom may be shaped by police presence in schools, the relationship between police and families or community broadly, students' interactions with police and other prevalent authority figures, and discourse and current events related to policing or other state authorities. Starting educators with an application of Bronfenbrenner's socio-ecological model draws attention to the multiple forces and dynamic interactions within which students are embedded. From there, a move into PVEST's core tenets—for example, all humans are vulnerable, environmental factors are interpreted and experienced as supports and challenges, coping is a bidirectional process tied to identity—facilitates deeper understanding of students' challenges, learning, and psychosocial dynamics.

To offer concrete utility for educators, a next step is providing examples of applying PVEST. The studies above offer one entryway into connecting the theory and educational contexts. Other examples span individual level issues like mental health and impostor syndrome (McClain et al., 2016) and systemic inequities in urban education (Lodato et al., 2021). While academic language and methodological complexity can be challenging, instructors can present studies to demonstrate, as we have sought to do, how PVEST can be applied to deconstruct racialized systemic and interpersonal inequities in education. Educators in development can be challenged to develop similar questions related to their contexts: "What processes could be informed by attention to students' meaning making processes?"; "How could a focus on students' contextualized coping change their own orientation as educators?"

PVEST IN ACTION: STRATEGIES AND TOOLS TO ADDRESS INEQUITY

Above, we outlined how to use PVEST as a developmental frame within teaching and learning contexts. This foundation leads to a deeper goal: concrete strategies and applicable tools to address inequity, promote social justice, and implement anti-racist teaching. This section provides examples of employing PVEST to deconstruct various factors underlying inequity in education: encouraging reflexivity in educators' positionality, addressing behavioral standards, reframing achievement gaps and culturally-biased standards for "success" in schools, and seeing learning as relational. We describe these applications across micro, meso, exo, and macrosystems to provide contextualized ways of thinking about students and engaging with them as educators.

Educators' Positionality

PVEST can provide a critical entryway into reflection on educators' own positionalities, cultural perspectives, and/or biases. This concrete application entails introspection at an individual level (for teachers), but is rooted in the norms, expectations, and institutions that have influenced their individual development and then plays out in the interpersonal interactions they have with students. Even as many teachers consciously hold egalitarian ideals about their learners, explicit and implicit attitudes about race/ethnicity pervade teaching behaviors and interactions with students. To this end, a recent analysis of national datasets found no significant difference between teachers and non-teachers on measures of implicit and explicit bias; both demonstrated pro-White preferences at similar levels (Starck et al., 2020).

Learning PVEST can concretely challenge educators to reflect on their assumptions, ideas about learning and learners, and actions by considering different perspectives and experiences of the world. Students act out, are unmotivated, or struggle to comprehend a concept not simply because of individual failing or pathology, but rather as part of coping processes as they respond to their environment. Further exploration can involve examining the disconnect between what the educators value or expect of their students and the students' own thinking, acting, and feeling. By more deeply understanding the student perspective and meaning-making processes, educators can reflect on what systems and modes of education they were socialized into and how their identities and orientations as educators emerged from these contexts. For example, hierarchical structures in which teachers hold classroom authority have predominated historically in the United States (e.g., Franklin, 1986; Hurn, 1985). A first step in curriculum could be providing material laying out the historical development of these systems, providing critiques (such as Freire, 1970/1993), and then asking educators in training to reflect on their own experiences of authority and relationships with teachers in their schooling experiences. Given that historical and prevailing models of education have been based in a hegemonic Whiteness, a genuine openness to explore this disconnect can lead not only to appreciating student experiences and meaning making, but also to the greater valuing of other cultural knowledge and perspectives on learning, growth, and success. PVEST can thus generate individual change (e.g., attitudes) that shapes interpersonal dynamics (e.g., orientations and actions toward students).

Behavioral Standards

Inequities in school discipline have been well documented and there is growing awareness that punitive systems have disproportionate and negative effects on students from marginalized groups (e.g., Hoffman, 2014). Zero tolerance approaches in the United States have been partly motivated by macrosystemic events (e.g., the mass incarceration movement, school shootings, and the push to "secure" educational settings via policing). There are also, however, historical roots that are reenacted in interpersonal interactions; within prevailing dominant frameworks, educators are authority figures who must mold students in their knowledge and moral development (e.g., Brubaker, 2009). Students are held to behavioral standards that fit broader social purposes of education, as it is demanded that they are able to follow directions, listen, and obey the instructor and other adults in schools. These expectations are culturally specific and yet are treated as objective and universal; many educators have been socialized into White norms of interaction and hierarchy how students should behave and act (and connected disciplinary policies and procedures (e.g., Leonard, 2009; Matias & Mackey, 2016). To this end, inequities in expulsions, suspensions, and disciplinary infractions can be understood systemically, but are also tied to interpersonal dynamics.

To address this issue of behavioral expectations, PVEST highlights several developmental processes that can reframe how educators think and act toward students. First, it draws attention at an individual level to the underlying mechanisms of behavior (including coping and resilience). Educators are challenged not simply to see the surface level action, words, or attitude, but to contextualize this within a process of interpretation and response. Such complexity also pushes beyond essentialized or homogenized categories, such as racial/ethnic prejudices and biases. For example, a disengaged student may not simply be lazy, uninterested, or hyperactive, but rather responding to expectations that family, educators, and peers have conveyed to them about their inability to meaningfully engage in these spaces.

Deconstructing surface behaviors and dynamics entails understanding how young people experience and actively respond to school environments. A second concrete application is using PVEST as a tool to consider the complexity of socio-ecological contexts and how they are interpreted by young people. Many curricula, programs, and interventions are designed, implemented, and evaluated by adults, whose understanding of what qualifies as "helpful," "positive," or "necessary" may not match students' experience. PVEST challenges educators to (re)examine how such supports—from small interpersonal moments of attempted connection to adapted intervention programs or disciplinary policies—are experienced by students. Applying PVEST means considering and analyzing these interpretive processes, which requires a genuine openness to students' perspectives and voices. For example, a school district could examine its disciplinary practices not simply through a focus on outcomes (e.g., disciplinary incidents, suspensions, and expulsions), but also engage students in conversations through focus groups and surveys about why they see the underlying conflicts arising, how they experience the rules and responses to such incidents, and how they and their peers respond to these processes.

Ultimately, this application of PVEST can strengthen educators' equity lens to their work and educational settings. While the amount of control educators have over systems of discipline may vary widely, interpersonally they have the power to build supportive environments, deconstruct behaviors, and intervene in ways that promote positive identity-based outcomes. Educators can work to understand how students experience their learning environments and how behaviors are coping strategies embedded within broader developmental processes. This lens inherently pushes back on zero-tolerance and punitive approaches and compels educators to consider other positionalities beyond their own (which may come loaded with implicit or explicit prototypes, like the "teacher's pet" or "class clown," and stereotypes).

Success in School

As detailed above, PVEST opens space for critical reflection of the disconnect between students' thinking about educational trajectories and dominant, historically rooted, and often unequal frameworks of success. There may be dissonance between what society and schools (at the systemic and institutional levels) value in an education and what individual students hope for in their futures and from their schooling (informed by parents, cultural backgrounds, peers, and communities). Modes of learning, what is valued in learning, and performances of learning are constructed within socio-ecological contexts. While grades and standardized tests are privileged indicators within our current educational system, PVEST can facilitate a more expansive view of different ways of holding, building, and expressing knowledge. In addition, PVEST can illuminate why diverse students may feel alienated when encountering curricula that only values White male scholarship while ignoring the contributions of other groups.

The modes through which educational institutions evaluate learning also need to change to address racial injustice. Standardized testing has long been identified as a barrier to the higher education of racially minoritized students (Sackett et al., 2001; Solórzano et al., 2000), and studies have shown that standardized testing is "normed to white, upper middle-class performance" (Guinier, 2015, p. 20). Standardized tests that claim to objectively measure aptitude perpetuate racial biases and, despite widespread criticism of these measures, commercialized testing continues to expand (Clarke et al., 2000). Efforts to "close the achievement gap" between racial-ethnic groups often disproportionately privilege training students to perform better on standardized testing, rather than ensuring an increased capacity to learn or the internalization of more content knowledge (Stewart & Haynes, 2015). By allowing a greater recognition of different forms of cultural knowledge, PVEST points to the need for greater diversity in the way learning can be demonstrated and evaluated to better reflect the diverse backgrounds and objectives of students within educational institutions. Educational institutions should shift away from the over-privileging of standardized tests towards more inclusive measurements of learning and evaluation that are attentive to their students' identities and backgrounds.

PVEST can also help educators to understand how representation matters in the classroom to students' future identities as scholars and learners. Concretely, this could involve empathy-building thought experiments for future educators where they are asked to consider young people's experience of representation or lack of it. They could be then led through a discussion of each stage of PVEST: "How might a young person from a minoritized background interpret a school context where no one is like them?; "How might they cope?"; and "How might those coping strategies be interpreted and responded to by personnel?" The activity could first be done individually, and then shared collectively to identify diverse thinking and possibilities.

When educational institutions and educators favor White instructors, authors, and modes of being, students of color may cope with these feelings of difference by disinvesting from a system that does not represent them. For example, the "Common Core" texts historically exclude literary contributions by authors of color, which results in the neglect of racially, culturally, and ethnically diverse students (Gangi, 2008). The educational implications of these choices are deep. As Gangi (2008) noted: "Since children must be able to make connections with what they read to become proficient readers, White children whose experiences are depicted in books can make many more text to-self, text-to-text, and text-to-world connections than can children of color" (p. 30). Students need opportunities to engage with other cultures through content, but they also must find a place for themselves and the experiences of their community. PVEST helps us to understand how these experiences have implications for identity formation, and that experiences of exclusion can motivate disengagement and self-doubt among youth of color.

Learning as Relational

Socio-ecological approaches to education draw attention to the fact that learning and schools influence developmental processes beyond the concrete objectives of cognition or content transfer (in line with banking models of instruction). Individual intellectual and cognitive development matter, but are embedded within interpersonal dynamics. These processes drive individual-level identity development with implications across domains of life (e.g., career, family, mental health, etc.).

Although PVEST is not unique in highlighting the importance of relationships in teaching and learning, it does offer an equity framework that is useful for approaching issues of inequity in education. A fundamental tenet of the theory is that all humans are vulnerable, while all behavior and outcomes must be understood as resulting from the ways that individuals experience and cope with their socio-ecological context. These tenets demand seeing the humanity of all students, as well as eschewing the application of pathological explanations, internalized deviance, or deterministic thinking that imbues implicit and explicit bias playing out in the classroom. Furthermore, the onus moves from the student to the educator as the latter must work to understand the perspective of and connect with the former in order to support learning and growth. This implication stands in contrast to behavioral or purely cognitive theories that focus on individual traits, rewards and punishments, or static intellectual capabilities.

CONCLUSION

An intentional focus on the humanity and learning capabilities of all students is imperative for an equitable educational system to come to fruition. Educators need effective tools and training to better understand the full humanity of their students and the various contextual and developmental factors that contribute to learning and growth. In this chapter, we have argued that teaching human development through PVEST provides future educators with a framework to understand variance in student needs and respond in ways that attend to their capacity to learn and thrive. This socio-ecological framework considers students as active agents in making sense of their social and educational environments to shape their learning experiences and inform their identities as learners. Our chapter highlights applied strategies educators can use to deconstruct problematic dynamics in education that feed into racial/ethnic inequality as well as achievement gaps. In providing examples of how PVEST can be applied in classroom settings, we hope that our chapter will help educational psychologists gain: (a) an understanding of how student learning can be informed by a socio-ecological framework on development, (b) a theoretical orientation that can motivate more effective supports for students from marginalized backgrounds, and (c) concrete strategies to connect this framework to anti-racist teaching strategies. Our efforts are to help future educators support the resilience of marginalized students by providing them with tools to understand the role of human development in teaching and learning.

PVEST focuses educators' attention to the mechanisms underlying young people's development. Learning is not simply a process of content acquisition, but entails understanding of the social world, cultural frameworks, coping strategies, and developing identities. The interpretive element is deeply shaped by relationships: as people, we understand our worlds, our place in them, and who we are through bidirectional influence with others and with our socio-ecological contexts. Educators may want to intervene in these processes in multiple ways, such as convincing students that they are capable of learning new material or concepts, motivating their engagement in the classroom, unpacking and counteracting stereotypes, and fostering critical consciousness about their social worlds. Each of these possibilities targets different parts of the developmental process laid out by PVEST, but a common element is that to intervene in meaning making (i.e., interpretation and response), there must be trust and connectedness between the educator and the student. The individual must receive the intervention as supportive and respond productively, which requires a relational connection and thoughtfulness to the positionalities and identities of both the educator and learner.

Even as many teacher education programs move away from a focus on human development, they also aim to provide students with more tools for anti-racist, social justice teaching. Recent social events and empirical research make it clear that a greater emphasis on equity and justice in education is needed. Revamping educational systems and the processes by which educators learn to teach and build relationships with their students is no small matter.

Teaching human development helps future educators to understand that the most effective learning processes are relational and holistic. A key aspect of relational teaching is recognizing the full humanity of students by acknowledging contextual factors that contribute to their development within and outside of the classroom and creating classroom climates that embrace various forms of learning (Gross & Lo, 2018). Furthermore, a holistic approach to teaching and learning facilitates the development of students as critical thinkers by granting space for experiential knowledge in the classroom and recognizing the importance of social context in learning processes (Patel, 2003). In this vein, educators can use the PVEST framework to advance effective teaching methods through relational and holistic approaches to teaching. PVEST allows for individual student experiences to be considered and valued within larger socio-ecological systems such as those that operate within educational institutions. Throughout the second half of the chapter, we have sought to provide concrete examples, and end with a reflection on future directions given the complexity and challenges of the COVID-19 pandemic.

Future Directions and the COVID-19 Pandemic

Our chapter provides the PVEST framework as a tool for future educators to engage in equitable and effective teaching strategies designed to dismantle systemic educational inequalities. The basic premise of the theory is that all humans develop within social systems and are susceptible to vulnerabilities. The COVID-19 pandemic presents an opportunity to thoughtfully consider access to quality education and effective teaching strategies for multifaceted developmental processes. It is important to consider the various risks students of all ages and backgrounds have encountered during the world health crisis including inequitable access to technology, exacerbated physical and mental health risks, and disruption to targeted instructional approaches for those with differential learning needs (Becker et al., 2022). The sociohistorical context of COVID-19 shapes the learning experiences of students and is not exempt from bias or disproportionate inequities tied to race/ethnicity, socioeconomic status, and other social categories. Due to financial hardship and limited access to Wi-Fi for distance learning, the COVID-19 pandemic has exacerbated systemic and cyclical educational challenges that disproportionately affect marginalized students such as educator bias, inequitable disciplinary practices and special education referrals, and limited access to secondary and postsecondary educational opportunities (Newman et al., 2021).

Clearly, the challenges are many for educators as schools enter their third academic year dealing with the COVID-19 pandemic. Significant institutional and systemic forces drive inequity and injustice, particularly for students from marginalized identities, while the lasting developmental impacts of this crisis will influence a generation of students in their academic, social, and personal trajectories. Developmental theory, and PVEST in particular, is not a panacea, but offers educators (both those in development and those currently teaching) the opportunity to make sense of the complexity of students' lives and learning, situating these processes within interlocking systems including current environmental and health crises. Just as PVEST itself highlights the agency of individuals in making meaning and coping with the socio-ecological systems within which they are embedded, it can strengthen educators' understanding of their agency to address inequity and injustice.

KEY CHAPTER TAKEAWAYS

Summary	Description
Examining ecosystems for classrooms and schools	Exploring the different factors across levels that influence students in the educational Setting (such as societal values, politics, community changes, family dynamics)
Focusing on student interpretation	Working to understand how students experience interventions or programming adults considered to be supportive
Reframing success in school	Being attentive to what success in school and intellectual development means to students and within their cultural contexts
Understanding behavior	Considering how behaviors labeled as "problematic" may be students' adaptive ways of coping with stressors and needs

KEY WORDS

Behavioral standards
Emergent identities
Intersectionality
Phenomenological variant of ecological systems theory (PVEST)
Positionality
Social justice
Socio-ecological theory

AUTHOR NOTE

Correspondence concerning this article should be addressed to Gabriel Velez, College of Education, Marquette University, P.O. Box 1881, Milwaukee, WI 53201-1881, United States. Email: Gabriel.velez@marquette.edu

REFERENCES

Anderson, J., Boyle, C., & Deppeler, J. (2014). The ecology of inclusive education: Reconceptualising Bronfenbrenner. In H. Zhang, P. Chan, & C. Boyle (Eds.), *Equality in education* (pp. 23–34). Brill Sense.

Becker, S. P., Breaux, R., Cusick, C. N., Dvorsky, M. R., Marsh, N. P., Sciberras, E., & Langberg, J. M. (2020). Remote learning during COVID-19: Examining school practices, service continuation, and difficulties for adolescents with and without attention-deficit/hyperactivity disorder. *Journal of Adolescent Health, 67*(6), 769–777. https://doi.org/10.1016/j.jadohealth.2020.09.002

Bowman, B. T., Comer, J. P., & Johns, D. J. (2018). Addressing the African American achievement gap: Three leading educators issue a call to action. *Young Children, 73*(2), 14–23. https://www.naeyc.org/resources/pubs/yc/may2018/achievement-gap

Bronfenbrenner, U. (1973). Social ecology of human development. In F. Richardson (Ed.), *Brain and intelligence: The ecology of child development* (pp. 113–129). National Education Press.

Bronfenbrenner, U. (1976). The experimental ecology of education. *Educational Researcher, 5*(9), 5–15. https://doi.org/10.3102/0013189X005009005

Brubaker, N. D. (2009). Negotiating authority in an undergraduate teacher education course: A qualitative investigation. *Teacher Education Quarterly, 36*(4), 99–118. https://eric.ed.gov/?id=EJ870217

Chambers, T. V. (2009). The "receivement gap": School tracking policies and the fallacy of the "achievement gap." *The Journal of Negro Education*, 417–431. https://eric.ed.gov/?id=EJ878489

Chaney, C. (2014). Bridging the gap: Promoting intergenerational family literacy among low-income, African American families. *The Journal of Negro Education, 83*(1), 29–48. https://doi.org/10.7709/jnegroeducation.83.1.0029

Clarke, M. M., Madaus, G. F., Horn, C. L., & Ramos, M. A. (2000). Retrospective on educational testing and assessment in the 20th century. *Journal of Curriculum Studies, 32*(2), 159–181. https://doi.org/10.1080/002202700182691

Condly, S. J. (2006). Resilience in children: A review of literature with implications for education. *Urban Education, 41*(3), 211–236. https://doi.org/10.1177/0042085906287902

Daro, D., & Dodge, K. (2009). Creating community responsibility for child protection: Possibilities and challenges. *The Future of Children, 19*(2), 67–93. https://doi.org/10.1353/foc.0.0030

De Wet, C. (2010). Victims of educator-targeted bullying: A qualitative study. *South African Journal of Education, 30*(2), 189–201. https://doi.org/10.4314/saje.v30i2.55481

Fish, J., & Syed, M. (2018). Native Americans in higher education: An ecological systems perspective. *Journal of College Student Development, 59*(4), 387–403. https://doi.org/10.1353/csd.2018.0038

Franklin, B. (1986). *Building the American community: The school curriculum and the search for control.* Falmer Press.

Freire, P. (1993). *Pedagogy of the oppressed.* Continuum. (Original work published 1970)

Gangi, J. M. (2008). The unbearable Whiteness of literacy instruction: Realizing the implications of the proficient reader research. *Multicultural Review, 17*(1), 30–35.

Gergen, K. (2009). *Relational being: Beyond self and community.* Oxford University Press.

Gross, N., & Lo, C. (2018). Relational teaching and learning after loss: Evidence from Black adolescent male students and their teachers. *School Psychology Quarterly, 33*(3), 381–389. https://psycnet.apa.org/record/2018-46653-004

Guinier, L. (2015). *The tyranny of the meritocracy: Democratizing higher education in America.* Beacon Press.

Harris, J. A., Spencer, M. B., Kruger, A. C., & Irving, M. A. (2019). An examination and interrogation of African American males' racial identity, prosocial behaviors and aggression. *Research in Human Development, 16*(1), 76–91. https://doi.org/10.1080/15427609.2018.1556068

Hoffman, S. (2014). Zero benefit: Estimating the effect of zero tolerance discipline polices on racial disparities in school discipline. *Educational Policy, 28*(1), 69–95. https://doi.org/10.1177/0895904812453999

Hurn, C. (1985). Changes in authority relationships in schools: 1960–1980. *Research in Sociology of Education and Socialization, 5,* 31–57.

Jussim, L., & Harber, K. D. (2005). Teacher expectations and self-fulfilling prophecies: Knowns and unknowns, resolved and unresolved controversies. *Personality and Social Psychology Review, 9*(2), 131–155. https://doi.org/10.1207/s15327957pspr0902_3

Kotok, S. (2017). Unfulfilled potential: High-achieving minority students and the high school achievement gap in math. *High School Journal, 100*(3), 183–202. https://www.jstor.org/stable/90024211

Kuhfeld, M., Gershoff, E., & Paschall, K. (2018). The development of racial/ethnic and socioeconomic achievement gaps during the school years. *Journal of Applied Developmental Psychology, 57,* 62–73. https://doi.org/10.1016/j.appdev.2018.07.001

Leonardo, Z. (2009). *Race, Whiteness, and education.* Routledge.

Lodato, B. N., Harris, K., & Spencer, M. B. (2021). Human development perspectives on public urban education. In H. R. Milner & K. Lomotey (Eds.), *Handbook of urban education* (pp. 84–96). Routledge.

Matias, C. E., & Mackey, J. (2016). Breakin' down Whiteness in antiracist teaching: Introducing critical whiteness pedagogy. *The Urban Review, 48*(1), 32–50. https://doi.org/10.1007/s11256-015-0344-7

McClain, S., Beasley, S. T., Jones, B., Awosogba, O., Jackson, S., & Cokley, K. (2016). An examination of the impact of racial and ethnic identity, impostor feelings, and minority status stress on the mental health of Black college students. *Journal of Multicultural Counseling and Development, 44*(2), 101–117. https://doi.org/10.1002/jmcd.12040

Newman, D. S., Albritton, K., Barrett, C., Fallon, L., Moy, G. E., O'Neal, C., & VanMeter, S. (2021). Working together towards social justice, anti-racism, and equity: A joint commitment from Journal of Educational and Psychological Consultation and School Psychology International. *Journal of Educational and Psychological Consultation, 31*(1), 8–12. https://doi.org/10.1080/10474412.2021.2015645

Okonofua, J. A., & Eberhardt, J. L. (2015). Two strikes: Race and the disciplining of young students. *Psychological Science, 26*(5), 617–624. https://doi.org/10.1177/0956797615570365

Patel, N. V. (2003). A holistic approach to learning and teaching interaction: Factors in the development of critical learners. *International Journal of Educational Management, 17*(6/7), 272–284. https://doi.org/10.1108/09513540310487604

Sackett, P. R., Schmitt, N., Ellingson, J. E., & Kabin, M. B. (2001). High-stakes testing in employment, credentialing, and higher education: Prospects in a post-affirmative-action world. *American Psychologist, 56*(4), 302–318. https://doi.org/10.1037/0003-066X.56.4.302

Solórzano, D., Ceja, M., & Yosso, T. (2000). Critical race theory, racial microaggressions, and campus racial climate: The experiences of African American college students. *Journal of Negro Education, 69*(1), 60–73. https://eric.ed.gov/?id=EJ636426

Spencer, M. B. (1999). Social and cultural influences on school adjustment: The application of an identity-focused cultural ecological perspective. *Educational Psychologist, 34*(1), 43–57. https://psycnet.apa.org/record/1999-10047-004

Spencer, M. B. (2007). Phenomenology and ecological systems theory: Development of diverse groups. In R. Lerner & W. Damon (Eds.), *Handbook of child psychology* (pp. 829–893). Wiley.

Spencer, M. B., Dupree, D., & Hartmann, T. (1997). A phenomenological variant of ecological systems theory (PVEST): A self-organization perspective in context. *Development and Psychopathology, 9*(4), 817–833. https://doi.org/10.1017/S0954579497001454

Spencer, M. B., Offidani-Bertrand, C., Harris, K., & Velez, G. (2020). Examining links between culture, identity, and learning. In N. Suad Nasir, C. Lee, & R. Pea (Eds.), *Handbook of the cultural foundations of learning* (pp. 44–61). Routledge.

Spencer, M. B., & Tinsley, B. (2008). Identity as coping: Assessing youths' challenges and opportunities for success. *The Prevention Researcher, 15*(4), 17–21. https://eric.ed.gov/?id=EJ823353

Stewart, S., & Haynes, C. (2015). An alternative approach to standardized testing: A model that promotes racial equity and college access. *Journal of Critical Scholarship on Higher Education and Student Affairs, 2*(1), 123–137. https://ecommons.luc.edu/jcshesa/vol2/iss1/9

Sullivan, L., Meschede, T., Dietrich, L., & Shapiro, T. (2016). *The racial wealth gap: Why policy matters.* DEMOS.

Tinsley, B., & Spencer, M. B. (2010). High hope and low regard: The resiliency of adolescents' educational expectations while developing in challenging political contexts. *Research in Human Development*, 7(3), 183–201. https://doi.org/10.1080/15427609.2010.505780

Thompson, K. V., Harris, K., & Clauss-Ehlers, C. S. (2013). The racial/ethnic identity development of tomorrow's adolescent. In C. S. Clauss-Ehlers, Z. N. Serpell, & M. D. Weist (Eds.), *Handbook of culturally responsive school mental health* (pp. 157–175). Springer.

Velez, G., & Spencer, M. B. (2018). Phenomenology and Intersectionality: Using PVEST as a frame for adolescent identity formation amid intersecting ecological systems of inequality. *New Directions for Child and Adolescent Development*, *161*, 75–90. https://doi.org/10.1002/cad.20247

CHAPTER 4

INTENTIONALLY INTEGRATING DEVELOPMENTAL THEORY AND RESEARCH INTO TEACHER EDUCATION

Examples From the Field

Sarah M. Kiefer
University of South Florida

Raven Robinson
University of North Florida

Rebecca West Burns
University of North Florida

Kerrijo Ellis
University of South Florida

Educators' knowledge and beliefs about human development, conceptions of teaching and learning, and perceptions of education-related theory and research play a central role in their instructional practices (Guilfoyle et al., 2020; Moser et al., 2021; Tezci et al., 2016). Despite their familiarity with the age group they teach, many educators hold misconceptions about their students' development as well as the teaching and learning process (McDevitt & Ormrod, 2008; Steinberg, 2015). Although educational psychology is not widely recognized as a central part of educators' professional practice (Moser et al., 2021), incorporating it within teacher education is critical for developing educators' research-based knowledge to inform their beliefs and practices regarding human development. This may help educational psychology instructors to effectively prepare teacher candidates and practicing educators to be responsive to the diverse developmental and learning needs of their PK–12 learners.

The aim of this chapter is to advocate for intentionally integrating knowledge of human development and teacher education research into teacher education. We begin by providing a rationale for the strategic integration of developmental theory and research as well as research in teacher education into teacher education programs. Next, we discuss innovative methods, strategies, and assignments that instructors can use to apply theory and research in human development and teacher education to their instructional practices, including: (a) developing signature assignments interconnected across courses and clinical experiences, (b) engaging in collaborative teacher inquiry, and (c) partnering with PK–12 schools to provide graduate coursework to practicing teachers as professional development (see Key Chapter Take-Aways). We provide examples from our own professional experiences as teacher educators. We conclude by considering ways educational psychology instructors can advocate for the integration of knowledge of human development and teacher education research into their own programs.

STRATEGICALLY INTEGRATING DEVELOPMENTAL THEORY AND RESEARCH INTO TEACHER EDUCATION

We advocate for the purposeful incorporation of developmental theory and research as well as research in teacher education (e.g., how teachers learn, teacher development, research in clinical practice, and school–university collaboration) across coursework and clinical experiences in ways that recognize and value the knowledge bases in both disciplines. This is done best when educational psychology instructors and teacher educators build sustainable collaborations and work together to develop a shared understanding of teacher education that promotes a mindset shift from thinking about "my course" to "our students." Educational psychology instructors and teacher educators can meet regularly to share program aims, course information, and develop a mutual sense of trust and respect. It may be necessary to address tensions and concerns regarding integration and ways to adopt or strengthen an inclusive approach to teacher education. This can include having conversations about what integrating developmental theory and research into teacher education means to different stakeholders, how it can support teacher candidates' learning, and what might be possible within a specific context. These conversations can lead to transformative points in collaboration, where educational psychology instructors and teacher educators share the same students and look for points of synergy across coursework. This may include assigning common readings and assessments, as well as seeking ways to meaningfully integrate courses and clinical experiences. We encourage educators to collectively question what constitutes a teacher education course and to consider changing the nature of coursework to allow for co-teaching or a team approach to the development and delivery of courses.

Through building sustainable collaborations and by integrating human development and teacher education across the curriculum, educational psychology instructors and teacher educators can prepare teacher candidates and practicing educators to be responsive to the diverse developmental and learning needs of PK–12 learners. In this section, we discuss how integrating developmental theory and research as well as research in teacher education across coursework may provide teacher candidates and educators with multiple opportunities to (a) identify misconceptions about student development as well as the teaching and learning process, (b) foster conceptual change and correct any misunderstandings about learning and development, and (c) engage in culturally responsive beliefs and practices that foster equitable learning environments.

Identify Misconceptions

Integrating knowledge of human development and teacher education may help teacher candidates and practicing teachers to identify and break down misconceptions about student development as well as the teaching and learning process and to be responsive to the diverse developmental and learning needs of PK–12 learners. For example, child development coursework for teacher candidates often does not consistently provide realistic examples of developmental concepts or connect concepts to the classroom (National Institute of Child Health and Human Development & National Association for the Accreditation of Teacher Education, 2007). Such coursework may not provide candidates with opportunities to reflect on the complexities of learning and development and to make deep and lasting connections to their students. In addition, developing a deeper understanding of adult learning and development, and specifically teacher candidate and teacher learning and development, may prepare candidates to be effective teachers, persist when facing challenges, and remain in the profession (see Bordewyck et al., this volume).

Integrating developmental theory and research as well as teacher education research across coursework may allow teacher candidates multiple opportunities to identify misconceptions, stereotypes, and overly simplistic ideas that they have about learning and development (McDevitt & Ormrod, 2008). For example, some teacher candidates and practicing teachers believe that (a) intelligence is inherited and fixed, rather than being shaped by the environment; (b) students learn best from teacher-centered practices, rather than from active and collaborative student-centered practices; and (c) that inadequate parenting is at the root of student behavior problems, rather than resulting from multiple factors including those involving the home, school, and student behavior (McDevitt & Ormrod, 2008; Reyna, 2000). Teacher candidates may have cognitive biases that influence how they interpret new information, including confirmation bias, or the tendency to look for information that confirms one's preexisting beliefs (De Lisi & Golbeck, 1999). They may also have ethnocentric biases and consider their own cultural teachings about child development and teaching as truths about best practices (McDevitt & Ormrod, 2008; Rogoff, 2003). In addition, it is important to identify teacher candidates' and practicing educators' beliefs about the nature of knowledge and learning that may be misleading or inaccurate (Hofer & Pintrich, 2002; King & Kitchener, 2004). For example, one may believe that knowledge in a discipline does not change rather than being subject to revision, that learning is a collection of isolated facts rather than complex and interrelated ideas, or that learning is something that happens relatively easily and effortlessly rather than taking significant time and cognitive effort (McDevitt & Ormrod, 2008; Patrick & Pintrich, 2001). Although individuals may not always be aware of these beliefs, they may influence educators' behaviors and interactions with their students (Patrick & Pintrich, 2001).

Foster Conceptual Change

Many beliefs are not readily available for reflection and revision and are interconnected with larger understandings of how the world works. Given that individuals' beliefs about children as well as teaching and learning may be resistant to conceptual change (McDevitt & Ormrod, 2008), it is unlikely that isolated coursework will be sufficient for lasting and meaningful change. Teacher educators can incorporate ongoing opportunities to engage in reflective practice, where teacher candidates reflect on their assumptions of the population(s) they serve and how to best support their learning, as well as how knowledge of human development and teacher education may inform and improve their instructional practices (Hogan et al., 2003; Larrivee, 2006). This may help teacher candidates and practicing teachers to become more aware of their understandings of development and engage in conceptual change, as well as apply their revised understandings to their clinical or professional experiences (McDevitt & Ormrod, 2008).

Curriculum that integrates fundamental knowledge of development into teacher preparation can allow teacher candidates to apply theory and research to correct any misunderstandings about learning and development and inform their educational practice in a meaningful way (Armstrong, 2006; McDevitt & Ormrod, 2008). Some teacher candidates believe research is not relevant to classroom practice or are skeptical of psychological research (Joram, 2007). This belief can have implications for their future teaching practice, as they may minimize the usefulness of theory and knowledge to inform their practice and rely more on trial and error (McDevitt & Ormrod, 2008). Teacher educators can combat this by demonstrating how theory and research, as well as teacher inquiry, can be used to address complexities and issues in development and learning that teacher candidates observe in their clinical experiences. This approach may help to bridge the research to practice gap and encourage teacher candidates to use research-based knowledge and strategies to inform their practice.

Promote Culturally Responsive Practitioners and Transform Teacher Identity

Through integrating theory and research in human development and teacher education, educators can engage in culturally responsive beliefs and practices that foster equitable learning environments in PK–12 schools to support the diverse experiences and developmental needs of all learners (Kahn et al., 2014; Miller Dyce & Owusu-Ansah, 2016; Sleeter & Owuor, 2011). Educators who understand foundational theories of human learning and development and engage in reflective practice are introduced to various forms of diversity regarding how people learn and grow. Ongoing reflection and critical classroom experiences have the potential to expand teachers' identities to one that defies place, time, and self-concept, as well as promote a culturally responsive teaching stance and practices that maximize educational outcomes for all learners (Miller Dyce & Owusu-Ansah, 2016; Sleeter & Owuor, 2011). For instance, teachers who incorporate culturally responsive practices into their teaching, aided in part by their previous educational experiences, made changes in their classrooms. Such changes include resolving linguistic conflicts among learners by engaging in class discussions about the importance of all languages (Miller Dyce & Owusu-Ansah, 2016). Knowledge of culturally responsive techniques allows practitioners to become more socially conscious and understanding, acknowledging that student differences are a byproduct of their ethnic, linguistic, and cultural backgrounds and should never be seen as foibles (Sleeter & Owuor, 2011).

To promote culturally responsive teaching and the transformation of teacher identity, teacher candidates must be willing to think deeply about their identity and biases. Through engaging in ongoing critical reflection and teacher inquiry, educators may transform how they think about their engagement in instructional practices. Such critical reflection can help shape their identities as teachers (Gay & Kirkland, 2003; Liu, 2015). Teacher candidates can analyze controversial issues on how diversity differences influence the teaching and learning process as well as closely scrutinize the educational system and society at large (Miller Dyce & Owusu-Anash, 2016). By engaging in critical consciousness and personal reflection, teacher candidates may become more aware of aspects of diversity and embrace the need to be reflective practitioners. The ability to question one's worldview is central to transforming teacher identity, as revising personal epistemologies can result in a lasting shift in how one perceives oneself (Miller Dyce & Owusu-Ansah, 2016). Teacher candidates may learn to understand their students' experiences and involve them in the process of developing, dissecting, and recreating constructs in the learning process by first understanding themselves. An increased understanding of developmental theories can help candidates to be confident in their ability to develop close relationships, establish positive student-centered learning environments, and instill trust and belonging in all learners—especially those who have been historically marginalized (Sleeter & Owuor, 2011).

APPLYING DEVELOPMENTAL THEORY AND RESEARCH TO INSTRUCTIONAL PRACTICES

Instructors can integrate knowledge of human development and teacher education research into their coursework and clinical experiences through (a) collaborating on signature assignments across courses within the teacher education program, (b) engaging in collaborative inquiry, and (c) partnering with PK–12 schools to provide graduate coursework to practicing teachers as professional development and to transform educators into teacher leaders.

Signature Assignments Within the Teacher Education Program

Educational psychology instructors can collaborate with teacher educators by discussing course goals, assessments, and needs of their learners as well as developing assignments integrated across coursework and clinical experiences. We share three signature assignments that integrate knowledge of human development and teacher education research into teacher preparation curriculum: (a) a reflective blog, (b) a case study paper, and (c) a lesson plan.

Signature Assignment 1: Reflective Blog

Instructors can develop a reflective blog assignment that is integrated across multiple courses and clinical experiences. Teacher candidates observe a child or children in their field placement classroom as they go through the learning process, interact with the child(ren) to determine their thinking process, and document the child(ren)'s abilities. Candidates then write reflective blog entries based on their observations informed by their understanding of human development and learning from course readings, lessons, and discussions. Candidates include reflective questions to deepen their understanding of human development in education, critically reflect on their personal ideologies and teaching philosophy, and consider multiple aspects of diversity and development encountered in courses and clinical experiences. For instance, teacher candidates can analyze their own involvement working with students in a clinical setting, as well as analyze their mentor teacher's instruction. Reflective prompts may include: (a) "Why did you choose this specific student interaction or instruction to reflect on?"; (b) "To what extent did you observe student(s') learning or the teacher's instruction according to your chosen theoretical lens?"; (c) "How was the interaction or instruction developmentally and culturally responsive to individual students?"; and (d) "How could you have enhanced student learning and/or engagement based on what you know about learning, development, and the classroom context?" Reflective prompts are designed to inform ways that teacher candidates could enhance their practice, based on what they observed and learned as well as their knowledge of human development and learning.

By regularly reflecting on how coursework informs clinical experiences, reflective blogs can help teacher candidates construct a robust understanding of human development, learning, and aspects of diversity that they experience in a classroom or school setting. Candidates can identify and break down misconceptions about student development and learning that they may have and revise their understandings. Candidates may become more responsive to using knowledge of human development and teacher education to inform and improve their instructional practices. In addition, reflective blogs may serve as a platform for candidates to analyze and deconstruct nuances of the educational system within the wider sociological and historical context by promoting an analysis of difficult subjects such as how diversity disparities impact teaching and learning.

Teacher candidates can think deeply about their identities as educators by writing reflective blogs on a personalized website. While self-reflection is a critical exercise, the experience is enhanced when teacher candidates engage in conversation with and receive feedback from their instructors and peers. Educational psychology and teacher educator instructors can engage candidates in digital conversations to stimulate thinking, confront misconceptions or deeply held beliefs, and deepen understanding of and learning about concepts of human development. The blog can also be used as a portfolio, allowing candidates to identify development and changes in their teacher identity and professional practice over time. Candidates often generate work that reflects their own unique voice, reflecting on their identities, how they felt, and what they learned from their clinically rich experiences.

Based on teacher candidate feedback, the reflective blog was one of the most enjoyable and meaningful course activities. Candidates were challenged to understand and assess developmental theories and the complexities of applying them to working with real students. Candidates shared they were more aware of, mindful, and appreciative of learner differences, as well as more confident in supporting their students. As instructors, we found that reflective blogs promoted authentic candidate–teacher interactions and increased critical consciousness among candidates. The blog is a unique public platform that can afford conversations among instructors and teacher candidates as well as members of the public.

Signature Assignment 2: Case Study Paper

Instructors can develop a case study assignment for teacher candidates that incorporates content from multiple courses to focus on an individual learner as a part of their clinical experiences rather than assigning a hypothetical vignette. For instance, at two of the coauthors' institutions, instructors in ESOL, reading, and educational psychology worked together to develop a case study assignment that incorporated content from their three respective courses and clinical experiences for teacher candidates in the elementary education program. Guidelines for the case study include discussing relevant human development and learning theories as well as teaching strategies from educational psychology to support a specific ESOL student's reading performance and overall learning. Candidates analyze the cultural, institutional, social-emotional, moral, behavioral, cognitive, linguistic, and metacognitive components of their development as a capstone project, which is under program-wide institutional research board approval, for multiple courses.

This capstone project can help candidates to gain a more nuanced and holistic understanding of student growth and learning. Candidates gain a deeper sense of the complexities of human development as they closely examine each developmental component of one child within the classroom environment. Based on course feedback, teacher candidates appreciated that the case study paper was integrated into multiple courses and their clinical experiences, as it served as a wrap-around, 360-view of an individual student in a real-world classroom. This authentic assignment allowed candidates to connect developmental theory to a specific learner as well as to knowledge from other coursework and clinical experiences.

Signature Assignment 3: Lesson Plan

In conjunction with other courses, teacher candidates develop and administer a lesson tailored to a small group of students throughout a semester at their clinical-based assignment. Candidates use developmental theories and research to inform their lesson plan, including learning objectives and expectations for student learning. Drawing upon human development and learning theories, candidates design a lesson plan that considers children's individual needs, developmental levels, and other applicable differences and provide a rationale for selecting specific instructional methods. Candidates incorporate differentiated instruction to support individual and group differences, evaluate the lesson's effectiveness, and develop a way to engage in teacher inquiry based on the lesson. Throughout the process, candidates can become aware of any misconceptions they may have regarding instruction and student learning. For instance, candidates explore differentiation based on their students' language, culture, abilities, and exceptionalities in multiple courses and their clinical experiences. This approach allows candidates to view developmental theories through multiple lenses and how they may be used to support the learning of a specific group of students. The lesson plan may also encourage conceptual transformation and modify teacher identities. As teacher candidates have ownership over the development, implementation, and assessment of their lesson plan, they may serve as advocates for their students and develop as culturally inclusive educators.

In course feedback, candidates reflected on how their lesson plan accomplished the objectives that were informed by developmental and learning theories. This may be instrumental in candidates using knowledge of human development to inform instruction in their future teaching practice. Candidates greatly benefitted from discussing each component of the lesson plan with their instructor and classmates, as it provided them opportunities to critically reflect on their beliefs about teaching and learning and to improve their lesson plan and support diverse types of learners. Distributing the assignment across the semester gave instructors an opportunity to provide candidates ongoing feedback to improve their incorporation of developmental theories within a lesson plan, promote culturally inclusive practices, and encourage candidates to advocate for their students.

Collaborative Teacher Inquiry

Teacher inquiry is the systematic and intentional study of one's own practice and is a stance through which educators can view their practice (Cochran-Smith & Lytle, 1993; Dana & Yendol-Hoppey, 2020). Teacher inquiry can be a powerful vehicle for educators to advocate for instructional practices to meet PK–12 students' developmental and learning needs (Currin, 2019; Wolkenhauer & Hooser, 2017). In this section, we share three collaborative teacher inquiry activities instructors may use that integrate knowledge of human development and teacher education research into the classroom: (a) discussions and simulations, (b) small groups, and (c) an inquiry paper. Educational psychology instructors and teacher educators can support students throughout the teacher inquiry process through collaboration across their respective courses, or through co-teaching or working together in teams.

Collaborative Teacher Inquiry Strategy 1: Discussions and Simulations

Instructors can provide safe spaces for teacher candidates to address tensions and/or issues in applying knowledge of human development and teacher education research to their instructional practice in their clinical experiences. Classroom discussions and simulated classroom activities allow candidates to problem solve in ways that promote their cognitive, moral, social, and emotional development as well as support their transition into becoming effective educators (McKeachie & Svincki, 2013; Warren, 2018). Discussions and simulations may also help candidates to make connections between coursework and clinical experiences by identifying relationships, applications, and analyses of developmental theories within their clinical contexts.

Discussions. Classroom discussions can allow teacher candidates to develop an increased awareness and insight into their teaching philosophy and practices, and to apply their learning to an immediate situation or educational context. This can help candidates to become aware of the "need to know" by making an intellectual case for the value of the learning in improving their teaching effectiveness in their field experiences (Merriam & Bierema, 2014). Focusing on common experiences in clinically based settings provides a solid basis for candidates to apply theories to real-world experiences as well as foster conceptual change through identifying and addressing misconceptions. Digital technology as well as written and oral dialogue are useful tools for creating discussions that foster critical thinking, problem solving, and collaboration.

Instructors can provide an overarching, equity-based inquiry question as a discussion prompt to probe teacher candidates' thinking about human developmental theory and research to help them make relevant connections to their practice. Open-ended questions allow for multiple responses and avenues for inquiry to promote a learner-centered classroom. For instance, discussion prompts—"How do our own backgrounds and belief systems impact our ability to create equitable learning environments for K–12 students?" and "How can we implement culturally responsive teaching practices to provide equitable learning environments for K–12 students?"—allowed candidates to reflect on the role of their own beliefs and practices in promoting equitable learning environments. Candidates have appreciated engaging in conversations that connect course content to their practice. For example, a discussion prompt such as "How can students know they are being treated fairly in your classroom?" allowed candidates to contemplate the role of teachers and students in the learning process, which connected to theory and research in human development and learning from their coursework.

Teacher educators can be intentional in fostering and guiding equity-based discussions. Educators can communicate a clear purpose for the discussion; this allows teacher candidates to know why the discussion is occurring and how it is useful for their ability to make connections between theory and practice. Presenting leading question(s) that are the focal point of discussion enables the class to focus on a specific topic or issue, rather than individual people—creating a safe platform for candidates to share their perspectives. Educators can set clear facilitation parameters and expectations for participation. Students want to know what role educators will have in helping them to guide their thinking throughout the discussion—"Will the teacher remain in a neutral position or provide constructive criticism to challenge students' thought processes?" Educators can also share the process for how the discussion will unfold, provide structure for discussion, and allow candidates to take co-ownership of the process to further value the purpose of the discussion. Allowing equitable time for candidates to share their perspectives can help to ensure that all voices are heard in a fair, consistent manner. Educators can provide time, immediately following the discussion, to debrief and allow candidates to reflect on their experiences and next steps as a result of the discussion.

Teacher educators can bring in artifacts to help guide equity-based discussions and link them to practice. Prior to classroom discussions, teacher candidates can post or share artifacts based on their clinical experiences, including an explanation about why they chose their artifact and include questions that the discussion prompt may have spurred for them. This may allow instructors to address issues of critical social justice or equity by identifying problems and conceptualizing solutions that lead to fundamental changes in teaching beliefs and practices (Sensoy & DiAngelo, 2017). This can provide opportunities for candidates to discuss ways to support the learning and development of diverse students, strengthen culturally inclusive pedagogy, and further develop their inquiry skills.

Simulations. Instructors can engage teacher candidates in simulations, or role-play, to practice perspective-taking of multiple educational stakeholders within their respective educational contexts. Simulations aim to recreate certain aspects of reality to gain information, clarify values, understand other perspectives and cultures, as well as to develop respect and sensitivity vital for effective teaching in a multicultural society (Cruz & Patterson, 2005; Zeichner et al., 2015). Simulations may provide teacher candidates transformative, solution-centered collaborative opportunities to learn from peers and to apply newly gained knowledge and skills to their clinical experiences. Candidates can refine their ability to identify misconceptions and why they need to learn, as well as recognize how their learning impacts their teaching experiences in relation to human development and learning. Through simulations, candidates can learn how to frame problems—specifically their own problems—and choose how to act on them. This is a central feature of enacting change in teaching beliefs and practices (Loughran, 2007).

Instructors can use simulations to meet the needs of PK–12 students within a culturally and socioeconomically diverse school. In this example, the instructor assigns roles to candidates as educational stakeholders, such as teacher, principal, parent, a school psychologist or guidance counselor, resource teachers, and other roles depending on the focus of the simulation, even playing the role of the PK–12 student. During simulations, the instructor poses a scenario that elicits ongoing critical thinking as the "stakeholders" share their ideas from their assigned roles, accompanied by a reenactment of the group reaching a solution with the PK–12 student. Following the simulations, the instructor debriefs with candidates about their experience by addressing any points of misunderstanding and provides further clarification about issues uncovered during the simulation. The instructor can also provide explicit connections to human development and research for teacher candidates to apply to their respective educational contexts. Candidates find simulations highly engaging, and often reconsider how they think about course material in relation to real world educational issues.

Collaborative Teacher Inquiry Strategy 2: Small Groups

Teacher candidates can investigate a topic related to human development and teacher education through reflective dialogue and collaboration in small groups. In small groups, candidates identify a topic that aligns with other clinically based assignments in their teacher education program through an inquiry question co-constructed by the instructor and candidates. Candidates collect data during their clinical experiences and use coursework to inform and analyze the inquiry process, and then share what they learned with their colleagues and reflect on ways to improve the inquiry process. Instructors can create small group assignments that foster purposeful collaboration with colleagues, mentor teachers, or others in planning for clinical or professional experiences through blogging and lesson planning to address their inquiry topic. Instructors can become active participants in the initial stages of teacher inquiry and encourage candidates to engage in inquiry that is embedded in their own teaching experiences (Bates et al., 2011). Instructors may use these assignments to guide classroom discussions and other activities to make further connections between theory and practice.

To begin collaborative dialogue and reflection in small groups, instructors can start class with a 5-minute, free-write activity based on an open-ended thinking stem (e.g., "I believe," "I think," "I understand," etc.) about what they believe about teaching based on acquired knowledge from coursework and clinical experiences. Next, candidates share their writing with peers in small groups based on school reform initiative (SRI) protocols that provide structure for purposeful, reflective dialogue and collaboration (School Reform Initiative, n.d.). For example, the SRI protocol, *gap analysis protocol*, is one of several within the *emphasizing equity and excellence* protocol category that builds candidates' awareness of their beliefs and practices to enhance K–12 student achievement. Candidates begin by individually reflecting on a core belief and the extent of its manifestation in their practices. Then, they gather in peer groups to share their individual analyses of alignment and gaps of their beliefs and practices by asking each other questions and providing ideas for future implementation. Candidates continue in rounds until each person has had a chance to share and receive feedback from their peers. As a result of the protocol, candidates are able to make stronger connections between their beliefs and practices. Additional SRI protocol categories that best fit small group needs include *exploring professional dilemmas, examining data, extending practice, observing one another,* as well as *investigating teaching, learning, and assessment.*

Structured protocols encourage teacher candidates to be attentive listeners and offer specific, constructive feedback that allows them to challenge each other to think in innovative ways, shifting their beliefs and practices toward supporting PK–12 student achievement (Kagle, 2014). To enhance collaboration, candidates can observe each other through videotaping and/or co-teaching in their clinical settings for continued brainstorming and reflection to develop next steps toward their inquiry. Teacher candidates report that learning with their peers, instructor, and other stakeholders through collaborative assignments and discussions improves their practice and they have more ownership of their inquiry process. Instructors find the incorporation of small group dialogue and reflection allows them to build trusting relationships with candidates by providing opportunities for continuous collaboration and feedback.

Collaborative Teacher Inquiry Strategy 3: Practitioner Inquiry Project

Instead of a traditional research paper, teacher candidates engaged in a collaborative practitioner inquiry project addressing a problem or issue that they identified in their professional practice that was informed by human development as well as teacher education theory and research. This inquiry project reinforces expectations of advocating questioning and problematizing present conditions and practices in schools to foster greater equity in one's living spaces (Glickman et al., 2017; Jacobs, 2006). To share their inquiries, teacher candidates wrote a paper that included seven components adapted from a step-by-step guide on how to effectively learn and teach through practitioner inquiry (Dana & Yendol-Hoppey, 2020). In the first three components, teacher candidates convey the significance of their inquiry in relation to their clinical context in the title of the paper, background/rationale for the inquiry and how it is situated within one's clinical or professional experiences and state the inquiry topic as a wondering (e.g., "I wondered...", "How can I..."). In the fourth component, teacher candidates discuss the methods for data collection and analysis, including how the inquiry was conducted and any change, intervention, innovation, or procedures introduced into practice. In the fifth component, teacher candidates discuss the findings in terms of what was learned and connect this to human development and teacher education theory and research. In the sixth component, teacher candidates connect the findings to their teaching beliefs and philosophy and reflect on what was learned about their identities as teachers. In the seventh and final component, teacher candidates discuss plans for practice/dissemination and how the inquiry may inform future educational practices. Teacher candidates can consider implications of the findings for their content area, their own teaching, and any new wonderings. The inquiry papers are evaluated using a rubric; the seven components comprised the categories of evaluation along with mechanics and clarity as two additional categories. If desired, select teacher candidates could work with their instructor to revise their inquiry papers for publication in journals such as *Networks* or *The Journal of Practitioner Research* (see Thomas & Polly, 2020 as an example).

PK–12 School Partnerships

Educational psychology instructors can partner with clinical educators to create authentic, meaningful, job-embedded experiences for teachers in schools that integrate knowledge of human development theory and research as well as research on teacher education such as teacher development and approaches to high-quality teacher professional learning. Two such examples are (a) creating a teacher leader academy and (b) engaging in teacher-led professional learning communities (PLCs) for equity.

Teacher Leader Academy

Instructors can partner with PK–12 schools to provide graduate coursework to practicing teachers as professional development to transform educators into teacher leaders. We share an innovative example of how instructors and teacher educators collaborated to integrate research-informed practices regarding human development throughout a master's degree program delivered at a partnership school through a teacher leader academy (TLA). This school has a long-standing relationship with the university as one of its professional development schools. These are school–university partnerships that have a comprehensive mission dedicated to: advancing educational equity for all students; preparing teachers through clinical practice; sharing boundary-spanning roles and governance structures; attending to the professional learning of all; committing to reflective and innovative practice; and engaging participants in teacher inquiry, research, and dissemination (NAPDS, 2021).

The program in the TLA uses a practice-to-theory approach where teacher leaders bring problems of practice from teaching and leading in a turnaround elementary school to "class," use theory to understand the issues, and identify research-informed practices to address the problems. Each year, the TLA involves approximately 1/3 of the school's staff. These teacher leaders enroll in one graduate course in the fall and spring semester. Both courses are integrated into one year-long experience co-taught at the school by an instructional team consisting of the professors of each course, school district representatives, and doctoral students (for more specifics on the program's award-winning design see Burns, Jacobs et al., 2019; Burns, Johnson, & Hardin-Roberts, 2017).

As part of their coursework, teacher leaders design and facilitate job-embedded professional learning for the rest of the school staff. They create a year-long professional learning unit for their peers and monthly lesson plans for each professional development session, which serve as graduate course class assignments. Prior to implementing the professional development sessions, the instructional team provides feedback to the teacher leaders. As part of their lesson plans, teacher leaders must know the peers who they will be working with. Teacher leaders must also be able to articulate and incorporate theories of adult development to meet those teachers' needs. The teacher leaders' abilities to successfully carry out the lesson plans and facilitate the monthly professional development sessions with their colleagues serve as performance assessments for the graduate courses. In this way, teachers' professional learning is transformed at the school site to meet their development needs. Teacher leaders become empowered to use theories of human development and research-informed practices for high-quality professional learning that improves instructional practice and supports student learning.

In addition to designing and leading professional learning for their peers, teacher leaders had the opportunity to engage in research and dissemination. Each year, the instructors (who are also research faculty) convene a voluntary collaborative research group of interested faculty, doctoral students, school administrators, and teacher leaders to inquire into how well the program met the annual goals to prepare equity-driven teacher leaders who could facilitate change at the school. Being a professional development school meant that there was a standing institutional research board to engage in research. The collaborative research team disseminated the research at national conferences and published their research and innovative practices in book chapters and academic journals (see Burns, Allsopp, et al., 2020; Burns, Haraf, et al., 2020; Burns et al., 2019; Burns, Johnson, & Hardin-Roberts, 2017; Jacobs et al., 2020; Porter & Burns, 2020). This partnership has elevated what constitutes professional learning at a school site while simultaneously rethinking what graduate coursework looks like and for what purpose graduate coursework serves. The results of this TLA program have resulted in significant changes in the school culture and climate, teacher professional learning, equity-driven practices to support student learning, and improved student achievement on state standardized tests (Burns, Allspp et al., 2020; Burns, Haraf et al., 2020; Jacobs et al., 2020).

Teacher-Led Professional Learning Communities for Equity

Instructors can support teachers' application of human development theory and research through teacher-led PLCs that discuss and demonstrate equity in their school contexts. PLCs are a highly structured process where teachers work together to examine and enhance their classroom practice and promote student achievement through ongoing cycles of questions (DuFour, 2014). Instructors can collaborate with teacher educators to design professional development structures where teachers plan and facilitate PLCs with their colleagues at their school sites as job-embedded professional development. Instructors, teacher educators, and teachers work together to develop equity-based inquiry topics for PLCs, such as fostering inclusive classroom culture and environments, promoting a caring classroom disposition, as well as pedagogy and instructional practices. Teachers may work in professional development small groups for an entire school year, identifying and refining their beliefs and practices through intentional and purposeful collaboration with colleagues. As a result, teachers often approach their classrooms with enhanced knowledge of student dynamics and stigmas, and work to promote equitable learning environments (hooks, 2014).

An example of a teacher-led PLC for equity involves two teacher leaders from the TLA who co-facilitated a PLC focused on the inquiry topic of pedagogy and instructional practices. To maintain a focus on equity, teachers were encouraged to integrate concepts of equity literacy such as recognizing, responding to, and redressing bias (Gorski, 2018). The teachers were required to create a lesson plan for their PLC facilitation based on a learning objective, written as: "Teachers will be able to think about how learning about their own backgrounds and cultures affects their own teaching practices and interactions with their students and colleagues." Other components of the lesson plan included a step-by-step detailed plan for the PLC session (including an ice breaker activity, cultural artifact protocol, debriefing, exit ticket, and follow-up), explanation about how the plan reflects what teachers learned after implementing the last round of the PLC, planned facilitation strategies, and connections to literature regarding culture and culturally responsive teaching. The PLC groups encouraged teachers to "think aloud," in which their discussion of questions, issues, and concerns associated with the changes to their pedagogy and instructional practices helped them to make their tacit learning experiences more explicit (Loughran, 2007). Through this collaboration, instructors and teacher educators actively engaged teachers in the continued application of concepts around human development based on their lived experiences as practicing teachers. Similar teacher-led PLCs for equity may support the social nature of knowledge construction for teachers to foster the development of knowledge that embraces harmonious and cooperative learning opportunities as the foundation for PK–12 student achievement (Newman & Latifi, 2021).

ADVOCATING FOR THE INTEGRATION OF DEVELOPMENTAL THEORY AND RESEARCH INTO TEACHER EDUCATION

Incorporating knowledge of human development and teacher education within teacher education is critical for developing educators' research-based knowledge to inform their beliefs and practices and to effectively prepare them to be responsive to the diverse developmental and learning needs of PK–12 learners. It is important for educational psychology instructors and teacher educators to advocate for the strategic integration of developmental theory and research as well as research in teacher education into teacher education curriculum. In this section, we discuss ways they can advocate for this integration in their own programs.

First, educational psychology instructors and teacher educators can advocate for the integration of human development and teacher education research within teacher education programs to promote opportunities for engagement in cross-curricular collaboration. Instructors can meet to discuss course goals, assessments, and teacher candidates' needs to foster synergy across coursework and clinical or professional experiences. These meetings have the potential to develop transformative, collaborative partnerships where instructors work together to support the needs of their candidates throughout a program. This may include co-teaching to intentionally integrate knowledge of human development and teacher education. Instructors can also inform and improve their own instructional practices by applying knowledge of human development and teacher education in support of teacher candidates' and practicing teachers' capacities to meet PK–12 learners' needs. We encourage instructors to reflect on their beliefs and understandings, individually and collectively, regarding PK–12 student development and learning, as well as the professional development of teachers. We urge instructors to question what constitutes a teacher education course and the nature of coursework in their program to allow for co-teaching or a team approach to the development and delivery of courses.

Second, incorporating knowledge of human development and teacher education research may help instructors to prepare teacher candidates and practicing teachers to identify misconceptions and foster their conceptual change (Gay & Kirkland, 2003; Liu, 2015). Instructors can offer ongoing opportunities for candidates to critically reflect on their development as teachers and their beliefs about teacher learning and human development. Instructors can do this by providing realistic examples of developmental concepts in educational settings. Opportunities to apply developmental theories to real-world experiences through assignments such as a cross-discipline reflective blog, a clinically based case study, and administered lesson plan are useful tools. We encourage instructors to incorporate teacher inquiry that draws upon knowledge of human development and teacher education by engaging in activities such as discussions, simulations, and collaborative teacher inquiry. Teacher inquiry provides teacher candidates with opportunities to systematically rethink their practice as well as their PK–12 students' development, learning, and achievement (Athanases & de Oliveira, 2008; Merino & Holmes, 2006). The teacher inquiry process can help educators to go beyond a superficial or initial understanding and promote a research-based practice and advocacy mindset in their teaching

(Athanases & de Oliveira, 2008). We encourage instructors to consider how they can provide practicing teachers with professional development opportunities to become teacher leaders through research-informed practices. Instructors can brainstorm ways to utilize a practice-to-theory approach in their own program. Such an approach provides practicing teachers opportunities to use theory to gain an understanding of issues and practices to address problems related to meeting PK–12 students' needs.

Third, intentionally integrating human development and teacher education research into teacher education allows instructors to effectively prepare teachers to be responsive to the diverse learning and developmental needs of their PK–12 learners. Instructors can help candidates to explore human development using an equity lens and cultural perspective to enhance their awareness and understanding of diverse learners. This knowledge is vital for transforming teacher identity (Kahn et al., 2014; Miller Dyce & Owusu-Ansah, 2016) as it allows individuals to construct a critically reflective understanding of learning and human development and its role in their professional practice. Research-based knowledge of human development allows teacher educators to purposefully bridge connections between theory and practice that support candidates' clinical experiences to build equitable learning environments. Instructors can prepare candidates to enact culturally responsive beliefs and practices by making connections between knowledge of developmental theories and learners' backgrounds. We encourage instructors to find ways to increase their cultural awareness and responsiveness to the teacher candidates and practicing teachers they work with in their program, as well as the PK–12 communities that they serve. We urge instructors to consider ways to support development and diversity among learners through assignments such as a cross-curricular reflective blog, clinical case study, and lesson plan, and by facilitating equity-based discussions, simulations, and teacher inquiry. We also encourage instructors to consider ways to sustainably promote teacher-led PLCs for equity among practicing educators (Gorski, 2018; Newman & Latifi, 2021).

In conclusion, this chapter advocates for the intentional, systematic integration of knowledge of human development and teacher education into teacher preparation curriculum. Such efforts aim to equip educational psychology instructors and teacher educators with the knowledge necessary to advocate for change in their own programs. Instructors can critically reflect on ways to help teacher candidates—and themselves—to identify misconceptions and foster conceptual change, as well as promote culturally responsive practices and the transformation of teacher identity. Teacher education programs can provide teacher candidates with a strong understanding of developmental theory and application to their practice by implementing signature assignments such as a cross-curricular reflective blog, clinical case study, and an administered lesson plan. Teacher education programs can also provide teacher candidates and practicing teachers with opportunities to engage in collaborative teacher inquiry, as well as provide teacher-led PLCs that focus on equity issues and promote teacher leaders through PK–12 and university partnerships.

KEY CHAPTER TAKEAWAYS

Teacher candidates can collaborate on signature assignments across courses and clinical experiences within the teacher education program. Examples include:	• A reflective blog in which teacher candidates observe a child(ren) in the field placement classroom, then write reflective blog entries based on their observations. • A case study paper in which candidates focus on an individual learner as a part of their clinical experiences. • A lesson plan in which candidates develop and administer a lesson at their clinical-based assignment informed by developmental theories and research in teacher education.
Teacher candidates engage in collaborative teacher inquiry through the uses of:	• Discussions and simulations in response to instructor's provision of equity-based inquiry questions that probe candidates' thinking about developmental theory and research. • Small groups in which candidates investigate a topic related to human development and teacher education through reflective dialogue and collaboration. • A practitioner inquiry project in which candidates write a paper on their role in a collaborative practitioner inquiry project and how it is informed by human development and teacher education theory and research
Faculty partner with PK–12 schools to provide graduate coursework to practicing teachers as professional development and to transform educators into teacher leaders through:	• A teacher leader academy. • Teacher-led professional learning communities for equity where instructors support teachers' application of human development theory and research.

KEY WORDS

Cognitive bias
Collaborative teacher inquiry
Conceptual change
Culturally responsive teaching
PK–12 school partnerships
Practitioner inquiry project
Professional learning communities
Signature assignments
Simulations
Teacher education research
Teacher leader academy

REFERENCES

Armstrong, T. (2006). *The best schools: How human development research should inform educational practice.* Association for Supervision and Curriculum Development.

Athanases, S. Z., & de Oliveira, L. C. (2008). Advocacy for equity in classrooms and beyond: New teachers' challenges and responses. *Teachers College Record, 110*(1), 64–104. https://doi.org/10.1177/016146810811000101

Bates, A. J., Drits, D., & Ramirez, L. A. (2011). Self-awareness and enactment of supervisory stance: Influences on responsiveness toward student teacher learning. *Teacher Education Quarterly, 38*(3), 69–87. https://files.eric.ed.gov/fulltext/EJ940634.pdf

Burns, R. W., Allsopp, D., Johnson, W. W., III, Stuart, C., Saia, H., Brown, L., & Carswell, K. (2020). Mort Elementary Community Partnership School: Making a twenty-five year commitment. In E. Garin & R. W. Burns (Eds.), *Clinically based teacher education in action: Cases from professional development schools* (pp. 159–165). Information Age Publishing.

Burns, R. W., Haraf, S., Perrone-Britt, F., Porter, M., Bellas, A., & Johnson, W. (2020). Making a difference: The influence of teacher leadership in an urban PDS on elementary students. *School–University Partnerships, 12*(4), 67–85.

Burns, R. W., Jacobs, J., Allsopp, D., Haraf, S., Baker, W., Johnson, W. W., Bellas, A., Perrone-Britt, F., Izzo, M., Hailey-Brown, L., Krein, D., & Wichinsky, L. (2019, September). Mort Elementary Community Partnership School 2019 Exemplary professional development school award winner. *School–University Partnerships, 12*(2), 3–11. https://files.eric.ed.gov/fulltext/EJ1234566.pdf

Burns, R. W., Johnson, W. W., III, & Hardin-Roberts, S. (2017). The Mort Teacher Leader Academy: Developing teacher leaders for urban schools together. In D. Yendol-Hoppey, D. A. Shanley, D. C. Delane, & D. Hoppey (Eds.), *Working together: Enhancing urban educator quality through school-university partnerships* (pp. 129–148). Information Age Publishing.

Cochran-Smith, M., & Lytle, S. (1993). *Inside/outside: Teacher research and knowledge.* Teachers College Press.

Cruz, B. C., & Patterson, J. (2005). Cross-cultural simulations in teacher education: Developing empathy and understanding. *Multicultural Perspectives, 7*(2), 40–47. https://doi.org/10.1207/s15327892mcp0702_7

Currin, E. (2019). From rigor to vigor: The past, present, and potential of inquiry as stance. *Journal of Practitioner Research, 4*(1), 1–21. https://doi.org/10.5038/2379-9951.4.1.1091

Dana, N. F., & Yendol-Hoppey, D. (2020). *The reflective educator's guide to classroom research: Learning to teach and teaching to learn through practitioner inquiry* (4th ed.). Corwin Press.

De Lisi, R., & Golbeck, S. L. (1999). Implications of Piagetian theory for peer learning. In A. M. O'Donnell & A. King (Eds.), *Cognitive perspectives on peer learning* (Chapter 1). Erlbaum.

DuFour, R. (2014). Harnessing the power of PLCS. *Educational Leadership, 71*(8), 30–35. https://eric.ed.gov/?id=EJ1043762

Gay, G., & Kirkland, K. (2003). Developing cultural critical consciousness and self-reflection in preservice teacher education. *Theory Into Practice, 42*(3), 181–187. https://doi.org/10.1207/s15430421tip4203_3

Glickman, C. D., Gordon, S. P., & Ross-Gordon, J. M. (2017). *Supervision and instructional leadership: A developmental approach* (10th ed.). Allyn & Bacon.

Gorski, P. C. (2018). *Reaching and teaching students in poverty*. Teachers College Press.

Guilfoyle, L., McCormack, O., & Erduran, S. (2020). The 'tipping point' for educational research: The role of pre-service science teachers' epistemic beliefs in evaluating the professional utility of educational research. *Teaching and Teacher Education, 90*, 1–15. https://doi.org/10.1016/j.tate.2020.103033

Hofer, B. K., & Pintrich, P. R. (Eds.). (2002). *Personal epistemology: The psychology of beliefs about knowledge and knowing*. Erlbaum.

Hogan, T., Rabinowitz, M., & Craven, J. A., III. (2003). Representation in teaching: Inferences from research of expert and novice teachers. *Educational Psychologist, 38*, 235–247. https://doi.org/10.1207/S15326985EP3804_3

hooks, b. (2014). *Teaching to transgress*. Routledge.

Jacobs, J. (2006). Supervision for social justice: Supporting critical reflection. *Teacher Education Quarterly, 33*(4), 23–39. https://files.eric.ed.gov/fulltext/EJ795224.pdf

Jacobs, J., Burns, R. W., Haraf, S., Bellas, A., Perrone-Britt, F., & Holt, M. (2020). Equity-based teacher leaders facilitating change within an urban professional development school. *School–University Partnerships, 13*(3), 102–123.

Joram, E. (2007). Clashing epistemologies: Aspiring teachers', practicing teachers' and professors' beliefs about knowledge and research in education. *Teaching and Teacher Education, 23*, 123–135. https://doi.org/10.1016/j.tate.2006.04.032

Kagle, M. (2014). Professional learning communities for pre-service teachers. *National Teacher Education Journal, 7*(2), 21–25.

Kahn, L. G., Lindstrom, L., & Murray, C. (2014). Factors contributing to preservice teachers' beliefs about diversity. *Teacher Education Quarterly, 41*(4), 53–70. https://www.jstor.org/stable/10.2307/teaceducquar.41.4.53

King, P. M., & Kitchener, K. S. (2004). Reflective judgment: Theory and research on the development of epistemic assumptions through adulthood. *Educational Psychologist, 39*, 5–18. https://doi.org/10.1207/s15326985ep3901_2

Larrivee, B. (2006). The convergence of reflective practice and effective classroom management. In C. M. Evertson & C. S. Weinstein (Eds.), *Handbook of classroom management: Research, practice, and contemporary issues* (pp. 983–1001). Erlbaum.

Liu, K. (2015). Critical reflection as a framework for transformative learning in teacher education. *Educational Review, 67*(2), 135–157. https://doi.org/10.1080/00131911.2013.839546

Loughran, J. (2007). Enacting a pedagogy of teacher education. In T. Russell & J. Loughran (Eds.), *Enacting a pedagogy of teacher education* (pp. 11–25). Routledge.

McDevitt, T. M., & Ormrod, J. E. (2008). Fostering conceptual change about child development in prospective teachers and other college students. *Child Development Perspectives, 2*(2), 85–91. https://doi.org/10.1111/j.1750-8606.2008.00045.x

McKeachie, W., & Svinicki, M. (2013). *McKeachie's teaching tips.* Cengage Learning.

Merino, B. J., & Holmes, P. (2006). Student teacher inquiry as an "entry point" for advocacy. *Teacher Education Quarterly, 33*(3), 79–96. https://www.jstor.org/stable/23478895

Merriam, S. B., & Bierema, L. L. (2014). *Adult learning: Linking theory and practice.* John Wiley & Sons.

Miller Dyce, C., & Owusu-Ansah, A. (2016). Yes, we are still talking about diversity: Diversity education as a catalyst for transformative, culturally relevant, and reflective preservice teacher practices. *Journal of Transformative Education, 14*, 327–354. https://doi.org/10.1177/1541344616650750

Moser, S., Zumbach, J., Deibl, I., Geiger, V., & Martinek, D. (2021). Development and application of a scale for assessing pre-service teachers' beliefs about the nature of educational psychology. *Psychology Learning & Teaching, 20*(2). https://doi.org/10.1177/1475725720974575

National Association for Professional Development Schools. (2021). *What it means to be a professional development school: The nine essentials* (2nd ed.). https://napds.org/nine-essentials/

National Institute of Child Health and Human Development & National Association for the Accreditation of Teacher Education. (2007, April). *Child and adolescent development research and teacher education: Evidence-based pedagogy, policy, and practice.* National Association for the Accreditation of Teacher Education.

Newman, S., & Latifi, A. (2021). Vygotsky, education, and teacher education. *Journal of Education for Teaching, 47*(1), 4–17. https://doi.org/10.1080/02607476.2020.1831375

Patrick, H., & Pintrich, P. R. (2001). Conceptual change in teachers' intuitive conceptions of learning, motivation, and instruction: The role of motivational and epistemological beliefs. In B. Torff & R. J. Sternberg (Eds.), *Understanding and teaching the intuitive mind: Student and teacher learning* (pp. 117–143). Erlbaum.

Porter, M., & Burns, R. W. (2020). Beyond survival: Three tips for thriving your first year of teaching. In A. Quinzio-Zafran & E. A. Wilkins (Eds.), *The new teacher's guide to overcoming common challenges: Curated advice from award-winning teachers.* Taylor & Francis Publishing.

Reyna, C. (2000). Lazy, dumb, or industrious: When stereotypes convey attribution information in the classroom. *Educational Psychology Review, 12,* 85–110. https://doi.org/10.1023/A:1009037101170

Rogoff, B. (2003). *The cultural nature of human development.* Oxford University Press.

School Reform Initiative. (n.d.). *Protocols.* https://www.schoolreforminitiative.org/protocols/

Sensoy, O., & DiAngelo, R. (2017). *Is everyone really equal? An introduction to key concepts in social justice education.* Teachers College Press.

Sleeter, C. E., & Owuor, J. (2011). Research on the impact of teacher preparation to teach diverse students: The research we have and the research we need. *Action in Teacher Education, 33*(5–6), 524–536. https://doi.org/10.1080/01626620.2011.627045

Steinberg, L. (2015). How to improve the health of American adolescents. *Perspectives on Psychological Science, 10*(6), 711–715. https://doi.org/10.1177/1745691615598510

Tezci, E., Erdener, M. A., & Atici, S. (2016). The effect of pre-service teachers' epistemological beliefs on teaching approaches. *Universal Journal of Educational Research 4*(12A), 220–215. https://doi.org/10.13189/ujer.2016.041326

Thomas, M., & Polly, D. (2020). The influence of visually rich technology on the writing process of elementary students. *Journal of Practitioner Research, 5*(1), Article 4. https://doi.org/10.5038/2379-9951.5.1.1104

Warren, C. A. (2018). Empathy, teacher dispositions, and preparation for culturally responsive pedagogy. *Journal of Teacher Education, 69*(2), 169–183. https://doi.org/10.1177/0022487117712487

Wolkenhauer, R., & Hooser, A. (2017). "Inquiry as confidence": How practitioner inquiry can support new teachers. *Journal of Practitioner Research, 2*(1), Article 5. http://doi.org/10.5038/2379-9951.2.1.1028

Zeichner, K., Payne, K. A., & Brayko, K. (2015). Democratizing teacher education. *Journal of Teacher Education, 66*(2), 122–135. https://doi.org/10.1177/0022487114560908

CHAPTER 5

THE WHY AND HOW OF WHAT WE DO

Using Case Studies to Understand Adolescent Development for Teacher Education

Dana L. Haraway
James Madison University

Ann Allred
James Madison University

Teachers face great challenges as they provide for the educational and mental health needs of students during and (optimistically) after the COVID-19 pandemic. In addition, the political climate, racial unrest, curriculum debates, and concerns of parents create a challenging milieu for teaching. As such, it seems logical and prudent to rely on educational psychology as a valuable resource to ground and inform teachers' instruction and decision-making practices (Anderson et al., 1995; Carter & Doyle, 1996).

Teaching Human Development for Educators, pages 95–113
Copyright © 2024 by Information Age Publishing
www.infoagepub.com
All rights of reproduction in any form reserved.

Yet, ironically, colleges and universities across the nation are continuing to phase out educational psychology programs, while faculty strive to establish relevance and produce evidence of the benefits of educational psychology in teacher education (Patrick et al., 2011). The crux of the debate regarding relevance seems to center on two main themes. First, there is discussion of the balance between theory and practice (Anderson et al., 1995; Chizhik & Chizhik, 2003; Crozier, 2009) and the domain that should be responsible for disseminating the knowledge to inform practice (Carter & Doyle, 1996). Second, there is the challenge to redefine the significance of educational psychology within teacher preparation programs given the fluid role of content standards (Woolfolk, 2000).

FOUNDATIONS IN EDUCATIONAL PSYCHOLOGY

Educational psychology provides a foundation for understanding and evaluating curriculum, teachers' decision-making, students' learning and development, and the effects of schooling structures on student learning. The field helps bring meaning to complex and multidimensional classroom events (Anderson et al., 1995; Carter & Doyle, 1996). Surveys of teacher educators reveal a consensus that educational psychology is important for preservice teachers in many areas, including "motivation and management, diversity, instructional strategies, assessment, emotions and relationships" (Hanich & Deemer, 2005, p. 189). Internationally, leaders in educational psychology ranked knowledge about cognitive and motivational development and the influence of social contexts as the highest needs in teacher preparation programs in addition to learning about child development (Lohse-Bossenz et al., 2013). In their future professions, preservice teacher candidates will need to "draw on knowledge of child development to nurture children's and adolescents' academic and creative skills, physical and emotional wellbeing, and productive peer relationships" (McDevitt & Ormrod, 2008, p. 85). Educational psychology guides preservice teacher candidates in developing "interested, motivated, self-regulated, and confident learners" while they in turn build their "own sense of self-efficacy as a teacher" (Woolfolk, 2019, p. 23).

Accrediting bodies and state licensure requirements recognize the importance of human growth and development coursework for teacher preparation (Woolfolk, 2000). The Council for the Accreditation of Educator Preparation and the Interstate Teacher Assessment and Support Consortium professional standards identify knowledge and skills for teacher candidates that directly descend from educational psychology. These include understanding individual differences among learners, approaches to creating safe and supportive learning environments, and employing an array of instructional strategies that result in equitable and inclusive learning experiences for diverse learners.

The purpose of this chapter is to share the rationale, development, and impact of one teacher leadership course that has a substantial focus on educational psychology and is part of a middle education Master of Arts in teaching (MAT) program. Preservice teacher candidates enroll in the course during their final semester, after having completed student teaching the previous semester. We write from two perspectives, one as the professor and one as a graduate student in the course. The revised Association for Middle Level Education (AMLE, 2012) accreditation standards were required to be implemented in all middle level teacher education preparation programs in 2015. Our teacher preparation program responded by engaging in self-study, identifying needs, and developing curriculum and assessments. A case study assignment for teacher candidates enrolled in the course was derived from the self-study work and intended to meet identified needs.

A main point of this chapter is that teacher candidates' grounding in educational psychology is essential to their being able to understand and justify what educators do in schools. In other words, educational psychology provides the foundation to inform teachers and administrators in making decisions about appropriate school structures, organization, and instruction based on a variety of student developmental needs. School structures include interdisciplinary teaming, content teaming, scheduling, and incorporating an advisory period and other systems and processes pertinent to the efficient operations of middle schools. Learning about middle school structures while revisiting or relearning educational psychology helps teacher candidates to understand the qualities of the school environment beyond their classroom.

In this chapter, we describe the rationale for a case study assignment that is based on both accreditation requirements and identified weaknesses in candidate preparation specifically related to learning and applying educational psychology theories about learning and human development. For our purposes, the term *case study* is defined as a fictional representation of characters and a school environment. The case study is created by candidates to demonstrate their understanding of educational psychology, students' development, and the characteristics of effective middle schools. We explore the use of case studies in teacher education and discuss how we prepare candidates for the case study assignment. Next, we outline the requirements of the assignment and provide samples of candidate work and reflections. Finally we describe our conclusions and implications for preparing teachers using the case study assignment.

RATIONALE BASED ON ACCREDITATION REQUIREMENTS

The case study assignment is designed to focus on the following AMLE standards: (a) knowledge of young adolescent development including implications for student diversity, curriculum, and programs; (b) knowledge of middle level philosophy and school organization; and (c) teachers' professional roles, including culturally responsive instruction and developmentally responsive schooling and working with families and communities. Based on the AMLE mission statement, teacher education programs are required to prepare preservice teachers to be responsive to the growth and development of middle grades adolescents. Within the mission statement itself (Bishop & Harrison, 2021), there is an implicit assumption that educators are knowledgeable in the fundamentals of educational psychology that inform responsive practices.

Preservice teachers often complete educational psychology courses early in their course sequence and experience large, lecture-based classes, resulting in fewer opportunities for discussion and limited chances for application exercises related to school settings (Cuseo, 2007; McKeachie et al., 1986). Preservice teachers may have a difficult time later recalling the material once they embark on their coursework and field experiences because either they forgot previous learning or they remembered concepts incorrectly (Pascarella & Terenzini, 2005; Shulman, 1999).

PURPOSES OF CASE STUDIES FOR TEACHER LEARNING

There are several purposes that case studies serve in the preparation of teacher candidates. First, case studies are useful in helping preservice teacher candidates "bridge the gap between theory and practice and develop skills of reflection and close analysis" (Darling-Hammond & Baratz-Snowden, 2007, p. 127). Teacher candidates that have not yet analyzed the theoretical implications of teaching during their teacher preparation program may develop bad habits and will likely miss opportunities to promote learning for all of their students. Second, case studies provide opportunities for faculty to engage students in discussion, instruction, and guidance that can support candidates' learning. By reviewing cases together, instructors are able to clarify misconceptions that emerge and support candidates in generating appropriate responses to situations. Thus, by assigning case studies, teacher education "programs teach [preservice] teachers to do more than simply implement a particular technique; they help teachers learn to think pedagogically, reason through dilemmas, investigate problems, and analyze student learning" (Darling-Hammond & Baratz-Snowden, 2007, p. 119). Third, case studies can lead to opportunities for shared experiences when teacher candidates collaborate to analyze classroom situations, explore existing misconceptions about students' behavior and development, and strategize appropriate responses to challenging instructional situations.

Because preservice teacher candidates often have difficulty relating theories of learning, motivation, and behavior management to practice, McDevitt and Ormrod (2008) suggested the need for "active cognitive engagement with the subject matter [to] promote[s] conceptual change" (p. 88). Real learning occurs when learners are able to transfer their knowledge to novel situations (Anderson & Krathwohl, 2001; Bloom, 1956; Popham, 2020). In this vein, case studies can help preservice teachers reflect on their observations during practicum experiences and apply what they have learned to new situations (Shulman, 1999). Given a firm foundation in educational psychology's theories, preservice teachers will be better equipped to employ case studies to interpret complex classroom situations where they can discern appropriate teacher actions in response to students' behaviors (Anderson et al., 1995). Chizhik and Chizhik (2003) refer to this as "a transformative instructional attitude and approach," described as an "integration of psychological theory and educational practice," while incorporating "creative problem solving" (p. 183).

In addition to the purposes described above, case studies enable candidates to demonstrate their understanding of the whole child and the school environment by examining realistic scenarios. Candidates can explore multidimensional aspects of students, as informed by educational psychology theories, to analyze how the case study student interacts within the school environment. For example, a candidate's case study might include a situation involving Pavlov's classical conditioning (1927/1960) to demonstrate their understanding about how one failure experience on a test might lead to associations with other tests—resulting in test anxiety. More importantly, candidates can describe teacher actions that could diminish this association and help students overcome conditioned responses.

Depending on the parameters of the assignment, case studies can also help candidates understand the characteristics of effective school and classroom practices such as block scheduling, homework policies, or zero credit for missing work, so that they are better prepared to respond to future teaching situations in supportive ways (Eun, 2016; Patrick et al., 2011). Case studies enable preservice teachers to examine the ecology of classrooms, including teachers' behaviors and well-established cultural patterns displayed in teacher–student interactions (Bowers & Flinders, 1990). For example, preservice teachers may explore the *ecology of power* (Bowers & Flinders, 1990) perpetuated when teachers are nonresponsive to students, potentially conveying "rejection and invalidation of student's thoughts and values" (1990, p. 163). As Darling-Hammond and Baratz-Snowden (2007) describe, students can read published case studies to gain understanding, but they can also write their own case studies, "learning to represent their experiences and analyze them through the lens of theory" (p. 128).

Gay and Kirkland (2003) make an argument for the importance of culturally responsive teaching being a focal point in teacher training programs. They contend that "teachers knowing who they are as people, understanding the contexts in which they teach, and questioning their knowledge and assumptions are as important as the mastery of techniques for instructional effectiveness" (p. 181). To that end, our case study assignment requires teacher candidates to develop and describe fictitious teachers who demonstrate ways of engaging with adolescent students that value and affirm the students' *cultural capital*, that is, the dispositions, knowledge, and competencies students bring to school (Bourdieu, 1986). Candidates create fictitious teachers who display planning skills and who implement specific teaching strategies that promote respectful interactions with diverse students and demonstrate cultural inclusivity in curriculum decisions and instructional strategies (e.g., assigning readings from diverse authors, incorporating instructional activities that encourage students to share their stories, cultures and experiences, and using illustrations that depict a variety of learners (Love, 2019). Candidates may further illustrate culturally relevant teaching practices by describing teachers in their case studies who, for example: demonstrate high expectations for student success; employ strength based approaches that value and incorporate diverse student cultures and experiences; and foster respectful classroom climates based on students' understandings of themselves and others (Benson, 2003; Byrd, 2016; Ladson-Billings, 1995; Zeichner, 1993).

PREPARING CANDIDATES FOR THE CASE STUDY

Prior to the introduction of the case study assignment, the teacher candidates work on developing the skills necessary to be developmentally responsive teachers. Weekly class discussions about various educational psychology theories help candidates strengthen their understanding by replacing forgotten learning, clarifying misconceptions, and activating inert knowledge (Shulman, 1999). After discussing and analyzing theories of learning and of child and adolescent development, candidates create scenarios with teacher characters whose actions and behaviors are responsive to student needs and supportive of student growth. They also read and discuss classroom vignettes that illustrate behavioral and developmental concepts, while reflecting on situations from their practica and student teaching experiences. For example, candidates might understand an "unmotivated" student by applying Erikson's (1968) ideas about the industry vs. inferiority stage of psychosocial development in which children are learning how to work and persist at tasks. Thus, the candidates can consider how different instructional scaffolds might assist future students to stay on task, work toward different goals, and gain confidence in their abilities.

Additional assigned readings include topics on special education interventions, the impact of socioeconomic factors on students' learning and achievement, teaching in diverse classrooms, promoting equity and fairness, and responding to students that have experienced trauma. Candidates explore the interconnections among educational psychology theories and recommended practices and strategies pertinent to these topics. For example, a candidate might describe an adolescent who, upon being placed in the foster care system, struggles in school. The candidate might then discuss the difficulty for the student in developing a sense of trust in self or others (drawing upon Erikson's developmental stage of trust vs. mistrust) or the role of various "systems" that influence the individual's life circumstances (drawing upon Bronfenbrenner's [1970] bioecological systems theory).

Following the introduction to theories or learning and development, candidates learn about the characteristics of effective middle schools as described by AMLE and the schools to watch (STW) program. Candidates read and analyze AMLE's mission statement (Bishop & Harrison, 2021), "The Successful Middle School: This We Believe" (TWB) and examine the essential school attributes (i.e., responsive, challenging, empowering, equitable, and engaging) and characteristics of effective schools. These characteristics comprise three categories: (a) culture and community; (b) curriculum, instruction, and assessment; and (c) leadership and organization. The STW program, developed by the National Forum to Accelerate Middle-Grades Reform, encourages middle schools to engage in a thorough self-study and seek designation for being academically excellent, developmentally responsive, and socially equitable (middlegradesforum.org, 2018). As part of the designation process, a team of evaluators conducts a comprehensive school visit to determine if a school meets STW's criteria for recognition. The preservice teachers replicate this work and engage in a mock STW site visit. Candidates then convene to discuss their impressions and generate a report describing how well the school's environment, personnel, and practices align with STW's criteria for an "exemplary" middle school. Using this process, candidates apply what they learn to develop their own fictitious case study school and characters.

By combining field experiences, such as those for the STW mock site visits, with class discussions of educational psychology and child and adolescent development theories, we have observed that the preservice teachers increase their understanding of developmentally appropriate school structures and practices. For example, during one STW mock visit, candidates learned of a middle school's mandate that all students pass Algebra I prior to promotion to ninth grade. Candidates applied Piaget's (1970) theory of cognitive development to understand why some students need concrete examples to learn abstract algebraic concepts. After examining assessment data provided by the school as part of the STW application, candidates drew from Vygotsky's (1986) theory, commenting that Algebra I concepts might be beyond some students' "zone of proximal development" (i.e., what students can learn with the support of a more capable peer or teacher). Candidates concluded that requiring Algebra I for all students was neither an equitable nor a developmentally appropriate practice for eighth grade.

THE CASE STUDY

Drawing from Blumenfeld et al.'s (1996) work, where preservice teachers apply concepts from educational psychology to justify unit and lesson plans, our case study assignment requires preservice teachers to create fictional scenarios that illustrate both the developmental challenges that young adolescents confront and the responsive school environments that support these students' development and learning. Teacher candidates draw evidence from course readings and discussions to establish a foundation for their "story" and provide justification for the elements of their story. After developing the case, candidates engage in peer review, analyze cases created by fellow candidates, and communicate feedback according to the case study scoring rubric (Appendix A). Then, candidates review and revise their cases based on peer feedback. Finally, they present their work and lead class discussions on the analysis of their case study.

REQUIREMENTS

Candidates must describe both the principal characters (e.g., main student, siblings, friends, parents, and teachers) and the school environment, including a variety of classroom situations and theoretical perspectives to meet two essential requirements of the assignment. First, candidates must describe relevant theories of adolescent development that "explain" their case study subject(s) including thoughts, interactions, and behaviors. Second, they must describe the school structures that address the diverse intellectual, social-emotional, and academic needs of students. Candidates can write their case study either independently or with a partner. The following is an excerpt from the assignment instructions:

> Begin with a detailed and creative description of your young adolescent. Sometimes combining characteristics of several students you know and/or have worked with helps you "see" the student and bring life to your description. Write your case study with the eventual analysis in mind but remember

you are writing a description of a young adolescent and telling a story... the analysis is separate. It may be helpful to include details about friends, classmates, and family to deepen your case and capture all the required aspects. Thus, be sure to provide enough details that you or a peer could identify evidence of your understanding about the unique challenges adolescents face and include examples and justifications of the following:

1. Physical development
2. Social and emotional development—Erikson
3. Moral development—Kohlberg
4. Bioecological systems theory—Bronfenbrenner
5. Cognitive development—Piaget and Vygotsky
6. Behaviorism and social cognitive theory—Bandura, Pavlov, Skinner
7. Two examples of adolescent dialogue

The assignment requires candidates to create authentic characters that illustrate the above requirements. Candidates must also include examples and descriptions of classroom and school situations that demonstrate their understanding of the middle school structures (as espoused by TWB and STW) that affect adolescent learners. The components of the case study that must be included and analyzed are: (a) the learning environment, (b) curriculum and instruction, (c) work with students with special needs, (d) the racial/ethnic diversity of the school/classroom, and (e) the relationship of family and school socioeconomic status (SES) to adolescents' academic achievement. The excerpt from one case study story (Figure 5.1), depicts the balance between narrative and analysis where candidates provide examples as well as justification to meet the requirements of the assignment.

Language Arts

Over the past few weeks Alex has noticed that Hannah likes to take Cornell notes during Mr. Davis' instruction. She explained how key questions or main ideas were listed to the left of the page and detailed information was recorded on the right. Alex loved this idea and wanted to incorporate it for himself. On the bus ride to school one day, Julio also showed Alex how he highlighted key terms in his language arts notes. Today, during Mr. Davis' instruction Alex tried taking notes using both the Cornell notes style and by highlighting key terms from class. He loved how organized his notes were and decided to use this method again tomorrow (25).

After today's lesson on similes and metaphors, Mr. Davis explained that each group was going to make a playlist of 5 songs of their choice. Each song needed to contain at least one simile or metaphor. Then groups were going to analyze the lyrics, highlight the examples they found, and explain why those examples were either a simile or a metaphor (26). Before sending groups off to work, Mr. Davis played one of his favorite songs and verbally demonstrated his thought process for identifying a metaphor within the lyrics (27). Finally, he gave students the rest of the class period to work and walked around the room monitoring their progress. Alex and Hannah get right to work. They talk briefly about what they learned in class and Hannah realizes that she has been mixing up the definitions of simile and metaphor. She loves talking with her classmates because it helps her better understand what they learned in class (28). The two spend the rest of their time looking up their favorite songs and completing the assignment.

25. Behaviourism: Bandura - Alex's combination of using Cornell notes, which he observed from Hannah, and highlighting key terms, which he observed from Julio, is an example of Bandura's **synthesized modeling**.

26. Curriculum and instruction - Mr. Davis uses music and songs to help students relate the concepts of similes and metaphors to real-world examples. Additionally, Mr. Davis uses modeling to show his students how to identify examples within the songs they select. He is providing students with a high-quality example. STW Academic Excellence: "All students are expected to meet high academic standards. Teachers provide students with exemplars of high quality work."

27. Vygotsky-By verbalizing his thought process for identifying a metaphor within a song, Mr. Davis is **scaffolding** his students through a think-aloud model.

28. Piaget - Hannah's discussion of content with her peers allows her to test her schemes against those of others. When their schemes don't match, her equilibrium is disrupted and she is motivated to adapt.

Figure 5.1 Case study excerpt.

CASE STUDY EXCERPT

For each requirement, candidates can choose to present either positive or negative examples. They are required to justify how their scenario illustrates the target theory (e.g., Piaget) or associated concept (e.g., formal operations), with citations, as applicable. If a negative example is given, candidates must also suggest methods to improve the practice, setting, or behavior. Candidates can describe culturally responsive teaching practices by creating situations within their story where teacher characters "modify curriculum content, instructional strategies, [or] learning climates to make them more responsive to ethnic and cultural diversity" and support student success (Gay & Kirkland, 2003, pp. 185–186).

Candidates must also devise two quotations for their case study characters that represent an adolescent's everyday speech and point of view. For example, a character remembers his mother's warning as he travels to school:

> "Please, don't get yourself in trouble again, alright, Mijo? Te amo y mas." His mom's parting words echoed in his head as his backpack vibrated to the bus's roll. "Easy for her to say... she doesn't understand... she doesn't have to go to school." Alex thinks to himself grumpily.

Candidates draw from their own classroom experiences, reflections of their interactions with adolescents, and other personal memories to develop authentic adolescent dialogue for their case study. One preservice teacher candidate reflected,

> The quotes we used in our study came from personal experiences both with students we worked with and our own middle school experiences. I think middle schoolers often go through a common experience of maturing and questioning the world around them, but many of the circumstances which lead them to and through that time are unique. So we used a quote that applied uniquely to our student's situation but still addressed the common themes of the middle students' life.

Once the candidates have curated their narratives, they exchange cases with another pair to conduct an independent analysis and provide suggestions for improvements. Using what Eisner (2002) terms "practical knowledge," candidates engage in "reflection and deliberation" in an iterative process of negotiating changes to revise their case study to include all of the required elements within the written document. One candidate reflected on this process, stating, "I learned a lot from the ideas of my peers. I heard new perspectives that I had not considered as well as thoughts and ideas that aligned with my own beliefs."

Following peer review, candidate pairs collaborate to make further revisions and develop a presentation. The partners alternate between reading the case study and stating justifications for each required component. At the conclusion of each presentation, class members ask questions about the case. The instructor also probes candidates' understanding of relevant theories and related concepts. Through these interrogations of their work, candidates are helped to develop their own "distinctive signature" for teaching (Eisner 2002, pp. 383–384). Candidates are given the case study scoring rubric, with detailed instructor feedback, following the presentation so that they can make final revisions before submitting the case study paper for grading.

CONCLUSION

Several conclusions can be drawn from the preservice teacher candidates' experiences in creating, discussing, and presenting fictional case studies of young middle school adolescents. First, practice at applying different learning and/or developmental theories and school organizational structures to explain their case study characters' behaviors improved when candidates first practiced with individual theories separately. Such practice was more effective when candidates received direct instruction for each educational psychology theory and middle school structure, practiced applying to school settings, and then integrated the theories and frameworks into the larger context of their case studies. This additional instruction allowed candidates to activate previous instruction in educational psychology and provide meaningful connections to school settings. The reflection below from one preservice teacher shows how this process was beneficial to the outcome of their study.

> Throughout the semester, [my partner] and I had practiced writing several examples of theorists, learning environment, and curriculum and instruction. When it came time to write our case study, it made it easier to modify our existing examples into the storyline we were creating.

Second, the quality of the final products, developed collaboratively, consistently exceeded those developed when teacher candidates worked alone. And, teacher candidates reported having more meaningful experiences when they worked together. For example, one candidate shared, "Working in pairs to complete a case student helped me to understand the content." The required peer discussions generated from the pre-case study work and the processes of writing, peer reviewing, and presenting the case study also helped candidates develop greater appreciation for the challenges of teaching young adolescents. One stated,

> When we sat down to create our case study student, we discussed what we personally had imagined our student to be like. Many of our ideas aligned and it was easy to create a character we both were excited to write about.

Third, our candidates' peer discussions of their student teaching experiences and their abilities to weave these experiences into their case study student's "story" brought life to their writing and produced case studies that demonstrated their understanding of adolescent development, educational psychology theories and related concepts, and how middle school characteristics and organizational structures influence young adolescents' growth, development, and academic achievement. Because candidates completed their student teaching prior to enrolling in this final seminar course, they were able to talk about their teaching experiences with peers who had also recently completed student teaching (Mather & Hanley, 1999).

Teacher candidates learned to appreciate the foundation educational psychology provides as they learned to recognize the essential characteristics of middle school classrooms and how schools should be organized to meet the needs of young adolescents. As one candidate commented, "I had not fully thought about the importance of having a healthy school environment." Another wrote, "[W]hat helps create a great school culture is what also creates a great classroom culture... I am now able to relate what I read into my own practices... I now know what I need to do, as a teacher."

Candidates' reflections on their case study work, along with course survey data, revealed several positive outcomes including deeper understanding of students as individuals and greater ability to view classrooms as part of a whole school context. Candidates gained insights into meeting the needs of students through strategies such as culturally responsive teaching (Gay & Kirkland, 2003) and they gained confidence for making the transition from teacher candidate to teaching professional. This transition is one of the most challenging aspects of teacher preparation for candidates. The case study assignment supported the candidates' growth and, in some cases, served as a catalyst for change. One candidate reflected, "[This case study experience] really makes you think critically about whether or not what you are doing is good for kids. If what we are doing as teachers is good for kids, we're doing something right." Another candidate offered this perspective,

> Doing the case study is new and groundbreaking and REALLY helped me understand that I could probably write a case study for every single one of my future students to understand them better, and understand how to better teach them, and help them just deal with life.

Candidates were able to reflect on the importance of culturally relevant teaching as part of their case study project. The case study experience, alongside coursework, helped candidates to integrate descriptions of specific teaching strategies into their fictitious—yet realistic—scenarios to demonstrate their knowledge of appropriate instructional materials, activities, and teachers' communication patterns that support diverse learners. Gay and Kirkland (2003) recommend providing "frequent and genuine opportunities for students to practice being multiculturally reflective and critically conscious" through projects that are "designed to allow students to bring to consciousness, cultural values and beliefs embedded in U.S. schools and society that are taken for granted or assumed to be universal" (pp. 185–186). The case study assignment helped candidates to engage in such critical consciousness. One preservice teacher stated, "I was given the opportunity to expand my knowledge of culturally responsive teaching and learn what that looks like within the classroom... these experiences will allow me to better support students both emotionally and academically." Another candidate stated, "The goal of a middle school teacher is not to always relate to students and their home life and experiences... but rather create a space where they feel both psychologically and physically safe, to matter."

Implications

Preservice teacher candidates need deep exposure to and opportunities to apply theories to "cases" to explain developmental change, student behavior, and school structures and instructional practices. Case studies can help teacher candidates look "more systematically at the different influences on learning and understand how theory relates to specific practice, and, in turn, to [student] outcomes" (Darling-Hammond & Baratz-Snowden, 2007, p. 128). Such assigments help candidates develop a strong foundation in theories of human development. Connecting these theories to authentic classroom practices is worthwhile for teacher candidates because such work helps them understand their students' developmental tasks and needs and inform methods for meeting those needs.

Writing collaboratively and engaging in peer review are powerful practices for candidate learning (Cabrera, et. al., 2002; Chace, 2014; Cockrell et al., 2000). Creating fictional case studies incorporating real-life characters and situations—rather than requiring candidates to find a "live" case study subject—is less time consuming and allows candidates greater latitude to describe, address, and analyze many aspects of adolescent behavior and development. Candidates can then describe teachers who demonstrate the kinds of effective instructional behaviors that they are striving to develop for themselves.

Candidates' success in conducting collaborative case studies was aided by several factors. First, candidates were part of a cohort that had learned together for over a year and whose members liked and trusted each other. Second, the case study assignment was designed to promote meaningful interactions with opportunities for structured peer dialogue. Third, the AMLE standards for teacher preparation were shared with the candidates at the beginning of the course, thus, they were aware of the purpose of the assignment.

By reviewing, reteaching, and clarifying educational psychology theories at the end of the candidates' preparation program, teacher educators can help candidates make important connections between and among educational theories. Guided field experiences focusing on effective school organizations and structures, as well as having opportunities to analyze classroom practices and interactions, will likely result in more positive outcomes for the students that candidates will teach. Requiring candidates to make explicit connections to the ways in which middle schools are organized and the different kinds of supports that these schools provide for young adolescents allows candidates to consider the effects of school environments on students. Subsequently, candidates are prepared to participate in shared decision making at both the classroom and school level. Finally, one of the teacher candidates provided an incentive to assigning case study work: "I think by the end, we could explain 'why we do things' well."

KEY CHAPTER TAKEAWAYS

- Education psychology provides the theoretical foundations that can help preservice teachers understand and interpret the diverse learning, developmental, and behavioral needs of students.
- The case study assignment helps preservice teacher candidates develop and express their knowledge of the complexity of the middle school environment and its effects on adolescent learners.
- Through class discussions and peers' collaborative work on the case study assignment, preservice teachers gain helpful insights on culturally responsive teaching, the characteristics of a healthy school environment, and the realities of teaching young adolescents.
- Revisiting educational psychology theories at the end of the teacher preparation program may help candidates better understand connections between theory and practice and result in more informed decisions that support the best interests and developmental needs of students.

KEY WORDS

Accreditation
Case study
Cultural capital
Culturally responsive teaching
Ecology of power
Middle education
School organization

The Why and How of What We Do • 109

APPENDIX A Case Study Scoring Rubric

	Target	Feedback
Case Study Developmental Descriptions	• Describe and identify characteristics • Provide specific examples • Provide rationale/justification with connection to readings	
Physical Development (5)	Provides a thorough description of the young adolescent's physical development. Description reflects understanding and empathy for adolescent development.	
Cognitive Development—Piaget (10) Cognitive Development—Vygotsky (10) Social and Emotional Development—Erikson (10) Moral Development Kohlberg (10) Behaviorism and Social Cognitive Theory—Bandura, Pavlov, Skinner 10) Bio-Ecological Systems Theory—Bronfenbrenner (10)	Identifies and provides thorough description of 2–3 specific concepts for each theorist. Description reflects thorough understanding of concepts employing appropriate vocabulary.	
Quote (5)	Case study includes 2 developmentally appropriate and realistic quotes and includes a rationale for its inclusion as part of the presentation.	
Cohesion (10)	Case study flows and tells a cohesive, realistic story. Includes an introduction and conclusion. Writing quality consistent with graduate level work.	

(continued)

APPENDIX A Case Study Scoring Rubric (continued)

Organizational Structures and Professional Practice	Description of Target	Feedback
Learning Environment (25)	Provides description/analysis of at least 3 learning environments/attributes/characteristics/practices appropriate and to ensure successful school experiences for all and meet the individual needs of your student and/or supporting characters. These can overlap with characteristics of theories. Description/analysis clearly conveys understanding of organization and structures of TWB/STW We Believe/STW and unique needs of young adolescents.	
Curriculum and Instruction (25)	Provides rich description of at least 2 specific instructional strategies related to curriculum and instruction for your student and/or supporting characters. Your analysis should include a rationale based on TWB/STW criteria. These examples should be in addition to the learning environment examples described above.	
Special Needs (25)	Provides description/analysis that conveys 2 examples of learners with special needs (IEP, 504) and structures/interventions/actions to meet their needs.	
Racial/Ethnic Diversity (25)	Provides description/analysis that conveys 2 examples that reflect understanding of challenges/events affecting racially, ethnically, and/or culturally diverse students. The analysis should discuss positive structures/interventions/actions to disrupt and repair harm.	
Impact of SES (25)	Provides description/analysis that conveys 2 examples that reflect understanding of challenges/events affecting students struggling with SES issues. The analysis should discuss positive structures/interventions/actions to support student/family needs.	
Presentation (25)	• Rich description and clarity/accuracy of your analysis; evoke empathy • Convey mastery adolescent development • Convey mastery of exemplary middle school practices intended/designed to address the unique needs of young adolescents	

REFERENCES

Anderson, L. W., & Krathwohl, D. R. (Eds.). (2001). *A taxonomy for learning, teaching and assessing: A revision of Bloom's taxonomy of educational outcomes.* Longman.

Anderson, L. M., Blumenfeld, P., Pintrich, P. R., Clark, C. M., Marx, R. W., & Peterson, P. (1995). Educational psychology for teachers: Reforming our courses, rethinking our roles. *Educational Psychologist, 30,* 143–157. https://doi.org/10.1207/s15326985ep3003_5

Association for Middle Level Education. (2012). *Association for middle level education middle level teacher preparation standards.*

Benson, B. E. (2003). Framing culture within classroom practice: Culturally relevant teaching. *Action in Teacher Education, 25*(2), 16–22. https://doi.org/10.1080/01626620.2003.10463301

Bishop, P. A., & Harrison, L. M. (2021). *The successful middle school: This we believe.* Association for Middle Level Education.

Bloom, B. S. (1956). *Taxonomy of educational objectives, Handbook I: The cognitive domain.* David McKay Co, Inc.

Blumenfeld, P. C., Hicks, L., & Krajcik, J. S. (1996). Teaching educational psychology through instructional planning. *Educational Psychologist, 31*(1), 51–61. https://doi.org/10.1207/s15326985ep3101_7

Bourdieu, P. (1986). The forms of capital. In J. Richardson (Ed.), *Handbook of theory and research for the sociology of education* (pp. 241–258). Greenwood.

Bowers, C. A., & Flinders, D. (1990). *Responsive teaching: An ecological approach to classroom patterns of language, culture, and thought.* Teachers College Press.

Bronfenbrenner, U., & Condry, J. C., Jr. (1970). *Two worlds of childhood: US and USSR.* Russell Sage Foundation.

Byrd, C. M. (2016). Does culturally relevant teaching work? An examination from student perspectives. *Sage Open, 6*(3), 1–10. https://doi.org/10.1177/2158244016660744

Cabrera, A. F., Crissman, J. L., Bernal, E. M., Nora, A., Terenzini, P. T., & Pascarella, E. T. (2002). Collaborative learning: Its impact on college students' development and diversity. *Journal of College Student Development, 43*(1), 20–34. https://eric.ed.gov/?id=EJ642665

Carter, K., & Doyle, W. (1996). Educational psychology and the education of teachers: A reaction. *Educational Psychologist, 31*(1), 23–28. https://doi.org/10.1207/s15326985ep3101_3

Chace, J. F. (2014). Collaborative projects increase student learning outcome performance in nonmajors environmental science course. *Journal of College Science Teaching, 43*(6), 58–63. http://www.jstor.org/stable/43631761

Chizhik, E. W., & Chizhik, A. W. (2003). Teaching educational psychology to develop creative and transformative teachers. *The Journal of Educational Thought, 37*(2), 177–194. https://www.jstor.org/stable/23767414

Cockrell, K. S., Caplow, J. A. H., & Donaldson, J. F. (2000). A context for learning: Collaborative groups in the problem-based learning environment. *The Review of Higher Education, 23*(3), 347–363. https://eric.ed.gov/?id=EJ608337

Crozier, W. R. (2009). The psychology of education: Achievements and challenges. *Oxford Review of Education, 35*(5), 587–600. https://www.jstor.org/stable/27784587

Cuseo, J. (2007). The empirical case against large class size: Adverse effects on the teaching, learning, and retention of first-year students. *The Journal of Faculty Development, 21*(1), 5–21. https://eric.ed.gov/?id=EJ774391

Darling-Hammond, L., & Baratz-Snowden, J. (2007). A good teacher in every classroom: Preparing the highly qualified teachers our children deserve. *Educational Horizons, 85*(2), 111–132. http://www.jstor.org/stable/42926597

Eisner, E. (2002). From episteme to phronesis to artistry in the study and improvement of teaching. *Teaching and Teacher Education, 18*(4), 375–385. https://doi.org/10.1016/S0742-051X(02)00004-5

Erikson, E. H. (1968). *Childhood and society.* Norton.

Eun, B. (2016). Equipping every student with psychological tools: A Vygotskian guide to establishing the goals of education. *European Journal of Psychology of Education, 31*(4), 613–627. https://doi.org/10.1007/s10212-015-0280-7

Gay, G., & Kirkland, K. (2003). Developing cultural critical consciousness and self-reflection in preservice teacher education. *Theory Into Practice, 42*(3), 181–187. https://doi.org/10.1207/s15430421tip4203_3

Hanich, L. B., & Deemer, S. (2005). The relevance of educational psychology in teacher education programs. *The Clearing House, 78*(5), 189–191. https://doi.org/10.3200/TCHS.78.5.189-191

Ladson-Billings, G. (1995). But that's just good teaching! The case for culturally relevant pedagogy. *Theory Into Practice, 34*, 159–165. https://doi.org/10.1080/00405849509543675

Lohse-Bossenz, H., Kunina-Habenicht, O., & Kunter, M. (2013). The role of educational psychology in teacher education: Expert opinions on what teachers should know about learning, development, and assessment. *European Journal of Psychology of Education, 28*(4), 1543–1565. https://doi.org/10.1007/s10212-013-0181-6

Love, B. L. (2019). *We want to do more than survive: Abolitionist teaching and the pursuit of educational freedom.* Beacon Press.

Mather, D., & Hanley, B. (1999). Cohort grouping and preservice teacher education: Effects on pedagogical development. *Canadian Journal of Education/Revue Canadienne de l'éducation, 24*(3), 235–250. https://doi.org/10.2307/1585873

McDevitt, T. M., & Ormrod, J. E. (2008). Fostering conceptual change about child development in prospective teachers and other college students. *Child Development Perspectives, 2*(2), 85–91. https://doi.org/10.1111/j.1750-8606.2008.00045.x

McKeachie, W. J., Pintrich, P., Lin, Y., & Smith, D. (1986). *Teaching and learning in the college classroom: A review of the research literature.* University of Michigan, NCRIPTAL.

National Middle School Association. (1982). *This we believe: A position paper of the National Middle School Association.* https://eric.ed.gov/?id=ED226513

Pascarella, E., & Terenzini, P. (2005). *How college affects students, Volume 2: A third decade of research.* Jossey-Bass.

Patrick, H., Anderman, L. H, Bruening, P. S., & Duffin, L. S. (2011). The role of educational psychology in teacher education: Three challenges for educational psychologists. *Educational Psychologist, 46*(2), 71–83. https://doi.org/10.1080/00461520.2011.538648

Pavlov, I. P. (1960) [1927]. *Conditional reflexes*. Dover Publications. (Originally published 1927)

Piaget, J. (1970). *The science of education and the psychology of the child*. Orion Press.

Popham, W. J. (2020). *Classroom assessment: What teachers need to know* (9th ed.). Pearson.

Shulman, L. S. (1999). Taking learning seriously. *Change: The Magazine of Higher Learning, 31*(4), 10–17. https://doi.org/10.1080/00091389909602695

Vygotsky, L. (1986). *Thought and language*. MIT Press.

Woolfolk, A. (2019). *Educational psychology* (14th ed). Pearson.

Woolfolk, A. (2000). Educational psychology in teacher education. *Educational Psychologist, 35*(4), 257–270. https://doi.org/10.1207/S15326985EP3504_04

Zeichner, K. (1993). Connecting genuine teacher development to the struggle for social justice. *Journal of Education for Teaching, 19*(1), 5–20. https://doi.org/10.1080/0260747930190102

CHAPTER 6

STRATEGIES FOR CENTERING INCLUSION AND EQUITY IN HUMAN DEVELOPMENT COURSES FOR PRESERVICE EDUCATORS

Alison C. Koenka
Virginia Commonwealth University

Korinthia D. Nicolai
Virginia Commonwealth University

Richard Garries
Virginia Commonwealth University

It is essential that preservice educators leave their teacher preparation programs equipped to effectively and equitably teach all students in their classrooms. A strong background in educational psychology—including human development—is critical to this process. Despite its importance

Teaching Human Development for Educators, pages 115–136
Copyright © 2024 by Information Age Publishing
www.infoagepub.com
All rights of reproduction in any form reserved.

for preservice teachers, many literatures within these disciplines have concerning shortcomings. Prior work has noted, for example, the (a) dearth of educational and developmental psychology research that centers the impact of race and (b) predominantly White, middle-class samples that are represented in primary studies (Agger et al., 2022; DeCuir-Gunby & Schutz, 2014; Graham, 1992; Usher, 2018). Moreover, a large majority of educational psychology scholars (and thus instructors) mirror these sample demographics (DeCuir-Gunby & Schutz, 2014). As a result, without intentional focus and scaffolded strategies, many educational psychology and human development instructors are less likely to effectively center equity and representation in their courses (DeCuir-Gunby & Schutz, 2014). Taken together, despite noteworthy exceptions, educational and developmental psychology disciplines typically fall short of fostering diversity, equity, and inclusion. As a result, these limitations manifest in pedagogical principles and commonly used resources in human development courses. Therefore, in this chapter, we discuss strategies for instructors to promote equity and inclusion in their human development courses.

As two of the chapter authors prepared to teach an undergraduate human development course, they redesigned a course that centered on equity and inclusion. Therefore, we use our human development and learning course as a running example throughout the chapter. We also explain how each recommended strategy is theoretically and empirically grounded. Our recommendations include strategies for human development instructors to (a) create an inclusive class environment and (b) prepare preservice teachers to apply developmental principles that support diversity, equity, and inclusion in their future classes.

In the following sections, we discuss suggestions and examples based on three overarching categories. We first focus on recommendations related to curriculum content, which we ground in critical race theory ([CRT]; Ladson-Billings & Tate, 1995) and recent work in educational psychology on the importance of race-reimaged and race-focused research (e.g., DeCuir-Gunby & Schutz, 2014; Matthews & López, 2020). Second, we draw from the motivation, Vygostskian, and stereotype threat literatures to discuss suggestions for designing equitable and effective exams and assignments (Harackiewicz et al., 2016; John-Steiner & Mahn, 1996; Patall et al., 2008; Schunk & Zimmerman, 1997; Steele & Aronson, 1995). Third, grounded in CRT, social cognitive theory (SCT), feedback, and belonging literatures, we make recommendations for facilitating engaging and inclusive class discussions. The Key Chapter Takeaways (p. 131) presents a summary of recommended strategies, examples, and theoretical and/or empirical grounding.

Before discussing our recommendations and the literature we draw from, it is important to emphasize that much of the educational psychology and developmental literatures have not focused on the importance of race

(Agger et al., 2022; DeCuir-Gunby & Schutz, 2014) and research samples have often consisted of White, middle class students (Graham, 1992; Usher, 2018). Due to the potential shortcomings of the theories discussed, we intentionally draw from and apply race-reimaged ("traditional constructs that are reconceptualized to include racially influenced, sociocultural perspectives" [DeCuir-Gunby & Schutz, 2014, p. 244]) and race-focused research/perspectives (constructs that are "centered around issues of race" [DeCuir-Gunby & Schutz, 2014, p. 244]). We also address these shortcomings by drawing from CRT and the stereotype threat literature. Therefore, throughout the chapter, we highlight the potential shortcomings of the theories we draw from for historically marginalized students, which aligns with our suggestion for instructors when discussing the classical literature that we discuss later. Additionally, just as we are explicit about the shortcomings of the theories we are drawing from to inform our recommendations, it is important for human development instructors to be explicit with students about the theories instructors are using to inform their practices and their shortcomings: specifically, that they may not be as applicable to historically marginalized and understudied students. As a result, preservice educators can apply these practices to their own with knowledge of the shortcomings of the theories.

CURRICULUM CONTENT

Theoretical and Empirical Grounding

We ground our recommended strategies for decolonizing curriculum content in (a) empirical data on research focus and representation within many educational and developmental psychology literatures, (b) recent work in educational psychology on the importance of race-reimaged and race-focused research, (c) CRT, and (d) SCT. For example, it was noted earlier that the overwhelming majority of empirical studies in educational and developmental psychology center the experiences of White, middle-class samples (DeCuir-Gunby & Schutz, 2014; Graham, 1992; Usher, 2018). Moreover, when work in these literatures does include understudied populations (e.g., youth who belong to a racially or ethnically underrepresented group and/or the LGBT+ community), it often reflects a deficit focus (Agger et al., 2022). In contrast, relatively little work in both educational and developmental psychology literatures have conducted race-reimaged or race-focused research. Yet, doing so is essential for centering students' racialized experiences from an asset-based perspective. These trends in the literature have critical implications for how and what curricular content is covered, which inform the strategies we summarize below.

CRT centers race and racism and their continued implications for issues of power and equity (Delgado & Stefancic, 2017; Ladson-Billings, 1995). CRT was developed from critical legal studies and radical feminism to "combat the subtler forms of racism that were gaining ground" (Delgado & Stefanic, 2017, p. 4). It is composed of many different tenets. Below, we highlight the tenets we drew from to inform our recommendations in this chapter: (a) permanence of racism (i.e., racism is ordinary and embedded in the United States; Bell, 1992, 1995; Crenshaw, 1988); (b) the critique of liberalism/challenge to the dominant ideology (i.e., critiquing meritocracy, color blindness, neutrality; Cook, 1990; Crenshaw, 1988; Freeman, 1995); and (c) counter-story telling (i.e., highlight voices of people of color to challenge dominant narratives; Bonilla-Silva, 2002). Taken together, CRT is a useful perspective to center race and the impact of racism while attending to the dominant narrative of Whiteness (DeCuir & Dixson, 2004).

Finally, from a motivational perspective, SCT speaks to the importance of modeling and social comparisons for promoting *self-efficacy*—confidence that one can successfully complete a given academic task—and ultimately academic performance (Schunk & DiBenedetto, 2020). That is, if a student witnesses a model experiencing success in related academic activities, they are more likely to believe that they can successfully do so, too. However, perceived similarity between the student and model are essential: if students believe that they share similar identities and characteristics with the successful model, they are much more likely to be positively influenced by them (Schunk & Usher, 2019). The importance of model similarity thus has critical implications for fostering diversity, equity, and inclusion through the curriculum content: if students—particularly those from historically underrepresented and/or understudied populations—see themselves in the curriculum, they will be more likely to feel efficacious and ultimately succeed in the course (Schunk & DiBenedetto, 2020).

Strategies for Human Development Instructors

Strategy 1: Center and Celebrate Development of Youth From Diverse Populations Throughout the Curriculum

First, we suggest infusing and emphasizing the development of understudied and/or underrepresented youth throughout the course curriculum. For example, skimming through many human development educational psychology textbooks, diversity-related and/or cultural content is often relegated to a single chapter and/or presented separately from the other material within a given chapter (e.g., through "in depth" boxes). Perhaps as a result of these common structural trends, instructors may be inclined to relegate the development of understudied populations to a single topic within a course calendar. However, we argue that it is essential to infuse content throughout the curriculum that speaks to understudied youth's development and experiences. Doing so aligns with CRT by supporting the permanence of racism tenet (Ladson-Billings & Tate, 1995). That is, it reinforces the notion that racism is deeply embedded in all aspects of society within the United States and cannot be relegated to a single unit or chapter.

Beyond making a point to cover diversity-related topics throughout the curriculum, we also suggest that human development instructors center and celebrate (a) the development of youth from historically marginalized populations and (b) research conducted by scholars belonging to these populations. Drawing from our human development and learning course, for example, we prioritized discussing the development of youth who identify as transgender when discussing the development of gender identity (e.g., Sorbara et al., 2020). Similarly, we prioritized a great deal of our identity development lecture to adopting an asset-based approach of ethnic/racial identity development among historically marginalized youth (e.g., Umaña-Taylor et al., 2018). We also emphasized the work of scholars of color, women, and other underrepresented groups when presenting this and other lecture material.

These practices align with a tenet of CRT—the importance of counter-storytelling: the research centered historically minoritized students' experiences and voices, which presents a needed counter-story to opinions and myths upheld by White supremacy (Delgado & Stefancic, 2012; White et al., 2019). Additionally, the asset-based focus of the research challenged dominant narratives of deficits. Finally, SCT also grounds our recommendation. In particular, doing so promotes equity and inclusion by helping minoritized students in the course see themselves both in the course curriculum and in the scholars who conducted the research (Schunk & Usher, 2019).

Strategy 2: When Presenting "Classic" Developmental Literature, Explicitly Address Its Limits

Despite the abovementioned recommendation to center research focused on understudied populations' experiences and scholarship, much of the literature that universities expect human development instructors to cover fails to do so (DeCuir-Gunby & Schutz, 2014; Graham, 1992; Usher, 2018). As a result, when continuing to present this "classic" literature, we recommend explicitly addressing its shortcomings and generalizability limits. When covering the development of language in our human development and learning course, for example, we presented the "classic," frequently cited research documenting the unique language developmental trajectories across children in low, middle, and high socioeconomic status populations (Hart & Risley, 1995); however, we immediately followed this lecture content by discussing more recent research (e.g., Hirsh-Pasek et al., 2015) that adopts an asset-based approach.

In doing so, we talked about how this research illustrates the importance of an asset-based perspective. We also emphasized the much more nuanced nature of the relation between language development and socioeconomic status that it yielded. As another example, we completely reworked our lecture material on the development of intelligence: rather than covering in detail typical conceptions of intelligence (e.g., Spearman's *g* for "general intelligence"), we assigned a podcast that discussed the racism and inequities associated with traditional intelligence tests to communicate the dangers of administering these tests and implications for them as future teachers. We used this podcast as a springboard for explaining why we would be focusing on the development of two constructs that were related to, yet distinct from, intelligence: (a) *mindsets*, or implicit beliefs about the nature of intelligence (e.g., Dweck & Leggett, 1988) and (b) *funds of knowledge*, or the knowledge that students bring to the classroom that they develop through "everyday experiences, events, activities, observations... [from] children's own private worlds and home lives, [and] life experiences in general" (Varelas & Pappas, 2006, p. 221).

These examples and recommended practices underlying them also align closely with the abovementioned theoretical and empirical literature. Drawing again from CRT, for example, content such as the podcast episode reflect the importance of counter-storytelling by centering the experiences and voices of people of color taking IQ tests in contrast to White students and educators (Delgado & Stefancic, 2012; White et al., 2019). By explicitly and directly addressing the shortcomings and limits to generalizability of much "classic" developmental and educational psychology literature, these recommended practices also align with the challenge to the dominant ideology tenet within CRT by questioning the idea that achievement tests are based upon meritocracy (i.e., outcomes based on ability). Finally, these recommended practices also make preservice educators aware of some of the literature's shortcomings, which will encourage them to avoid misapplying it in their own teaching practices.

EXAMS AND ASSIGNMENTS

Theoretical and Empirical Grounding

Inspired by recent calls to "rethink assessment practices [in higher education] from a motivational perspective" (Daniels et al., 2021, p. 15), we drew heavily from multiple literatures to (a) more effectively foster engagement through our exams and assessments and in doing so (b) make them more equitable, inclusive, and accessible for all students.

Motivation Research Literature

Beyond SCT (described in the previous section), three other theories of motivation inform our recommendations for fostering engagement and inclusiveness through exams and assignments. First, *achievement goal theory* distinguishes between different types of goals that students pursue in the classroom (Maehr & Zusho, 2009): students may adopt a *mastery goal orientation*, for example, which prioritizes the *development* of one's competence. That is, mastery-oriented students focus on learning the material deeply (Maehr & Zusho, 2009). Students may alternatively pursue a *performance goal orientation*, which prioritizes the *demonstration* of one's competence (or avoiding appearing incompetent; Maehr & Zusho, 2009). Students who adopt a mastery rather than performance goal orientation are typically more engaged, intrinsically motivated, cheat less, and persist more when confronted with challenges (Anderman & Koenka, 2017; Urdan & Kaplan, 2020). Instructor behaviors in general and their assessment practices, in particular, can play a critical role in fostering mastery goal orientations in students (Ames, 1992; Meece et al., 2006): if instructors develop assessments and communicate about them in a way that emphasizes the importance of deep understanding rather than grades and competition with classmates, for example, these behaviors should promote a mastery goal orientation in students (Ames, 1992; Anderman & Koenka, 2017).

Our recommendations are also grounded in *self-determination theory* (SDT) and *situated expectancy-value theory* (SEVT). According to decades of SDT-guided research, providing students with structured opportunities to make choices when engaging in academic tasks is essential for promoting *intrinsic motivation*, or the desire to engage in academic activities for their own sake (Ryan & Deci, 2020; Patall et al., 2008). Moreover, SEVT-guided intervention research has revealed the powerful motivational benefits of reflecting on the personal relevance of class material—especially those who belong to historically marginalized and underrepresented groups in higher education (e.g., Harackiewicz et al., 2016). However, despite the utility of these literatures, they are couched within educational and developmental psychology research, which often centers the experiences of White, middle-class samples and may be limited when applied to historically underrepresented students (DeCuir-Gunby & Schutz, 2014; Graham, 1992; Usher, 2018). Therefore, to ensure the relevance of our recommendations for students who are underrepresented, we also drew from sociocultural theory for Strategy 4 and stereotype threat literatures for Strategy 3, which are discussed next. Taken together, inspired by the abovementioned motivation literature, we share strategies for developing exams and assignments that: (a) emphasize mastery over performance, (b) promote student choice, and (c) encourage students to reflect on the personal relevance of the human development material. Drawing from the motivation literature and applying it to assessment practices and policies is valuable across a variety of courses and academic domains in higher education. However, doing so is especially useful in human development courses because it is directly related to the curricular content. As a result, applying the motivation literature to assessment practices provides human development instructors with an opportunity to model some of the curricular content being taught to students.

Developmental and Social Psychology Research Literature

Finally, we draw from the developmental and social psychology literature. For example, a Vygotskian (i.e., sociocultural) developmental perspective emphasizes the importance of *scaffolding* in fostering student learning (e.g., John-Steiner & Mahn, 1996). That is, especially when students work towards challenging and unfamiliar tasks, it is essential to provide them with the pedagogical support necessary to do so. Finally, and most directly relevant to creating assessments that are equitable, inclusive, and accessible to all students, the stereotype threat literature reveals how "traditional" assessments (e.g., timed, closed book, high stakes) often disproportionately and negatively affect the experiences and performance of students from historically marginalized populations. When negative, racialized, gendered and/or ableist stereotypes are made salient—which often occurs in traditional college testing contexts—minoritized students experience *stereotype threat*: heightened anxiety, which in turn undermines their performance (e.g., Murphy et al., 2007; Steele, 1997; Steele & Aronson, 1995). Therefore, drawing from these literatures, we discuss strategies for refining exams and assignments that (a) incorporate additional opportunities for scaffolding and (b) attenuate the likelihood that students from historically marginalized groups would have an inequitable experience when completing them.

Strategies for Human Development Instructors

Strategy 3: Give Open-Book, Untimed Exams

Drawing from the achievement goal theory and stereotype threat literatures, we recommend that instructors consider giving exams that are both open book and untimed. In our human development and learning course, for example, students took two exams across the semester. We modified these exams to be *open book*: that is, students were encouraged to draw from their notes, the lecture recordings, readings, and any other resources that would be useful to them as they were taking the exam. Furthermore, our exams were *untimed*. As a result, each exam was posted for approximately 10 days.

Within this window of time, students were welcome to (a) work on the exam whenever they desired, (b) take as much time as they wanted to complete it, and (c) return to it as many times as they wanted before turning it in.

These exam characteristics accomplished several objectives. First, they promoted a mastery goal orientation in students. The open book nature of the exams immediately removed the need to memorize and cram; instead, it encouraged students to think critically about and practice applying the material when studying. Relatedly, the untimed nature reduced perceived competition surrounding exams: a hallmark contextual factor that often promotes performance goal orientations and undermines mastery goal orientations (Ames, 1992; Meece et al., 2006). Second, open-book, untimed exams also made our assessments more equitable and accessible by removing classic characteristics of assessments that are especially likely to produce anxiety fueled by stereotype threat (Steele & Aronson, 1995). Third, we took one final step to ensure that our open-book, untimed exams fostered the equitable experiences and outcomes we desired: we included very explicit written and verbal guidelines to ensure that all students shared an understanding of expectations and what was meant by "open book" and "untimed." Especially with many being first-generation college students and/or transfer students, this was an essential step to disrupt inequitable advantage by making the "hidden curriculum" that often infiltrates higher education more explicit.

Strategy 4: Give Students Choice on Assignment Type and Timelines

Second, inspired by SDT, we recommend building in choice on assessments. For example, students had three options when completing their capstone project in our human development course: (a) collect case study data on a child or adolescent and apply it to the course material ("case study"); (b) choose a human development topic of particular interest and apply it to their own personal or professional lives ("application paper"); or (c) choose a human development topic of particular interest and create a brochure and brief paper to disseminate knowledge on the selected topic to a selected stakeholder in education ("brochure and paper"). This assignment choice promotes students' intrinsic motivation by supporting their need for autonomy (Patall et al., 2008; Ryan & Deci, 2020). Beyond motivation, the opportunity to focus on topics of interest in the latter two assignment options was instrumental in promoting inclusion and equity. Despite our abovementioned attempts to diversify and decolonize the curriculum content, we view overcoming one's blind spots as a career-long endeavor. As a result, providing students with opportunities to select and learn more about a topic that may not have been covered in our course material was instrumental in (a) affirming their individual interests and learning goals and (b) learning about one's blind spots as an instructor.

We also recommend building in student choice on assessment timelines. Beyond introducing the abovementioned broad window of time for completing exams, for example, we built in choice for assignment submission deadlines. For example, all students were required to submit weekly questions to guide our synchronous human development discussions. However, they were permitted to "skip" submitting several weeks in the semester and had complete autonomy to choose when they did so. Drawing again from SDT, this built-in agency over submission deadlines further promoted students' need for autonomy (Patall et al., 2008; Ryan & Deci, 2020) and thus further fostered their intrinsic motivation. Choice in assignment submission deadlines was also essential from an equity and inclusion perspective: it especially benefited students who had (a) just transferred from a community college and needed additional time and bandwidth to become situated at a new institution and/or (b) less financial security, and thus had less flexible outside-of-class schedules due to working long hours. Moreover, it is important to note that our course occurred in Fall 2020. As a result, the COVID-19 pandemic was a significant stressor for all students (and continues to be one during the writing of this chapter). However, it is arguably especially so for many students of color given that it was compounded with a national spotlight on racial injustice. Built-in assignment deadline flexibility thus created a more racially equitable experience and allowed students to avoid completing assignments in weeks that were disproportionately distressing for many students of color (e.g., the 2020 presidential election).

Strategy 5: Provide Scaffolding

Third, we suggest providing scaffolding on exams and assignments to promote efficacy and deep learning. For example, the abovementioned capstone assignment options typically feel quite daunting for students, and many lack efficacy about where to begin. As a result, we provide scaffolding by "chunking" the assignment into several different components. First, early in the semester, students completed a brief, low stakes "selection form" to indicate (a) which assignment option they would like to pursue, (b) other details about their idea (e.g., interest in a particular developmental stage and/or topic), and (c) any questions they would like to run by the instructors. Midway through the semester, students were required to submit some preliminary data from their project. Those who completed the case study, for example, were required to submit their interview notes; students who completed either the application paper or brochure and paper were required to submit a structured matrix that summarized key points from the literature they gathered. Third, at the end of the semester, students submitted the final product.

This assignment structure provided scaffolding to students in multiple ways. First, the mere act of "chunking" a major assignment into three broad components modeled to students how and what strategies they can use as future educators to help their students tackle seemingly daunting and overwhelming academic tasks (Schunk & DiBenedetto, 2020). Second, we provided feedback at each capstone juncture, which served as an additional scaffold. Drawing from the SCT and Vygotskian developmental (John-Steiner & Mahn, 1996; Schunk & DiBenedetto, 2020) literatures, students benefited from these scaffolding practices in multiple ways. Dividing up daunting tasks into a series of subtasks and the resulting experience of progress, is instrumental in fueling feelings of *self-efficacy*, for example (Schunk & DiBenedetto, 2020). Moreover, scaffolding opportunities allowed for students to learn the material much more deeply than would have been possible without it (John-Steiner & Mahn, 1996).

Strategy 6: Promote Personal Relevance

Fourth, drawing from the SEVT literature (Eccles, 2009; Eccles & Wigfield, 2020), we recommend building in as many opportunities as possible for students to identify personal relevance in the material. For example, by prioritizing student choice in assignment type, students also had an opportunity to tailor their learning to topics that were personally relevant and of particular interest to them. The emphasis on relevance was especially salient in the "application paper" and "brochure and paper" capstone options given that students were encouraged to select any human development topic that was of particular interest to them. Moreover, we directly drew from the relevant intervention literature when developing the "application paper" capstone assignment option (e.g., Harackiewicz et al., 2016; Lazowski & Hulleman, 2015): after reading and summarizing literature on a human development topic of the student's choosing, they reflected on how (a) the material was relevant to their personal life and/or professional goals and (b) they would apply it moving forward. One student, for example, chose to learn more about the literature on the development of academic motivation during middle school. She reflected on how this literature applied to her experiences observing middle school classrooms and discussed specific ways in which she would apply the material in her own practice as a future language arts middle school educator. This kind of built-in opportunity to reflect on personal relevance in the material is instrumental for promoting all preservice educators' interest, performance, and continued pursuit of teaching (Eccles; 2009; Eccles & Wigfield, 2020; Hecht et al., 2020). However, doing so was also central to our goals of promoting an inclusive and equitable environment given that it especially benefits students from historically marginalized populations in higher education (Harackiewicz et al., 2016).

ENGAGING AND INCLUSIVE CLASS DISCUSSIONS

Theoretical and Empirical Grounding

We ground our recommended strategies for facilitating engaging and inclusive class discussions in the CRT and SCT literatures, which are summarized in previous sections (e.g., Ladson-Billings & Tate, 1995; Schunk & DiBenedetto, 2020). In addition, we draw from the belonging literature (e.g., Baumeister & Leary, 1995; Goodenow, 1993; Gray, 2017; Gray et al., 2018). This work consistently indicates that a *sense of school belonging*, or one's "sense of being accepted, valued, included, and encouraged by others.... in the [academic]... environment" (Goodenow, 1993, p. 25) is a "fundamental human motivation" in and of itself (Baumeister & Leary, 1995, p. 497). A sense of belonging is also a critical precursor to sparking students' (a) confidence, (b) the value they attach to their academic work, (c) positive academic emotions, and (d) performance (Goodenow, 1992; Gray, 2017). Creating academic environments that support student belonging is a complex and nuanced endeavor; however, environments that allow students to feel that they fit in *and* stand out are core to doing so (Gray, 2017). Importantly, some students—including students of color and first-generation college students—experience disproportionate barriers to belonging due to the pervasive, systemic inequities in education (Gopalan & Brady, 2019; Gray et al., 2018; Walton & Cohen, 2007, 2011).

Therefore, to promote belonging and ultimately equity among students who identify with groups that have been marginalized in higher education, it is essential to acknowledge and address the broader structures that undermine it. Gray and colleagues (2018), for example, wrote about the importance of supporting belonging among Black students not only through interpersonal interactions, but also through instructional and institutional opportunities. As an example of an instructional opportunity, Gray et al. recommend that instructors adopt *cultural distinctiveness* practices to fuel belonging. That is, they illustrate the critical importance of practices that allow students—particularly Black students—to see that cultural values in the classroom "are compatible with the cultural values [students] bring with them" to school (p. 102). Taken together, the extant literature speaks to the importance of (a) not only fostering belonging in students, but also (b) attending to the broader structures to promote belonging in an equitable and inclusive manner.

Our recommendations for facilitating engaging and inclusive discussions are also informed by the feedback literature. *Academic feedback*, or information delivered to students about their capabilities or performance both verbally and on assessments, is one of the most powerful mechanisms for shaping students' learning and motivation (Hattie & Timperley, 2007;

Hattie, 2009). However, feedback is a double-edged sword: it can do just as much harm as it can good. Relatedly, an absence of feedback—including overlooking a student during a class discussion, for example—can also be quite motivationally damaging (Koenka et al., 2021; Tenenbaum & Ruck, 2007). To promote rather than undermine learning and motivation in students, the literature converges on providing feedback that (a) is specific and task focused (Koenka et al., 2021) and (b) makes suggestions for improvement, especially when the feedback is negative (Fong et al., 2019). Finally, just like opportunities to experience belonging, not all feedback is delivered equally. It is well-documented in the literature, for example, that educators often provide Black and Latiné[1] students with biased, motivationally inferior feedback (Harber et al., 2012; Tenenbaum & Ruck, 2007). Therefore, it is essential that instructors educate themselves and frequently check their biases when interacting with students. Like the previous theoretical sections, much of the work in these fields has focused on White students (DeCuir-Gunby & Schutz, 2014; Graham, 1992; Usher, 2018) and may not be representative of all students, especially those from historically marginalized populations. However, a race-reimaged approach (e.g., Gray, 2017; Gray et al., 2018) informed all three strategies, and CRT informed the latter two. Doing so makes the strategies more relevant to students who are underrepresented in motivation research.

Strategies for Human Development Instructors

Strategy 7: Get to Know Your Students

In the spirit of promoting a sense of belonging among students in the human development classroom space and ultimately facilitating engaging, inclusive discussions, we first recommend getting to know one's students as whole people. Doing so can begin before students even set foot into the classroom. In our human development and learning course, for example, we circulated a survey prior to our first classroom discussion. This survey included questions about their reason(s) for taking the course, background knowledge in human development (if any), and longer-term career objectives. Equally important, however, were questions that were completely unrelated to the course content, in which we asked about (a) students' hobbies and interests and (b) if there was anything more they wanted to share with us. Circulating a survey of this nature signaled to students our interest in getting to know them as people right from the beginning of the semester; and, consistent with the belonging literature, it communicated that their personal interests were welcome and celebrated in our learning space (Goodenow, 1993). Asking questions about interests and hobbies, in particular, was a helpful starting point for us as instructors to create opportunities for students to experience *cultural distinctiveness* during discussions. In particular, these survey responses were an important first step to raising questions during discussions that supported students' culturally infused interests, which is essential for promoting belonging in an equitable and inclusive manner (Gray et al., 2018).

Strategy 8: Affirm Students' Personal Experiences, Identities, and Cultural Backgrounds

Second, affirming students' personal experiences, identities, and cultural backgrounds is essential for creating engaging and inclusive discussions. One way that we did so in our human development and learning course was by regularly centering students' personal experiences in discussions. We began each discussion with a "Question of the Day," which related to the course material and always encouraged students to draw from their own experiences and funds of knowledge. When learning about the development of identity, for example, we began class by asking "What is core to your identity?" and "How do you think your identity has changed as you've matured?" Consistent with the abovementioned literature, these kinds of opportunities for cultural distinctiveness should (a) help students feel as though they both fit in and stand out (Gray, 2017) and (b) ultimately foster belonging in an inclusive manner (Gray et al., 2018). Moreover, many students who responded to these questions were from historically marginalized racial and/or ethnic groups in our course; when doing so, they frequently reflected on their own academic experiences as a student of color. As a result, this discussion practice also provided space for counter storytelling and thus aligns with this CRT tenet (Bonilla-Silva, 2002).

In addition, the way in which instructors interact with and respond to student contributions during discussions—particularly when students draw from their personal experiences and cultural identities to do so—is a crucial way to affirm students' experiences, identities, and backgrounds. In our human development and learning course, and consistent with the abovementioned feedback literature, we made a point to respond directly and specifically to every student's contribution and affirm their referenced personal experiences when doing so. For example, whenever possible, we identified something specific about the student's contribution to reinforce its value and connect it back to the course material. Doing so not only served as task-focused feedback for the student (Koenka et al., 2021), but it often also presented spontaneous opportunities for us to foster cultural distinctiveness within students (Gray et al., 2018). Moreover, as mentioned earlier, an absence of feedback or lack of acknowledgement (a) is a powerful mechanism for undermining motivation (Koenka et al., 2021) and (b) disproportionately occurs among Black and Latiné students compared to their White peers (Tenenbaum & Ruck, 2007). As a result, we prioritized acknowledging and affirming all students' contributions, including and especially contributions that can be easy to inadvertently overlook (e.g., comments via chat and/or via the Zoom whiteboard feature in an online course like ours).

Strategy 9: Invite Guest Scholars to Engage in Discussions

Finally, we recommend inviting guest scholars to engage in class discussions who vary across racial identity, gender identity, career type, and career stage. In our human development and learning course, for example, we invited four scholars to join discussions throughout the semester who were (a) diverse in their racial and gender identities; and (b) represented many and in some cases multiple career paths and stages (i.e., dean, faculty member, PhD student, social worker, former teacher). These scholars also had expertise in equity-focused topics in which students had expressed particular interest (e.g., supporting mental health in children and adolescents) and/or or were important but were not well-represented in our textbook (e.g., the development of ethnic/racial identity in mixed-race youth). Moreover, when scholars join discussions, we recommend providing space for students rather than the instructor to take the lead in determining the focus. In our course, for example, students read or listened to a background resource prior to the discussion (e.g., an article written by the guest scholar or podcast featuring them). Next, we encouraged students to submit questions ahead of time and to ask questions spontaneously during discussion. Doing so helped to center the discussion around the students' interests.

Drawing from SCT, the practice of inviting guest scholars to class discussions is a powerful mechanism for fostering efficacy, engagement, and inclusion. For example, we were very intentional in our human development and learning course about selecting scholars who varied widely in their demographic and career identities. We also prioritized inviting scholars of color. Given that models perceived by students to be similar are especially important for fostering efficacy and ultimately engagement (Schunk & DiBenedetto, 2020), we intended for this diverse group of scholars to serve as models for students who often do not see instructors who look like them in higher education, taking a race re-imaged approach by attending to racial identities. We viewed doing so as especially important in our course given that the instructor of record identifies as a White, cisgender woman and the teaching assistant identifies as mixed race, Latina and White, cisgender woman.

In addition, inviting demographically diverse scholars with expertise in equity-focused work often served as a catalyst for supporting several CRT tenets. One visit from a faculty member with expertise in identity development among youth who identify as mixed race is a particularly strong example: she devoted a great deal of her visit to not only centering the experiences of an understudied population of youth—those who identify as mixed race—but also emphasized how her own developmental experiences as someone who is mixed race inspired her research in this area. In doing so, this discussion both challenged dominant ideology (e.g., the norm of neutrality in conducting research; Cook, 1990; Freeman, 1995) and provided space for counter-storytelling to occur (Bonilla-Silva, 2002).

CONCLUSION

In this chapter, we provided strategies for instructors teaching human development courses to promote inclusion, equity, engagement, motivation, and ultimately learning. These recommendations—focused on curriculum content, exams and assignments, and facilitating discussions—are all grounded in a variety of research literatures and illustrated by examples from our human development and learning course. By adopting these strategies, preservice teachers will not only experience a more equitable and inclusive learning context; they will also learn (a) human development content in a way that allows them to thoughtfully and accurately apply it in their own classroom and (b) strategies for teaching equitably and inclusively through their instructors' modeling of these strategies. Furthermore, while adopting these strategies, we encourage instructors to be explicit with students about the theories that are informing their practices along with their shortcomings—specifically representing historically marginalized and understudied students—so that preservice educators can apply these practices to their own pedagogy.

NOTE

1. We use the term "Latiné" to refer to individuals of Latin American descent for two reasons. First, it is inclusive of gender neutrality and does not imply that gender identity is a dichotomous construct (similar to the term "Latinx"). Second, we do so because "Latiné" is more commonly used by circles within Latin America.

KEY CHAPTER TAKEAWAYS	
Big-Picture Takeaways	
Given the history of educational and developmental psychology, it is necessary to rethink how we teach human development courses Self-reflection is a necessary first step to fostering diversity, equity, and inclusion Fostering diversity, equity, and inclusion is an ongoing process and thus is never "finished."	
Takeaways for Practice	
Strategies for Instructors	Examples From Human Development Course
Strategy 1: Center and Celebrate Development of Diverse Youth Throughout the Curriculum	Prioritized youth who identify as transgender when discussing development of gender identity
Strategy 2: When Presenting "Classic" Developmental Literature, Explicitly Address Its Limits	Discussed inequities associated with traditional intelligence tests, mindsets, and funds of knowledge
Strategy 3: Give Open-Book, Untimed Exams	Modified exams to be open book and untimed; defined "open book" and "untimed"
Strategy 4: Give Students Choice on Assignment Type and Timing	Gave three options when completing the capstone project
Strategy 5: Provide Scaffolding	Divided capstone assignment into several different components
Strategy 6: Promote Personal Relevance	Prioritized student choice to tailor topics that were of personal relevance and interest
Strategy 7: Get to Know Your Students	Circulate a survey prior to the first discussion to learn about students
Strategy 8: Affirm Students' Personal Experiences, Identities, & Cultural Backgrounds	Intentional, motivationally-supportive affirmation of students during instructor–student discussions
Strategy 9: Invite Guest Scholars to Engage in Discussions	Invited scholars to join discussions who (a) varied in demographic identity, career type/stage and (b) had expertise in equity-focused literature

KEY WORDS

Belonging
Critical race theory
Feedback
Motivation
Race-focused research
Race reimaged research
Social cognitive theory
Stereotype threat

AUTHOR NOTE

Thanks to our thoughtful and resilient human development and learning students, who pushed our thinking every day and inspired this chapter. A special thanks to Breanna Easter, who provided insightful and valuable feedback as we began developing this chapter. Please send all correspondences to Dr. Alison C. Koenka: alison.koenka.2021@gmail.com

REFERENCES

Agger, C., Roby, R. S., Nicolai, K. D., Koenka, A. C., & Miles, M. L. (2022). Taking a critical look at adolescent research on Black girls and women: A systematic review. *Journal of Adolescent Research*. https://doi.org/10.1177/07435584221076054

Ames, C. (1992). Classrooms: Goals, structure, and student motivation. *Journal of Educational Psychology, 84*(3), 261–271. https://psycnet.apa.org/record/1993-03487-001

Anderman, E. M., & Koenka, A. C. (2017). The relation between academic motivation and cheating. *Theory into Practice, 56*(2), 95–102. https://www.doi.org/10.1080/00405841.2017.1308172

Baumeister, R. F., & Leary, M. R. (1995). The need to belong: Desire for interpersonal attachments as a fundamental human motivation. *Psychological Bulletin, 117*(3), 497–529. https://doi.org/10.1037/0033-2909.117.3.497

Bell, D. A. (1992). *Faces at the bottom of the well: The permanence of racism*. Basic Books.

Bell, D. A. (1995). Racial realism. In K. Crenshaw, N. Gotanda, G. Peller, & K. Thomas (Eds.), *Critical race theory: The key writings that formed the movement* (pp. 302–312). The New Press.

Bonilla-Silva, E. (2002). We are all Americans! The Latin Americanization of racial stratificatiion in the USA. *Race and Society, 5*(1), 3–16. https://doi.org/10.1016/j.racsoc.2003.12.008

Cook, A. (1990). Beyond critical legal studies: The reconstructive theology of Dr. Martin Luther King, Jr. *Harvard Law Review, 103*(5), 985–1044. https://doi.org/10.2307/1341453

Crenshaw, K. W. (1988). Race, reform, and retrenchment: Transformation and legitimation in anti-discrimination law. *Harvard Law Review, 101*, 1331–1387. https://harvardlawreview.org/print/vol-133/race-reform-and-retrenchment/

Daniels, L. M., Goegan, L. D., & Parker, P. C. (2021). The impact of COVID-19 triggered changes to instruction and assessment on university students' self-reported motivation, engagement and perceptions. *Social Psychology of Education, 24*, 299–318. https://doi.org/10.1007/s11218-021-09612-3

DeCuir, J. T., & Dixson, A. D. (2004). "So when it comes out, they aren't that surprised that it is there": Using Critical Race Theory as a tool of analysis of race and racism in education. *Educational Researcher, 33*(5), 26–31. https://doi.org/10.3102/0013189X033005026

DeCuir-Gunby, J. T., & Schutz P. A. (2014). Researching race within educational psychology contexts. *Educational Psychologist, 49*(4), 244–260. https://doi.org/10.1080/00461520.2014.957828

Delgado, R., & Stefancic, J. (2012). *Critical race theory: An introduction* (2nd ed.). NYU Press.

Delgado, R., & Stefancic, J. (2017). *Critical race theory: An introduction* (3rd ed.). NYU Press.

Dweck, C. S., & Leggett, E. L. (1988). A social-cognitive approach to motivation and personality. *Psychological Review, 95*(2), 256–273. https://doi.org/10.1037/0033-295X.95.2.256

Eccles, J. (2009). Who am I and what am I going to do with my life? Personal and collective identities as motivators of action. *Educational Psychologist, 44*(2), 78–89. https://doi.org/10.1080/00461520902832368

Eccles, J. S., & Wigfield, A. (2020). From expectancy-value theory to situated expectancy-value theory: A developmental, social cognitive, and sociocultural perspective on motivation. *Contemporary Educational Psychology, 61.* https://doi.org/10.1016/j.cedpsych.2020.101859

Fong, C. J., Patall, E. A., Vasquez, A. C., & Stautberg, S. (2019). A meta-analysis of negative feedback on intrinsic motivation. *Educational Psychology Review, 31*, 121–162. https://doi.org/10.1007/s10648-018-9446-6

Freeman, A. (1995). Legitimizing racial discrimination through antidiscrmination law: A critical review of supreme court doctrine. In K. Crenshaw, N. Gotanda, G. Peller, & K. Thomas (Eds.), *Critical race theory: The key writings that formed the movement* (pp. 29–46). The New Press.

Goodenow, C. (1993). Classroom belonging among early adolescent students: Relationships to motivation and achievement. *Journal of Early Adolescence, 13*(1), 21–43. https://doi.org/10.1177/0272431693013001002

Gopalan, M., & Brady, S. T. (2019). College students' sense of belonging: A national perspective. *Educational Researcher, 49*, 134–137. https://doi.org/10.3102/0013189X19897622

Graham, S. (1992). "Most of the subjects were White and middle class": Trends in published research on African Americans in selected APA journals, 1970–1989. *American Psychologist, 47*, 629–639. https://doi.org/10.1037/0003-066X.47.5.629

Gray, D. L. (2017). Is psychological membership in the classroom a function of standing out while fitting in? Implications for achievement motivation and emotions. *Journal of School Psychology, 61,* 103–121. https://doi.org/10.1016/j.jsp.2017.02.001

Gray, D. L., Hope, E. C., & Matthews, J. S. (2018). Black and belonging at school: A case for interpersonal, instructional, and institutional opportunity structures. *Educational Psychologist, 53,* 97–113. https://doi.org/10.1080/00461520.2017.1421466

Harackiewicz, J. M., Smith, J. L., & Priniski, S. J. (2016). Interest matters: The importance of promoting interest in education. *Policy Insights From the Behavioral and Brain Sciences, 3*(2), 220–227. https://doi.org/10.1177/2372732216655542

Harber, K., Gorman, J., Gengaro, F., Butisingh, S., Tsang, W., & Ouellette, R. (2012). Students' race and teachers' social support affect the positive feedback bias in public schools. *Journal of Educational Psychology, 104*(4), 1149–1161. https://doi.org/10.1037/a0028110

Hart, B., & Risley, T. R. (1995). *Meaningful differences in the everyday experience of young American children.* Paul H Brookes Publishing.

Hattie, J. A. C. (2009). *Visible learning: A synthesis of over 800 meta-analyses relating to achievement.* Routledge.

Hattie, J. A. C., & Timperley, H. (2007). The power of feedback. *Review of Educational Research, 77*(1), 81–112. https://doi.org/10.3102/003465430298487

Hecht, C. A., Grande, M. R., & Harackiewicz, J. M. (2020). The role of utility value in promoting interest development. *Motivation Science, 7*(1), 1–20. https://doi.org/10.1037/mot0000182

Hirsh-Pasek, K., Adamson, L. B., Bakeman, R., Owen, M. T., Golinkoff, R. M., Pace, A., Yust, P. K. S., & Suma, K. (2015). The contribution of early communication quality to low-income children's language success. *Psychological Science, 26*(7). https://doi.org/10.1177/0956797615581493

John-Steiner, V., & Mahn, H. (1996). Sociocultural approaches to learning and development: A Vygotskian framework. *Educational Psychologist, 31*(3–4), 191–206, https://doi.org/10.1080/00461520.1996.9653266

Koenka, A. C., Linnenbrink-Garcia, L., Moshontz, H., Atkinson, K. M., Sanchez, C. E., & Cooper, H. (2021). A meta-analysis on the impact of grades and comments on academic motivation and achievement: A case for written feedback. *Educational Psychology, 41*(7), 922–947. https://doi.org/10.1080/01443410.2019.1659939

Ladson-Billings, G., & Tate, W. (1995). Toward a critical race theory of education. *Teachers College Record, 97*(1), 47–68. https://doi.org/10.1177/016146819509700104

Lazowski, R. A., & Hulleman, C. S. (2015). Motivation interventions in Education: A meta-analytic review. *Review of Educational Research, 86*(2). https://doi.org/10.3102/0034654315617832

Maehr, M. L., & Zusho, A. (2009). Achievement goal theory: The past, present, and future. In K. R. Wenzel & A. Wigfield (Eds.), *Handbook of motivation at school* (pp. 77–104). Routledge.

Matthews, J. S., & López, F. (2020). Race-reimaging educational psychology research: Investigating constructs through the lens of race and culture. *Contemporary Educational Psychology, 61,* 101878. https://doi.org/10.1016/j.cedpsych.2020.101878

Meece, J., Anderman, E., & Anderman, L. (2006). Classroom goal structure, student motivation, and academic achievement. *Annual Review of Psychology, 57*, 487–503. https://doi.org/10.1146/annurev.psych.56.091103.070258

Murphy, M. C., Steele, C. M., & Gross, J. J. (2007). Signaling threat: How situational cues affect women in math, science, and engineering settings. *Psychological Science, 18*(10), 879–885. https://doi.org/10.1111/j.1467-9280.2007.01995.x

Patall, E. A., Cooper, H., & Robinson, J. C. (2008). The effects of choice on intrinsic motivation and related outcomes: A meta-analysis of research findings. *Psychological Bulletin, 134*(2), 270–300. https://doi.org/10.1037/0033-2909.134.2.270

Ryan, R. M., & Deci, E. L. (2020). Intrinsic and extrinsic motivation from a self-determination theory perspective: Definitions, theory, practices, and future directions. *Contemporary Educational Psychology, 61*, 101860. https://doi.org/10.1016/j.cedpsych.2020.101860

Schunk, D. H., & DiBenedetto, M. K. (2020). Motivation and social cognitive theory. *Contemporary Educational Psychology, 61*, 101832. https://doi.org/10.1016/j.cedpsych.2019.101832

Schunk, D. H., & Usher, E. L. (2019). Social cognitive theory and motivation. In R. M. Ryan (Eds.), *The Oxford handbook of human motivation (2nd ed.)*. Oxford University Press.

Schunk, D., & Zimmerman, B. (1997). Social origin of self-regulatory competence. *Educational Psychologist, 32*, 195–208. https://doi.org/10.1207/s15326985ep3204_1

Sorbara, J. C., Chiniara, L. N., Thompson, S., & Palmert, M. R. (2020). Mental health and timing of gender-affirming care. *Pediatrics, 146*, 1–10. https://doi.org/10.1542/peds.2019-3600

Steele, C. M. (1997). A threat in the air: How stereotypes shape intellectual identity and performance. *American Psychologist, 52*(6), 613–629. https://doi.org/10.1037/0003-066X.52.6.613

Steele, C. M., & Aronson, J. (1995). Stereotype threat and the intellectual test performance of African Americans. *Journal of Personality and Social Psychology, 69*(5), 797–811. https://doi.org/10.1037/0022-3514.69.5.797

Tenenbaum, H. R., & Ruck, M. D. (2007). Are teachers' expectations different for racial minorities than for European American students? A meta-analysis. *Journal of Educational Psychology, 99*(2), 253–273. https://doi.org/10.1037/0022-0663.99.2.253

Umaña-Taylor, A. J., Kornienko, O., Bayless, S. D., & Updegraff, K. A. (2018). A universal intervention program increases ethnic-racial identity exploration and resolution to predict adolescent psychosocial functioning one year later. *Journal of Youth and Adolescence, 47*(1), 1–15. https://doi.org/10.1007/s10964-017-0766-5

Urdan, T., & Kaplan, A. (2020). The origins, evolution, and future directions of achievement goal theory. *Contemporary Educational Psychology, 61*, 101862. https://doi.org/10.1016/j.cedpsych.2020.101862

Usher, E. L. (2018). Acknowledging the Whiteness of motivation research: Seeking cultural relevance. *Educational Psychologist, 53*(2), 131–144. https://doi.org/10.1080/00461520.2018.1442220

Varelas, M., & Pappas, C. C. (2006). Intertextuality in read-alouds of integrated science-literacy units in urban primary classrooms: Opportunities for the development of thought and language. *Cognition and Instruction, 24*(2), 211–259. https://doi.org/10.1207/s1532690xci2402_2

Walton, G. M., & Cohen, G. L. (2007). A question of belonging: Race, social fit, and achievement. *Journal of Personality and Social Psychology, 92,* 82–96. https://doi.org/10.1037/0022-3514.92.1.82

Walton, G. M., & Cohen, G. L. (2011). A brief social-belonging intervention improves academic and health outcomes of minority students. *Science, 331,* 1447–1451. https://doi.org/10.1126/science.1198364

White, A. M., DeCuir-Gunby, J. T., & S. Kim. (2019). A mixed methods exploration of the relationships between the racial identity, science identity, science self-efficacy, and science achievement of African American students at HBCUs. *Contemporary Educational Psychology, 57,* 54–71. https://doi.org/10.1016/j.cedpsych.2018.11.006

CHAPTER 7

CREATING CLARITY THROUGH UNDERSTANDING COMPLEXITY

Building a Case for Development as a Critical Component of Educator Preparation

Lisa Looney
California State University, San Bernardino

Andréa C. Minkoff
University of La Verne

Gabriela Wilson
University of La Verne

Those within educational contexts must see their role as spurring the self to imagine radically and actualize students' humanities more fully.
—Carey, 2020, p. 739

Messages conveyed by the United States' educational system are characterized by promises of opportunity and fulfillment (Isseks, 2017; Labaree, 2012; Mijs, 2016; Ruck et al., 2019). Education in this country is often touted as being a great equalizer, with promises of wisdom, social mobility, and economic security (Isseks, 2017; Ruck et al., 2019). Yet, despite the possibilities that education is promised to afford, much research has shown considerable declines in performance, motivation, and attendance as youth progress through school (Boykin, 2015; Eccles et al., 1993; Roeser & Eccles, 1998). Further, educational practices, programs, and policies have challenged the idea of education as an equalizing force, instead producing outcomes that point more toward a social stratification system (Isseks, 2017; Labaree, 2012; Mijs, 2016). Schools serve multiple purposes, including the acquisition of subject matter content; however, a more informal, nonacademic curriculum exists within the school setting. Specifically, the school system teaches children and adolescents rules, norms, and values pertinent in society (Brint, 2017; Hamilton, 1983; Peguero & Bondy, 2015). As a socializing context, a great deal is learned from teachers, peers, and others about acceptable behaviors, tolerable beliefs, which individuals and groups are deemed worthy of success, and who is relegated to failure (Brint, 2017; Byrd & Hope, 2020). Examinations of who thrives and who struggles in formal education reveal complex processes at play (Mijs, 2016; Peguero & Bondy, 2015), particularly by the time students enter secondary education (Hoffman et al., 2021).

Education as a point of excitement for young children in preschool and early elementary years becomes something many students dread by the time they reach middle school and high school (Eccles & Roeser, 2011; Roeser & Eccles, 1998). Secondary students report perceiving education as meaningless and show declines in commitment to school (Roeser et al., 2000). Much has been written about declines in adolescent academic motivation and performance as a function of school transitions (Midgley & Edelin, 1998), larger teacher–student ratios (Eccles et al., 1993), and an increased emphasis on assessment or performance goals (Midgley, 2002). The goal of this chapter is to take a step back from these more micro-level—albeit warranted and important—reasons for drops in educational motivation and performance. Instead, we focus on apparent mismatches between school contexts and the developmental needs of students as a potential catalyst for these declines. More specifically, we aim to show the importance of creating a student-environment fit by inserting more developmental content into teacher preparation programs, in order to provide educators with tools to better meet the needs (both academic and nonacademic) of their students. We assert that developmental knowledge offers future educators an explanatory framework for understanding the differences that students bring to the classroom. Using a systems lens, we review the existing research and make the case that the use of educational psychology in educator preparation programs offers a foundation that speaks to the complexity of human experience. When engaging in practice informed by developmental theory, educators are better able to contribute to the growth, learning, and well-being of an increasingly diverse student population, thereby contributing to a system that is more equitable in nature, rather than one that perpetuates dominant norms.

ADOLESCENCE AS A CRITICAL TIME

Adolescence is a significant time of change (Sawyer et al., 2018). The teen years are full of promise, transition, and self-discovery (Schwartz, 2006). This time of life brings with it cognitive changes that allow adolescents to think about what is possible (Oyserman & Fryberg, 2006), reason about abstract concepts (Yurgelun-Todd, 2007), and recognize the relative nature of worldviews (Keating, 1990). Identity formation begins as the adolescent considers possible selves and explores potential ideologies and occupations (Steinke et al., 2009). It is also a time when adolescents have the capacity to observe the world around them, evaluate the systems in which they develop, and form beliefs about themselves and others based on implicit and explicit messages received (Hughes et al., 2006).

These developmental changes are enhanced or hindered by surrounding contextual influences. Systems theories (e.g., Bronfenbrenner, 1979) have shown how the multiple, interrelated, complex environments surrounding developing children and youth impact developmental trajectories. More proximal systems, such as microsystemic and mesosystemic environments (e.g., home, school, church) have a more immediate direct effect, while more distal exosystemic and macrosystemic systems (e.g., parents' work environment, teachers' training and preparation, educational policies at the state and national level) lead to indirect outcomes (Bronfenbrenner, 1979). The complexity surrounding adolescent development and the systemic influences that help to characterize it cannot be ignored.

Given the enormous, documented influence various systems have on development, it follows that creating contexts that aim to support youth, develop meaningful interactions with youth, and implement policies and expectations that encourage and propel youth toward optimal developmental outcomes (where they feel seen, heard, and valued) is needed. However, when it comes to the educational setting—a setting where much time is spent—not all adolescents feel supported or that they belong (Cipriano et al., 2019; Darling-Hammond et al., 2020; Gray et al., 2018; Legette & Kurtz-Costes, 2021). Despite the positive growth and change that is taking place during this life stage, adolescents enter systems like the school setting where educators' stereotypical negative viewpoints about their age group abound (Hines & Paulson, 2006). Many teachers, for example, hold beliefs that students need to be controlled and monitored (Eccles & Roeser, 2011). Schools create contexts that limit the formation of meaningful relationships, and they often marginalize children who do not excel academically. Further, education systems typically focus on a set of normative standards and curricula that might not be representative of all students' lived experiences (Hayes & Juarez, 2012; Isseks, 2017; Yu et al., 2018).

For students of color, stereotypical attitudes and feelings of marginalization are often further exacerbated (Fasching-Varner & Dodo Seriki, 2012; Luna & Tijerina Revilla, 2013; Perez-Brena et al., 2018). Traditionally, school systems have perpetuated social inequities through use of curricula and strategies that foster achievement in dominant communities (i.e., White, ableist, gendered), leaving minoritized groups feeling lessened in the process. These approaches, coupled with inherent educator biases, tend to privilege cultural assimilation of ethnic youth (Hope et al., 2015) and disseminate a deficit perspective when achievement gaps are noted (Perez-Brena et al., 2018). For middle schoolers and high schoolers, this all comes at a time when they are developing the increased cognitive capacity to recognize and understand such abstract concepts as structural inequality (Hughes et al., 2006; Ruck et al., 2019). The extent to which students perceive inequity, and perhaps experience it firsthand, predicts their motivation, well-being, and behavior (Eccles & Roeser, 2011). These experiences and the perceptions of the systemic issues involved impact students' attributions about their worth, their academic capability, and their chances for academic and occupational success (Godfrey et al., 2019).

A CALL FOR CHANGE

Change is needed. One area that can have a significant impact on what happens in the school environment is teacher education. Educator preparation programs have long grappled with how to best prepare future teachers to effectively teach an increasingly diverse student population (Zeichner, 2017). Traditionally, preservice preparation programs have tended to prioritize subject matter content and pedagogical skill (Darling-Hammond, 2000). Recently, increased emphasis has been given to the teacher's role in fostering social-emotional growth and creating learning spaces where students feel safe and supported (Schonert-Reichl et al., 2015). Even more recently, movements toward creating educational spaces that foster achievement for students from nondominant and translingual communities have gained attention, calling for reform to the White, ableist, gendered curriculum often seen in educational contexts (Souto-Manning & Rabadi-Raol,

2018). Demands for recognition of diverse experiences and backgrounds have become more prominent (Howard & Milner, 2014), representing an increasing awareness of diversity and complexity in the human experience (Pugach et al., 2019).

While the profession has recognized that transformation in learning environments is essential, the need for change exists in tandem with a teacher education system tied to accountability demands, state regulations, and measurement (Kretchmar & Zeichner, 2016). While teacher education programs vary greatly (Zeichner, 2017), a large majority place emphasis on curriculum and instruction strategies, at the exclusion of greater emphasis on child and adolescent development (Schonert-Reichl et al., 2015). As teacher education wrestles with ways to best prepare democratic professionals (Zeichner, 2020), it is imperative that the field consider the complexity that occurs developmentally within the educational system. Students enter the classroom space with different home environments; personalities; skills; educational resources and supports; and cultural, linguistic, and economic backgrounds (Lin & Bates, 2014). These young learners interact with peers and teachers in the environment who also come to the space with diverse perspectives, biases, training, personalities, skills, and supports (Milner, 2003).

Rather than thinking about the classroom space as one made up of a homogeneous group of individuals to which various curricular and instructional strategies might apply, examining the complexity of the educational space has value. Beyond the well-documented diversity in learning capabilities, recognition that the *intersectionality* of social identities present in the classroom space is varied and complex (Pugach et al., 2019) is also critical. The term intersectionality highlights the importance of moving beyond the examination of a single marker of identity and, instead, recognizing the intersection of multiple social categories to which one might belong (e.g., race, gender, ethnicity; Anthias, 2013; Crenshaw, 1989; Cuba et al., 2021). A school classroom, therefore, is made up of both teachers and students who experience a combination of social categories that shape their identity development, social perspectives, views of education, and support systems. Institutional structures such as an educational system further influence intersectionality, as systems can advantage some identities while marginalizing others (Nunez, 2014). A teacher's understanding of this complexity (intersectionality), through the teaching of child and adolescent development, is a must for successful teaching and learning to occur (Howard & Milner, 2014).

Focusing on curriculum and instruction, at the exclusion of (or separate from) development, often creates a teacher education program that compartmentalizes developmental processes and educational practices (Darling-Hammond et al., 2020). This compartmentalization results in a centering of norms and processes that marginalize children and youth and compromise motivation and successful learning outcomes (Souto-Manning & Rabadi-Raol, 2018). To think about instructional practices as distinct and separate from the students that will experience them, and to consider children and teens as distinct and separate from the contexts within which they operate poses a detriment to the system as a whole (Darling-Hammond et al., 2020).

In the sections that follow, we highlight the importance of developmental and educational psychology training for educators, emphasizing its value in (a) facilitating preservice educators' understanding of the complexity of the intersectionality present in the educational environment, in order to allow for discussions of curriculum and instruction, centered on strategies within diverse and inclusive environments; and (b) helping to decenter dominate norms and create spaces that are inclusive of the lived experiences of marginalized youth. Moreover, we focus on the importance of these values in the preparation of secondary level educators (i.e., middle school and high school), as the developmental changes during the adolescent stage of life warrant special attention for educational practices.

THE INTERRELATED COMPONENTS OF TEACHING

Educator preparation programs must consider ways in which they can enhance preservice teachers' success when they enter the field (Zeichner, 2017). This task is not without difficulty, as the educational environment is not one that lends itself to situations and decisions that are clear cut (Ball, 2009). Essentially, teaching involves two interrelated components: one that is more academic and technical in nature (e.g., subject-matter content, pedagogical skills and strategies) and one that is more psychological (e.g., those aspects of the environment that accompany pedagogical practice—student background, student motivation, teacher beliefs, teacher expectations; Darling-Hammond, 2006; Eccles & Roeser, 2011). Preparing teachers for the interconnected nature of both components of the academic environment is essential to ensure success in the profession.

The preparation of preservice educators in the United States often involves a primary focus on the academic component of teaching (Kosnik & Beck, 2009; Darling-Hammond, 2000; Patrick et al., 2011; Schonert-Reichl et al., 2015), thus exacerbating a disconnect between theory and practice (Ketter & Stoffel, 2008; Taylor et al., 2014). In this model of preparation, preservice teachers (of all levels) spend most of their certification courses learning about teaching various subject matter content (e.g., mathematics, science, language arts), and acquiring knowledge about strategies to be used to enhance children's understanding of that content (Darling-Hammond, 2000; Kosnik & Beck, 2009; Patrick et al., 2011). This information is arguably valuable to success in the profession (Kosnik & Beck, 2009), providing preservice teachers with effective tools for imparting knowledge to children and youth. However, teaching is a complex profession (Davis, 2007; Ketter & Stoffel, 2008), and this standard of preparation (i.e., a primary focus on curriculum and instruction) lends itself to a variety of interrelated, unwarranted assumptions; namely, (a) that if certain approaches are utilized, children will learn; (b) that children learn in similar ways; and (c) that if teachers teach effectively (i.e., they employ effective pedagogical strategies), and students do not demonstrate successful learning outcomes, then the problem lies with the student (e.g., learning differences, motivation, inattention).

The psychological component involved in the teaching profession highlights that the above assumptions are not correct. Instead, that successful implementation of pedagogical practices depends, in part, on a variety of components related to the student, to the teacher, and to the environment itself (Darling-Hammond, 2006; Eccles & Roeser, 2011). This is not a new realization in the field. Systems theories (Bronfenbrenner, 1979) help to inform our understanding of the educational environment, demonstrating that what takes place in the classroom setting impacts, and is impacted by, several biological and contextual factors that are both proximal and distal to the individuals involved (Eccles & Roeser, 2011). A growing body of evidence has bolstered educators' understanding that social-emotional factors can help or hinder academic success (Taylor et al., 2017). To remedy increasing rates of school pushouts (Luna & Tijerina Revilla, 2013), decreased achievement, increased opportunity gaps, and wavering academic motivation, educators, researchers, and policy makers have implemented research-based strategies designed to enhance students' social-emotional growth (Battin-Pearson et al., 2000; Schonert-Reichl et al., 2015). In doing so, educators have demonstrated recognition that the psychological component of the teaching environment matters and that attention to this component is needed for student success (Darling-Hammond et al., 2020; Schonert-Reichl et al., 2015).

Even more recently, with a national focus on systemic racism and increased awareness of the marginalization of people of color, individuals invested in the educational system (e.g., parents, students, community members, scholars) are calling for educational curriculum and educational settings that are more diverse and inclusive and that reflect social justice initiatives (Hayes & Juarez, 2012; Souto-Manning & Rabadi-Raol, 2018). While the field of teacher education has made a commitment to preparing teachers for social justice (Pugach et al., 2019), understanding how best to train them is a continuing conversation. Some scholars assert that the profession has failed in its attempts to adequately train a predominantly White, female, and English-speaking teaching force to engage effectively with an increasingly diverse student population (Fasching-Varner & Dodo Seriki, 2012; Hayes & Juarez, 2012). At the center of these discussions lies a recognition that understanding the complexity of human experience (i.e., the intersection of both student and teacher experiences), and how it overlaps with pedagogical practices, is lacking in teacher preparation (Fasching-Varner & Dodo Seriki, 2012; Hayes & Juarez, 2012; Souto-Manning & Rabadi-Raol, 2018).

Some educator preparation programs have responded to these calls for teachers' increased understanding of social-emotional growth and recognition of diverse lived experiences by adding an area of psychological emphasis to their certification programs (Woolfolk Hoy, 2000). Teacher certification tests in many states now expect teacher candidates to demonstrate awareness of some of these more psychological components, requiring preservice teachers to be exposed to content related to psychological processes that factor into the educational environment (Patrick et al., 2011). These changes display a recognition for the need for transformation; however, the implementation of these changes warrants discussion.

Responses to calls for change typically have involved the addition of full courses or components of courses related to psychological processes (e.g., social-emotional development, child development, diversity and social justice) to the curriculum to supplement instruction content. While variance occurs from program to program and state to state, a large majority of preparation programs focus primarily on curriculum and instruction, with a more minor emphasis on psychological processes, resulting in a compartmentalization of educational practices and developmental processes (Darling-Hammond et al., 2020). Preservice teachers, therefore, learn about development and diversity separate from effective instructional strategies.

Given what we know about the complexity of the educational environment, the effectiveness of simply adding on psychological content is called into question. For more than 4 decades, the field of developmental psychology has known, through the discussion of ecological systems models (e.g., Bronfenbrenner, 1979), that the compartmentalization involved in examining developmental processes separate from contextual influences is incomplete (Darling-Hammond et al., 2020). The multifaceted interactions that occur between individuals' biological make-up and the various contexts and connections of contexts they encounter reveal that developmental paths are unique. While patterns might exist, human and contextual complexity create situations that are not entirely predictable. This unpredictability in the human developmental trajectory is somewhat counter to the narrative that educational institutions espouse. A focus on curriculum and instructional strategies promotes a more unidirectional focus of contexts rather than a bidirectional one (Eccles & Roeser, 2011).

Further, work within the last couple of decades on intersectionality (Crenshaw, 1989), provides us with a framework to demonstrate another layer of complexity in environments such as classrooms and schools (Pugach et al., 2019). A bidirectional systems lens reveals that even in a classroom with students that possess a singular group identity, an argument can be made for how contextual differences (e.g., home environments, socioeconomic statuses, peer relationships) can contribute to differences seen in academic outcomes. Intersectionality provides a further multidimensional lens, demonstrating that several social identifiers (e.g., class, race, ethnicity, gender, language, culture, sexuality) are at play (Pugach et al., 2019). Intersectionality provides educators with a way to contemplate classroom complexity, acknowledging that attributing similarities to certain groups of individuals is problematic, when multiple group identifiers are considered (Pugach et al., 2019).

Finally, a primary focus on curriculum and instruction assumes a "best practice" exists. Preservice teachers are provided with strategies, techniques, and approaches that are considered "best" for bringing children and youth from one level of understanding in a subject area to a more advanced level (Ball & Forzani, 2009). However, evidence on which educators base these strategies is often based on White, middle-class, gendered, abled participants, and represent a "normative" definition of quality (Souto-Manning & Rabadi-Raol, 2018) when, in reality, the intersectionality within and between the individuals present contributes to a lack of one "best" way to teach. The existence of intersections in the classroom—and the acknowledgement of those complexities—allows teachers the opportunity to evaluate and create instructional practices that go across and between identity markers, recognize the various assets that students across identity markers bring to the instructional environment, and maintain a social justice approach to their teaching—an approach that values and privileges complexity.

PREPARING TEACHERS FOR COMPLEXITY: REVERSING THE EMPHASIS

Understanding curriculum and pedagogical strategies is arguably valuable for educators. We do not deny that this information has a place in educator preparation programs. However, we argue for a reversal of emphasis in how educators are prepared for the workforce by positioning educational and developmental psychology as critical components of educator preparation. As argued above, the current primary focus of educator preparation is centered on the academic environment with a secondary focus on some aspects of the psychological environment in a compartmentalized fashion (Darling-Hammond et al., 2020; Patrick et al., 2011; Woolfolk Hoy, 2000). This training teaches educators to become *content and pedagogical experts* with an understanding that "best practices" exist, but differential outcomes might occur based on some aspects of the individual or environment (e.g., class size, culture, sex, motivation). What follows from this is a deficit perspective on student learning (Milner, 2010). When best practice approaches are based on White, middle-class standards, outcomes that deviate from those standards are framed through a deficit lens, with educators making the case that remediation is needed to move those children up to the desired standard (Hayes & Juarez, 2012; Perez-Brena et al., 2018; Souto-Manning & Rabadi-Raol, 2018).

Reversing the emphasis for educator preparation requires psychological processes to become the primary focus. A focus on the complexities of the educational system as a whole (e.g., the individual, the classroom, relationships, the school environment) coupled with information related to curriculum and instruction allows educators to become *developmental systems* experts. Rather than being able to evaluate how to teach a particular content area to a group of students (while potentially ignoring factors about the student, the teacher, or the environment that could impact learning), an educational and developmental psychology focus would allow educators to evaluate and make decisions regarding how to teach a particular content area *given what is needed for the particular students involved*. In other words, this approach to preparation teaches educators to understand the systems involved in education and to engage curricula in a way that will possibly reach a diverse group of students, recognizing that curricular efforts might shift, based on the developmental needs of the current student body. This removes the deficit lens and creates a much-needed shift in the conceptualization of normative development for historically underrepresented groups (Perez-Brena et al., 2018). When educators look at various paths and outcomes for academic success on a horizontal plane, rather than a vertical hierarchy (Gladwell, 2004), and recognize that success can be reached in various ways and within diverse timetables, groups that were traditionally marginalized or seen as deficient can be celebrated for their strengths (Fasching-Varner & Dodo Seriki, 2012; Perez-Brena et al., 2018).

Another advantage of reversing the emphasis puts a greater degree of importance on psychological health and well-being, rather than meeting content standards. The work of Abraham Maslow (1943) highlights the importance of this emphasis by noting that individuals do not meet their full potential until various psychological and safety needs are met. Based on this framework, children and youth might struggle with academic content if they feel unsafe, unsupported, or that they do not belong (Ibrahim & El Zaatari, 2020; Slade & Griffith, 2013). For all youth (and those in marginalized groups, in particular), feelings of being unsafe, unsupported, or of not belonging become especially important if they exist within a system that transmits messages of inferiority that become internalized, impacting their self-efficacy beliefs (Bandura, 1997; Uwah et al., 2008), academic motivation (Gillen-O'Neel & Fuligni, 2013; Slade & Griffith, 2013), self-esteem (Hernández et al., 2017), and academic performance (Allen et al., 2017; Slade & Griffith, 2013). Educator preparation that prioritizes knowledge of psychological health and well-being helps teachers to be successful at creating meaningful connections with students, enhancing students' feelings of self-worth while they move toward mastery of academic content (Woolfolk Hoy, 2000).

An emphasis on the psychological component of the educational environment can also inform teachers about the power of relationships. Much research has examined the teacher–student relationship, finding that students perceive effective teachers as those that show they care (Noddings, 1992; Wentzel, 1997; Yu et al., 2018). In a caring environment, students are shown that they matter (Bartell, 2011; Tucker et al., 2010), and in the educational context, teachers can show that students matter through making them feel that they are significant, meaningful, and that they belong (Carey, 2020; Gray et al., 2018; Tucker et al., 2010). Mattering and a sense of belonging can be fostered through relationships within the classroom (e.g., teacher–student, student–student) and from the context of the classroom or school environment (Carey, 2020; Gray et al., 2020; Wigfield & Wentzel, 2007), resulting in a students' internalization of their own self-value and significance (Carey, 2020). For adolescents identifying with underrepresented groups, when institutions such as schools perpetuate racial stereotypes, commit to a curriculum that is not representative of their lived experience, or look at their accomplishments (or lack thereof) through a deficit lens, this can result in feelings of insignificance (Carey, 2020; Gray et al., 2018). Educator preparation that highlights the importance of relationships can impact how future teachers interact with their students.

A FOCUS ON THE TEACHER'S ROLE

Another benefit to educator preparation that emphasizes educational psychology and creates developmental systems experts is the focus this preparation could give to the role of the teacher. Teachers, alongside students, are an integral part of the educational environment; therefore, preparation to be an educator should focus on this role as one that is above and beyond a facilitator of content knowledge. The beliefs teachers hold about students' ability (Dweck, 2006), the expectations they have for their students (Rosenthal & Jacobson, 1968), the thoughts they have about their ability to carry out teaching tasks (Katz et al., 2020), and their attitudes about the role they play in the classroom (Eccles & Roeser, 2011) are all pieces teachers bring to the educational setting that can factor into student outcomes. A focus on educational psychology (and the complexity of education as a system, in particular) sets educators up for understanding how they contribute to student learning (Eccles & Roeser, 2011).

This becomes especially important for secondary teachers. In comparison with their elementary counterparts, middle and high school teachers are more likely to see their role in relation to academic content, rather than to child development or the socialization of children (Eccles & Roeser, 2011). This has important implications for the secondary education environment. Specifically, if educators see their role as primarily imparting knowledge, they are likely to focus largely on instructional strategies and, more importantly, exclude (or diminish) a focus on psychological elements (e.g., teacher–student relationships, identity development, motivation) that intersect with instruction (Eccles & Roeser, 2011; Hamre & Pianta, 2001). While early childhood education and preparation of elementary educators has often emphasized a need for developmental knowledge more heavily (Copple & Bredekamp, 2009), the exclusion (or diminished emphasis) of this focus in secondary education is problematic. Teachers are socializing agents (Hamilton, 1983), no matter the grade level, and given the immense amount of physical, cognitive, social, and emotional changes that occur as children enter into (and move through) adolescence, it becomes imperative that secondary educators understand the development of middle school and high school students and recognize the role they play in socializing youth within the school context (Roeser et al., 2000; Schonert-Reichl, 2015).

Furthermore, complexity and diversity do not just exist within the student body. Teachers come to the educational context with intersecting social identifiers, intricate backgrounds, varied beliefs, and distinct personalities that might complement or conflict with those of their students (Pugach et al., 2019). Teachers' attitudes about their students (Glock & Kleen, 2019), beliefs about their own capabilities as a teacher (Bandura, 1997; Kim & Seo, 2018), and philosophies about the nature of student ability (Dweck, 2006; Matheis et al., 2017; Safrudiannur & Rott, 2021) have important implications in the classroom. As such, educator preparation programs that prepare teachers to examine the characteristics they bring to the classroom and how this interaction between teacher and student attributes might help or hinder learning, further aid in assisting teachers in their understanding of how complex systems can impact academic outcomes (Pugach et al., 2019). Requiring preservice teachers to understand their own personal narratives, including their own identities related to race, gender, and ability, allows them to reflect on how these identities exist in tandem with historically underrepresented groups and opens their eyes to working with diverse groups of students (Fasching-Varner & Dodo Seriki, 2012). Given that the workforce of teachers, the curricula used, and the strategies implemented often come from historically *over*represented populations, change in helping to make the education system an equalizer rather than a social stratifier comes from an understanding of how educators' personal narratives, pedagogical beliefs, and practices come from a place of privilege (Hayes & Juarez, 2012; Fasching-Varner & Dodo Seriki, 2012). Such change would make a focus on teacher complexity and the teacher role important elements of educator preparation.

DECENTERING OF DOMINANT NORMS

Perhaps one of the most compelling arguments for the creation of developmental systems experts through the teaching of educational and developmental psychology is the potential toward building equitable educational systems. When teacher education programs prepare teachers to be content matter and instructional experts (instead of developmental systems experts), the focus is centered on the pedagogy. When teacher education programs prepare teachers to be content matter and instructional experts, the focus is centered on strategies to "reach" different groups of students (Hayes & Juarez, 2012). When teacher education programs prepare teachers with instructional strategies rooted in White, gendered, ableist norms, this becomes the standard, and discussions of diversity center on the "other" that might have needs separate from the dominant standard (Hayes & Juarez, 2012). As a result, dominant norms that privilege historically overrepresented groups are perpetuated, thereby marginalizing those that fall outside those groups (Hayes & Juarez, 2012). Without teachers' awareness of complexity, without recognition of the intersectionality present in their students, without appreciation for developmental processes, and without the attentiveness to their own biases and expectations, teachers inevitably contribute to a system that affords some with educational opportunities and denies others. Without adequate preparation, teachers contribute to a system of social stratification. On the other hand, when teachers demonstrate value for a student's personhood and the complexity of their lived experience, when they critically examine how their own lived experiences shape the lens through which they view their students, and when they possess a disposition toward unlocking the value that each student brings to the classroom (regardless of race, class, gender, sexuality), a system of equity can be realized (Fasching-Varner & Dodo Seriki, 2012).

PREPARING SECONDARY LEVEL EDUCATORS

While developmental knowledge is important at all levels of teacher education for all the reasons discussed above, we highlight a need for change in secondary educator preparation, in particular. We place emphasis on secondary education, in part, because preparation for teaching children of younger ages has traditionally had a heavier developmental focus, particularly for infant, toddler, and preschool education (Copple & Bredekamp, 2009). Preservice teachers who will work within the elementary school environment can also benefit greatly from developmental understanding; however, we highlight middle school and high school teacher preparation for a number of reasons.

First, the physical, cognitive, and social-emotional changes that occur during the adolescent period are complex and varied (Steinberg & Morris, 2001). Physically, pubertal changes adolescents are experiencing can correlate with adolescent anxiety (Reardon et al., 2009), beliefs about the self (Martin, 2018), and peer acceptance (Conley & Rudolph, 2009). These changes come at a time when adolescent cognition heightens their sense of self-consciousness (Rankin et al., 2004), oftentimes leading to a focus on appearance and a fear of being noticed or singled out (Hawes et al., 2020; Zimmer-Gembeck et al., 2021). Changes in brain structure are also occurring with the brain reaching full maturation in the mid-20s, making the time of the adolescent life stage a critical one for brain growth (Dumontheil, 2016). The prefrontal cortex (responsible for planning, thinking ahead, controlling impulses and weighing risks and rewards of behavior) is still developing (Dumontheil, 2014). Cognitively, adolescents become more future-oriented; their thinking becomes more multidimensional as they consider issues from a variety of perspectives; they engage in more relative thinking; and they examine concepts that are more abstract in nature (Ruck et al., 2019; Yurgelun-Todd, 2007). Socially, adolescents enter a time when they have increased interest in spending time with friends (Hartup, 1993). Understanding all of the significant developmental changes that occur during this time can assist educators in creating learning spaces that are sensitive to, and representative of, developmental needs.

Of all the developmental changes that occur, perhaps the most significant from an educator standpoint is the development of identity (Meeus et al., 1999), coupled with increased cognitive capacities for abstract thought (Dumontheil & Blakemore, 2012). Middle school and high school students begin the introspective process of figuring out who they are and who they want to be (Oyserman et al., 2006). That self-development is informed by the messages they receive from those around them (Hope et al., 2015) and their cognitive capacity to understand higher-level abstract concepts and ideas (Yurgelun-Todd, 2007). Educators play an impactful role in identity development, as they contribute to youths' perception of themselves (Pugach et al., 2019). The potential for academic success, the attributions being formed, and the formation of future selves (e.g., occupations) can be influenced by the educational context (Hope et al., 2015). If adolescents perceive an educational system in which they can thrive, have teachers that believe in their capabilities, and experience a system that privileges the effort they put in, identity formation that results in meeting one's full self-potential can occur (Hope et al., 2015; Klem & Connell, 2004).

Research has noted declines in academic motivation and performance during the middle school and high school years. Transitions from elementary to secondary education (and all that entails, such as multiple teachers and an increased focus on grades) has led the educational psychology community to call for a greater emphasis on developmental knowledge (Darling-Hammond et al., 2020). Relatedly, various educational policies put in place for secondary schools exemplify a mismatch in the fit between developmental needs and school context. Adolescents strive for increased autonomy, competence, and connection; yet they enter a school system that engages in such practices as early school start times, implementation of rules that exert more control rather than offer independence, placement of students into various "tracks" (Legette & Kurtz-Costes, 2021), and the creation of class sizes that impede the development of meaningful teacher–student relationships (Eccles & Roeser, 2011). These practices are all counter to research evidence demonstrating what adolescents need for optimal developmental growth (Legette & Kurtz-Costes, 2021).

Finally, the teen years are fraught with perceptions of negativity (Hines & Paulson, 2006). Societal views of the adolescent life stage paint a picture of hormonal, moody, impulsive individuals, and this systemic interpretation of adolescence trickles down into various facets of the educational system, including the policies put into place and educator beliefs that middle school and high schoolers need to be controlled (Eccles & Roeser, 2011). Educator preparation programs that create true understanding of adolescents could create environments where negative perceptions are a minority.

PUTTING THE UNDERSTANDING OF COMPLEXITY INTO PRACTICE

Understanding the complex systems at play in the educational environment should be accompanied by a recognition that no concrete formula exists for the implementation of good teaching. Instead, understanding complexity provides educators with knowledge to guide reflections on actions to be taken to enhance learning, while considering the multifaceted characteristics of the students involved and the context in which learning takes place. As we have noted throughout the chapter, the educational environment, in and of itself, does not produce situations that are predictable, with methods that are clear cut (Ball, 2009), since what takes place in this setting is impacted by a myriad of biological and contextual factors (Bronfenbrenner, 1979; Eccles & Roeser, 2011). Given that no specific set of approaches exists to fit all variations of what a teacher might encounter, how can teacher educators put these ideas into practice and prepare preservice teachers for the complex task of teaching? To sum up some of the points made in this chapter, teacher educators can: (a) develop educator preparation curriculum steeped in understanding development, human experiences, and intersectionality, with opportunities to reflect on how these overlap with pedagogy; (b) reverse the emphasis of teacher education, bringing development and developmental systems to the forefront and discuss curriculum and instruction in light of developmental theory and research, thereby creating an understanding that pedagogical practices can (and should) shift based on developmental needs of the students involved; (c) give focus to the teacher's role in the educational environment by helping preservice educators to understand their own personal narratives and pedagogical beliefs, while increasing their ability to recognize their role as one that transcends mere facilitation of content; and (d) cultivate an appreciation for the power of relationships in the school environment, empowering teachers to recognize the importance of perceiving their students (and the experiences from which they come) as significant, meaningful, and valuable.

While the above summation is not a set of tangible methods per se, it is important to note that teaching is *not* a technical task with technical solutions (Bartolome, 1994; Davis, 2007). Thinking of teaching as such often leads to expectations for improving teaching and learning by focusing on practical implications and solution-focused methods to "correct" whatever obstacles or problems are identified (Bartolome, 1994; Davis, 2007). This is not to say that instructional methods are ineffective, but instead is meant to be a recognition that methods learned in teacher education should be thought of as malleable, and teachers should be equipped with ample developmental systems knowledge so as to reflect upon, modify, and recreate methods in consideration of the needs of the individuals involved (Bartolome, 1994). Encouraging educators to "humanize pedagogy" (Bartolome, 1994, p. 173) by understanding and respecting the complexity and intersectionality present in the classroom and school setting allows them to contribute to the building of equitable educational systems.

As we have argued in this chapter, a true understanding of the development of students, the educational environment in which they learn, and the intersectionality of identities at play in those learning environments (e.g., personalities, biases, lived experiences) allows developmentally appropriate solutions to follow. Understanding complexity frees teachers from more rigid, unidirectional methodologies that might work for some and not others and creates an appreciation for the bidirectional interactions at play in the educational system that can either enhance or hinder the learning process (Bartolome, 1994). Therefore, teacher educator methods that employ the use of reflection and discussion surrounding case studies and vignettes, along with a recognition that multiple avenues toward successful teaching and learning are possible, can enhance preservice educators' understanding of the complexity they will encounter in their profession. An emphasis on educational and developmental psychology can bridge the gap between theory and practice in a meaningful way, thereby promoting educators who understand developmental systems enough to use that framework as a lens through which to reflect upon and enhance their teaching. As Bartolome (1994) states, "Under ideal conditions, competent educators simultaneously translate theory into practice *and* consider the population being served and the sociocultural reality in which learning is expected to take place" (p. 179).

CONCLUSION

Educator preparation that emphasizes educational psychology and creates developmental systems experts, we argue, can have great benefits for the student population. The current emphasis on curriculum and instruction, without attending to the dynamics of learning and development, risks producing a profession of educators who lack understanding of the complexity involved in creating pedagogy that is meaningful and relevant to the diverse group of students present in today's educational space. As microcosms of society, schools are socializing units, and teachers within the educational system transmit socialization messages to children and youth within that setting (Brint, 2017). Teachers play a role in development, functioning, and overall socialization in a number of ways. From the discipline techniques used in the classroom to the development of teacher–student relationships, teachers impact more than just academic outcomes for their students (Martin et al., 2010; Rios-Aguilar, 2010). Self-esteem (Akin & Radford, 2018), peer acceptance (Hughes & Kwok, 2006), levels of self-efficacy (Bandura, 1997; Walker, 2010), and social behavior (Nowacek et al., 1990) are among some of the important outcomes that teachers influence. Perhaps most importantly, teachers have a role in shaping the academic identity of students; and this academic identity has an impact on feelings of worth and on various future trajectories these adolescents explore. The (conscious and unconscious) beliefs teachers form about their students (Staats, 2016) guide their student expectations (Chin et al., 2020) and drive whether a teacher calls on a student (Altermatt et al., 1998), whether a teacher overlooks certain behaviors or other performance outcomes (Gilliam et al., 2016), or the degree to which a teacher creates a warm, supportive relationship with a student (Gershenson & Papageorge, 2018), further contributing to feelings of worth and belongingness (or lack thereof) that become internalized.

The complex systems present in the school and classroom environment provide an informal curriculum that instructs students on who is valued and who is marginalized (Hayes & Juarez, 2012), potentially impacting the differential success rates of multiply minoritized students (Chin et al., 2020). As educator preparation programs contend with how best to train future teachers, we call on the field to place considerable emphasis on educational psychology and developmental knowledge, making these core components of teacher preparation. Doing so increases the likelihood that students will encounter educators who understand their developmental needs, respect and value their lived experiences, and are equipped to create classrooms and school communities that are academically stimulating and responsive to the realities of navigating school while coming of age. Further, this emphasis in teacher preparation equips teachers to enter into an educational context understanding their own biases, beliefs, expectations, and philosophies, which can have a significant impact on how teachers interact with a diverse student body. As schools are called upon to engage in more humanizing approaches in their work with students, we assert that a focus on educational psychology in teacher preparation will contribute to the production of educators who have clarity in how they can effectively support the learning and development of their students.

KEY CHAPTER TAKEAWAYS

- Educator recognition and understanding of the complexity of the human experience is needed, as is the translation of this understanding to pedagogical experiences.
- Educator preparation should focus more heavily on development and developmental systems, infusing discussions of curriculum and instruction as it relates to developmental needs.
- Educators would benefit from a complex understanding of the teacher's role in the educational environment, since appreciation and comprehension of how personal narratives, pedagogical beliefs, and life experiences shape teacher identity and effectiveness can strengthen the facilitation of content.
- Educators cultivate relationships in the educational setting, and educator preparation should help foster an appreciation for the power of those relationships, helping others to recognize and appreciate the intersectionality present in their students, with the goal of considering these experiences as valuable and significant to the learning process.

KEY WORDS

Academic motivation
Adolescent development
Content and pedagogical experts
Developmental systems experts
Identity development
Intersectionality
Social justice
Systems theory
Teacher identity
Teacher role

REFERENCES

Akin, I., & Radford, L. (2018). Exploring the development of student self-esteem and resilience in urban schools. *Contemporary Issues in Education Research, 11*(1), 17–24. https://doi.org/10.19030/cier.v11i1.10118

Allen, K. A., Kern, M. L., Vella-Brodrick, D., & Waters, L. (2017). School values: A comparison of academic motivation, mental health promotion, and school belonging with student achievement. *The Educational and Developmental Psychologist, 34*(1), 31–47. https://doi.org/10.1017/edp.2017.5

Altermatt, E. R., Jovanovic, J., & Perry, M. (1998). Bias or responsivity? Sex and achievement-level effects on teachers' classroom questioning practices. *Journal of Educational Psychology, 90*(3), 516–527. https://doi.org/10.1037/0022-0663.90.3.516

Anthias, F. (2013). Intersectional what? Social divisions, intersectionality and levels of analysis. *Ethnicities, 13*, 3–19. https://doi.org/10.1177/1468796812463547

Ball, A. F. (2009). Toward a theory of generative change in culturally and linguistically complex classrooms. *American Educational Research Journal, 46*(1), 45–72. https://doi.org/10.3102/0002831208323277

Ball, D. L., & Forzani, F. M. (2009). The work of teaching and the challenge for teacher education. *Journal of Teacher Education, 60*(5), 497–511. https://doi.org/10.1177/0022487109348479

Bandura, A. (1997). *Self-efficacy: The exercise of control.* WH Freeman/Times Books.

Bartell, T. (2011). Caring, race, culture, and power: A research synthesis toward supporting mathematics teachers in caring with awareness. *Journal of Urban Mathematics Education, 4*(1), 50–74. https://doi.org/10.21423/jume-v4i1a128

Bartolome, L. I. (1994). Beyond the methods fetish: Toward a humanizing pedagogy. *Harvard Educational Review, 64*, 173–194. https://doi.org/10.17763/haer.64.2.58q5m5744t325730

Battin-Pearson, S., Newcomb, M. D., Abbott, R. D., Hill, K. G., Catalano, R. F., & Hawkins, J. D. (2000). Predictors of early high school dropout: A test of five theories. *Journal of Educational Psychology, 92*, 568–582. https://doi.org/10.1037/0022-0663.92.3.568

Boykin, A. W. (2015). American k–12 education as gateway or gatekeeper: What must research tell us about how to secure educational opportunity for all? In *Opening the doors to opportunity for all: Setting a research agenda for the future* (pp. 29–34). American Institute for Research. Retrieved from http://www.air.org/sites/default/files/OpeningTheDoors-EquityProject-Jan2015.pdf#page=35

Brint, S. (2017). *Schools and societies* (3rd ed.). Stanford University Press.

Bronfenbrenner, U. (1979). *The ecology of human development.* Harvard University Press.

Byrd, C. M., & Hope, E. C. (2020). Black students' perceptions of school ethnic-racial socialization practices in a predominantly Black school. *Journal of Adolescent Research, 35,* 728–753. http://doi.org/10.1177/0743558419897386

Carey, R. L. (2020). Making Black boys and young men matter: Radical relationships, future oriented imaginaries and other evolving insights for educational research and practice. *International Journal of Qualitative Studies in Education, 33,* 729–744. https://doi.org/10.1080/09518398.2020.1753255

Chin, M. J., Quinn, D. M., Dhaliwal, T. K., & Lovison, V. S. (2020). Bias in the air: A nationwide exploration of teachers' implicit racial attitudes, aggregate bias, and student outcomes. *Educational Researcher, 49*(8), 566–578. https://doi.org/10.3102/0013189X20937240

Cipriano, C., Barnes, T. N., Pieloch, K. A., Rivers, S. E., & Brackett, M. (2019). A multilevel approach to understanding student and teacher perceptions of classroom support during early adolescence. *Learning Environments Research, 22,* 209–228. http://doi.org/10.1007/s10984-018-9274-0

Conley, C. S., & Rudolph, K. D. (2009). The emerging sex difference in adolescent depression: Interacting contributions of puberty and peer stress. *Development and Psychopathology, 21*(2), 593–620. https://doi.org/10.1017/S0954579409000327

Copple, C., & Bredekamp, S. (2009). *Developmentally appropriate practice in early childhood programs serving children from birth through age 8* (3rd ed.). National Association for the Education of Young Children.

Crenshaw, K. (1989). Demarginalizing the intersection of race and sex: A Black feminist critique of antidiscrimination doctrine, feminist theory, and antiracist politics. *University of Chicago Legal Forum, 1989,* Article 8. https://chicagounbound.uchicago.edu/cgi/viewcontent.cgi?article=1052&context=uclf

Cuba, M. J., Massaro, V. R., Waters, C., Watson, S., Cody, A. M., & Stemhagen, K. (2021). Beyond the label: Using a multilevel model of intersectionality to explore the educational experiences of Latino English learners. *Journal of Latinos and Education, 20,* 62–77. https://doi.org/10.1080/15348431.2018.1540351

Darling-Hammond, L. (2000). How teacher education matters. *Journal of Teacher Education, 51,* 166–173. https://doi.org/10.1177/0022487100051003002

Darling-Hammond, L. (2006). Constructing 21st century teacher education. *Journal of Teacher Education, 57*(3), 300–314. https://doi.org/10.1177/0022487105285962

Darling-Hammond, L., Flook, L., Cook-Harvey, C., Barron, B., & Osher, D. (2020). Implications for educational practice of the science of learning and development. *Applied Developmental Science, 24,* 97–140. https://doi.org/10.1080/10888691.2018.1537791

Davis, S. (2007). Bridging the gap between research and practice: What's good, and how can one be sure? *Phi Delta Kappan, 88*(8), 568–578. https://doi.org/10.1177/003172170708800804

Dumontheil, I. (2014). Development of abstract thinking during childhood and adolescence: The role of rostrolateral prefrontal cortex. *Developmental Cognitive Neuroscience, 10*(C), 57–76. https://doi.org/10.1016/j.dcn.2014.07.009

Dumontheil, I. (2016). Adolescent brain development. *Current Opinion in Behavioral Sciences, 10,* 39–44. https://doi.org/10.1016/j.cobeha.2016.04.012

Dumontheil, I., & Blakemore, S. J. (2012). Social cognition and abstract thought in adolescence: The role of structural and functional development in rostral prefrontal cortex. *BJEP Monograph Series II, Number 8-Educational Neuroscience, 1*(1), 99–113. htps://doi.org/10.1016/j.dcn.2014.07.009

Dweck, C. S. (2006). *Mindset: The new psychology of success.* Random House.

Eccles, J. S., & Roeser, R. W. (2011). Schools as developmental contexts during adolescence. *Journal of Research on Adolescence, 21*(1), 225–241. https://doi.org/10.1111/j.1532-7795.2010.00725.x

Eccles, J. S., Wigfield, A., Midgley, C., Reuman, D., Iver, D. M., & Feldlaufer, H. (1993). Negative effects of traditional middle schools on students' motivation. *The Elementary School Journal, 93*(5), 553–574. https://doi.org/10.1086/461740

Fasching-Varner, K., & Dodo Seriki, V. (2012). Moving beyond seeing with our eyes wide shut: A response to "There is no culturally responsive teaching spoken here." *Democracy & Education, 20,* 1–6. https://democracyeducationjournal.org/home/vol20/iss1/5

Gershenson, S., & Papageorge, N. (2018). The power of teacher expectations: How racial bias hinders student attainment. *Education Next, 18*(1), 64–70. https://eric.ed.gov/?id=EJ1162328

Gillen-O'Neel, C., & Fuligni, A. (2013). A longitudinal study of school belonging and academic motivation across high school. *Child Development, 84*(2), 678–692. https://doi.org/10.1111/j.1467-8624.2012.01862.x

Gilliam, W. S., Maupin, A. N., Reyes, C. R., Accavitti, M., & Shic, F. (2016). Do early educators' implicit biases regarding sex and race relate to behavior expectations and recommendations of preschool expulsions and suspensions? *Yale University Child Study Center, 9*(28), 1–16. https://marylandfamiliesengage.org/wp-content/uploads/2019/07/Preschool-Implicit-Bias-Policy-Brief.pdf

Gladwell, M. (2004, February). *Choice, happiness, and spaghetti sauce* [Video]. https://www.ted.com/talks/malcolm_gladwell_choice_happiness_and_spaghetti_sauce?utm_campaign=tedspread&utm_medium=referral&utm_source=tedcomshare

Glock, S., & Kleen, H. (2019). Attitudes toward students from ethnic minority groups: The roles of preservice teachers' own ethnic backgrounds and teacher efficacy activation. *Studies in Educational Evaluation, 62,* 82–91. https://doi.org/10.1016/j.stueduc.2019.04.010

Godfrey, E. B., Burson, E. L., Yanisch, T. M., Hughes, D., & Way, N. (2019). A bitter pill to swallow? Patterns of critical consciousness and socioemotional and academic well-being in early adolescence. *Developmental Psychology, 55*(3), 525–537. https://doi.org/10.1037/dev0000558

Gray, D. L., Hope, E. C., & Byrd, C. M. (2020). Why Black adolescents are vulnerable at school and how schools can provide opportunities to belong to fix it. *Policy Insights From the Behavioral and Brain Sciences, 7*(1), 3–9. https://doi.org/10.1177/2372732219868744

Gray, D. L., Hope, E. C., & Matthews, J. S. (2018). Black and belonging at school: A case for interpersonal, instructional, and institutional opportunity structures. *Educational Psychologist, 53,* 97–113. https://doi.org/10.1080/00461520.2017.1421466

Hamilton, S. F. (1983). The social side of schooling: Ecological studies of classrooms and schools. *The Elementary School Journal, 83,* 313–334. https://doi.org/10.1086/461320

Hamre, B., & Pianta, R. (2001). Early teacher–child relationships and the trajectory of children's school outcomes through eighth grade. *Child Development, 72,* 625–638. https://doi.org/10.1111/1467-8624.00301

Hartup, W. W. (1993). Adolescents and their friends. *New Directions for Child and Adolescent Development, 1993*(60), 3–22. https://doi.org/10.1002/cd.23219936003

Hawes, T., Zimmer-Gembeck, M. J., & Campbell, S. M. (2020). Unique associations of social media use and online appearance preoccupation with depression, anxiety, and appearance rejection sensitivity. *Body Image, 33,* 66–76. https://doi.org/10.1016/j.bodyim.2020.02.010

Hayes, C., & Juarez, B. (2012). There is no culturally responsive teaching spoken here: A critical race perspective. *Democracy & Education, 20,* 1–14. https://democracyeducationjournal.org/home/vol20/iss1/1

Hernández, M. M., Robins, R. W., Widaman, K. F., & Conger, R. D. (2017). Ethnic pride, self-esteem, and school belonging: A reciprocal analysis over time. *Developmental Psychology, 53*(12), 2384–2396. https://doi.org/10.1037/dev0000434

Hines, A. R., & Paulson, S. E. (2006). Parents' and teachers' perceptions of adolescent storm and stress: Relations with parenting and teaching styles. *Adolescence, 41,* 597–614.

Hoffman, A. J., Pullés, S. A., Medina, M. A., Pinetta, B. J., Rivas-Drake, D., Schaefer, D. R., & Jagers, R. J. (2021). Considering multiple levels of influence on adjustment in school: Ethnic-racial public regard, peer socialization, and social-emotional learning practices. *Social Development,* 806–832. https://doi.org/10.1111/sode.12501

Hope, E. C., Hoggard, L. S., & Thomas, A. (2015). Emerging into adulthood in the face of racial discrimination: Physiological, psychological, and sociopolitical consequences for African American youth. *Translational Issues in Psychological Science, 1,* 342–351. http://dx.doi.org/10.1037/tps0000041

Howard, T. C., & Milner, H. R. (2014). Teacher preparation for urban schools. In H. R. Milner, IV & K. Lomotey (Eds.), *Handbook of urban education* (pp. 199–216). Routledge. https://doi.org/10.4324/9780203094280

Hughes, D., Rodriguez, J., Smith, E. P., Johnson, D. J., Stevenson, H. C., & Spicer, P. (2006). Parents' ethnic-racial socialization practices: A review of research and directions for future study. *Developmental Psychology, 42,* 747–770. https://doi.org/10.1037/0012-1649.42.5.747

Hughes, J. N., & Kwok, O. (2006). Classroom engagement mediates the effect of teacher-student support on elementary students' peer acceptance: A prospective analysis. *Journal of School Psychology, 43*(6), 465–480. https://doi.org/10.1016/j.jsp.2005.10.001

Ibrahim, A., & El Zaatari, W. (2020). The teacher–student relationship and adolescents' sense of school belonging. *International Journal of Adolescence and Youth, 25*(1), 382–395. https://doi.org/10.1080/02673843.2019.1660998

Isseks, J. (2017). Hegemony of the "Great Equalizer" and the fragmentation of common sense: A Gramscian model of inflated ambitions for schooling. *Educational Studies, 52,* 49–62. https://doi.org/10.1080/00131946.2016.1261026

Katz, D., Mahfouz, J., & Romas, S. (2020). Creating a foundation of well-being for teachers and students with SEL curriculum in teacher education programs. *Northwest Journal of Teacher Education, 15*(2), Article 5. https://doi.org/10.15760/nwjte.2020.15.2.5

Keating, D. P. (1990). Adolescent thinking. In S. S. Feldman & G. R. Elliott (Eds.), *At the threshold: The developing adolescent* (pp. 54–89). Harvard University Press.

Ketter, J., & Stoffel, B. (2008). Getting real: Exploring the perceived disconnect between education theory and practice in teacher education. *Studying Teacher Education, 4,* 129–142. https://doi.org/10.1080/17425960802433611

Kim, K. R., & Seo, E. H. (2018). The relationship between teacher efficacy and students' academic achievement: A meta-analysis. *Social Behavior and Personality, 46*(4), 529–540. https://doi.org/10.2224/sbp.6554

Klem, A. M., & Connell, J. P. (2004). Relationships matter: Linking teacher support to student engagement and achievement. *Journal of School Health, 74,* 262–273. https://doi.org/10.1111/j.1746-1561.2004.tb08283.x

Kosnik, C., & Beck, C. (2009). *Priorities in teacher education: The 7 key elements of preservice preparation.* Routledge.

Kretchmar, K., & Zeichner, K. (2016). Teacher prep 3.0: A vision for teacher education to impact social transformation. *Journal of Education for Teaching, 42,* 417–433. http://doi.org/10.1080/02607476.2016.1215550

Labaree, D. F. (2012). School syndrome: Understanding the USA's magical belief that schooling can somehow improve society, promote access, and preserve advantage. *Journal of Curriculum Studies, 44,* 143–163. http://doi.org/10.1080/00220272.2012.675358

Legette, K. B., & Kurtz-Costes, B. (2021). Curricular tracking, students' academic identity, and school belonging. *Journal of Early Adolescence, 41*(7), 961–981. https://doi.org/10.1177/0272431620977659

Lin, M., & Bates, A. (2014). Who is in my classroom? Teachers preparing to work with culturally diverse students. *International Research in Early Childhood Education, 5*(1), 27–42. https://files.eric.ed.gov/fulltext/EJ1151003.pdf

Luna, N., & Tijerina Revilla, A. (2013). Understanding Latina/o school pushout: Experiences of students who left school before graduating. *Journal of Latinos and Education, 12,* 22–37. https://doi.org/10.1080/15348431.2012.734247

Martin, A. J., Marsh, H. W., Cheng, J. H. S., & Ginns, P. (2010). Fathers and male teachers: Effects on boys academic and non-academic development. *Childhood Education, 86*(6), 404–408. https://doi.org/10.1080/00094056.2010.10523178

Martin, K. A. (2018). *Puberty, sexuality, and the self: Boys and girls at adolescence.* Routledge.

Maslow, A. H. (1943). A theory of human motivation. *Psychological Review, 50*, 370–396. https://doi.org/10.1037/h0054346

Matheis, S., Kronborg, L., Schmitt, M., & Preckel, F. (2017). Threat or challenge? Teacher beliefs about gifted students and their relationship to teacher motivation. *Gifted and Talented International, 32*(2), 134–160. https://doi.org/10.1080/15332276.2018.1537685

Meeus, W., Iedema, J., Helsen, M., & Vollebergh, W. (1999). Patterns of adolescent identity development: Review of literature and longitudinal analysis. *Developmental Review, 19*(4), 419–461. https://doi.org/10.1006/drev.1999.0483

Midgley, C. (2002). *Goals, goal structures, and patterns of adaptive learning.* Lawrence Erlbaum Associates.

Midgley, C., & Edelin, K. C. (1998). Middle school reform and early adolescent well-being: The good news and the bad. *Educational Psychologist, 33*, 195–206. https://doi.org/10.1207/s15326985ep3304_4

Mijs, J. J. B. (2016). The unfulfillable promise of meritocracy: Three lessons and their implications for justice in education. *Social Justice Research, 29*, 14–34. http://doi.org/10.1007/s11211-014-0228-0

Milner, H. R. (2003). Teacher reflection and race in cultural contexts: History, meanings, and methods in teaching. *Theory Into Practice, 42*(3), 173–180. https://doi.org/10.1207/s15430421tip4203_2

Milner, H. R. (2010). What does teacher education have to do with teaching? Implications for diversity studies. *Journal of Teacher Education, 61*(1–2), 118–131. https://doi.org/10.1177/0022487109347670

Noddings, N. (1992). *The challenge to care in schools: An alternative approach to education.* Teachers College Press.

Nowacek, E. J., McKinney, J. D., & Hallahan, D. P. (1990). Instructional behaviors of more and less effective beginning regular and special educators. *Exceptional Children, 57*(2), 140–149. https://psycnet.apa.org/record/1991-25800-001

Nunez, A. (2014). Employing multilevel intersectionality in educational research: Latino identities, contexts, and college access. *Educational Researcher, 43*, 85–92. https://doi.org/10.3102/0013189X14522320

Oyserman, D., & Fryberg, S. A. (2006). The possible selves of diverse adolescents: Content and function across gender, race and national origin. In C. Dunkel & J. Kerpelman (Eds.), *Possible selves: Theory, research, and applications* (pp. 17–39). Nova Science Publishers.

Patrick, H., Anderman, L. H., Bruening, P. S., & Duffin, L. C. (2011). The role of educational psychology in teacher education: Three challenges for educational psychologists. *Educational Psychologist, 46*(2), 71–83. https://doi.org/10.1080/00461520.2011.538648

Peguero, A. A., & Bondy, J. M. (2015). Schools, justice, and immigrant students: Assimilation, race, ethnicity, gender, and perceptions of fairness and order. *Teachers College Record, 117*(7), 1–42. https://doi.org/10.1177/016146811511700706

Perez-Brena, N. J., Rivas-Drake, D., Toomey, R. B., & Umana-Taylor, A. J. (2018). Contributions of the integrative model for the study of developmental competencies in minority children: What have we learned about adaptive culture? *American Psychologist, 73*, 713–726. http://dx.doi.org/10.1037/amp0000292

Pugach, M. C., Gomez-Najarro, J., & Matewos, A. M. (2019). A review of identity in research on social justice in teacher education: What role for intersectionality? *Journal of Teacher Education, 70*(3), 206–218. https://doi.org/10.1177/0022487118760567

Rankin, J. L., Lane, D. J., Gibbons, F. X., & Gerrard, M. (2004). Adolescent self-consciousness: Longitudinal age changes and gender differences in two cohorts. *Journal of Research on Adolescence, 14*(1), 1–21. https://doi.org/10.1111/j.1532-7795.2004.01401001.x

Reardon, L. E., Leen-Feldner, E. W., & Hayward, C. (2009). A critical review of the empirical literature on the relation between anxiety and puberty. *Clinical Psychology Review, 29*(1), 1–23. https://doi.org/10.1016/j.cpr.2008.09.005

Rios-Aguilar, C. (2010). Measuring funds of knowledge: Contributions to Latina/o students' academic and nonacademic outcomes. *Teachers College Record, 112*(8), 2209–2257. https://doi.org/10.1177/016146811011200805

Roeser, R. W., & Eccles, J. S. (1998). Adolescents' perceptions of middle school: Relation to longitudinal changes in academic and psychological adjustment. *Journal of Research on Adolescence, 8*, 123–158. https://doi.org/10.1207/s15327795jra0801_6

Roeser, R. W., Eccles, J. S., & Sameroff, A. J. (2000). School as a context of early adolescents' academic and social-emotional development: A summary of research findings. *The Elementary School Journal, 100*, 443–471. https://doi.org/10.1086/499650

Rosenthal, R., & Jacobson, L. (1968). *Pygmalion in the classroom: Teacher expectations and pupils' intellectual development.* Holt, Rinehart & Winston.

Ruck, M. D., Mistry, R. S., & Flanagan, C. A. (2019). Children's and adolescent's understanding and experiences of economic inequality: An introduction to the special section. *Developmental Psychology, 55*, 449–456. http://doi.org/10.1037/dev0000694

Safrudiannur, & Rott, B. (2021). Offering an approach to measure beliefs quantitatively: Capturing the influence of students' abilities on teachers' beliefs. *International Journal of Science and Mathematics Education, 19*(2), 419–441. https://doi.org/10.1007/s10763-020-10063-z

Sawyer, S. M., Azzopardi, P. S., Wickremarathne, D., & Patton, G. C. (2018). The age of adolescence. *The Lancet Child & Adolescent Health, 2*(3), 223–228. https://doi.org/10.1016/S2352-4642(18)30022-1

Schonert-Reichl, K. A., Hanson-Peterson, J. L., & Hymel, S. (2015). SEL and preservice teacher education. In J. A. Durlak, C. E. Domitrovich, R. P. Weissberg, & T. P. Gullotta (Eds.), *Handbook of social and emotional learning: Research and practice* (pp. 406–421). The Guilford Press.

Schwartz, S. J. (2006). Predicting identity consolidation from self-construction, eudaimonistic self-discovery, and agentic personality. *Journal of Adolescence, 29*(5), 777–793. https://doi.org/10.1016/j.adolescence.2005.11.008

Slade, S., & Griffith, D. (2013). A whole child approach to student success. *KEDI Journal of Educational Policy, Special Issue, 10*(3), 21–35. https://www.proquest.com/docview/1430480780

Souto-Manning, M., & Rabadi-Raol, A. (2018). Re(centering) quality in early childhood education: Toward intersectional justice for minoritized children. *Review of Research in Education, 42*, 203–225. https://doi.org/10.3102/0091732X18759550

Staats, C. (2016). Understanding implicit bias: What educators should know. *The Education Digest, 82*(1), 29–38. https://www.aft.org/sites/default/files/ae_winter2015staats.pdf

Steinberg, L., & Morris, A. S. (2001). Adolescent development. *Annual Review of Psychology, 52*(1), 83–110. https://doi.org/10.1146/annurev.psych.52.1.83

Steinke, J., Lapinski, M., Long, M., VanDerMaas, C., Ryan, L., & Applegate, B. (2009). Seeing oneself as a scientist: Media influences and adolescent girls' science career-possible selves. *Journal of Women and Minorities in Science and Engineering, 15*(4), 279–301. https://doi.org/10.1615/JWomenMinorScienEng.v15.i4.10

Taylor, M., Klein, E. J., & Abrams, L. (2014). Tensions of reimagining our roles as teacher educators in a third space: Revisiting a co/autoethnography through a faculty lens. *Studying Teacher Education, 10*, 3–19. https://doi.org/10.1080/17425964.2013.866549

Taylor, R. D., Oberle, E., Durlak, J. A., & Weissberg, R. P. (2017). Promoting positive youth development through school-based social and emotional learning interventions: A meta-analysis of follow-up effects. *Child Development, 88*(4), 1156–1171. https://doi.org/10.1111/cdev.12864

Tucker, C., Dixon, A., & Griddine, K. (2010). Academically successful African American male urban high school students' experiences of mattering to others at school. *Professional School Counseling, 14*, 135–145. https://doi.org/10.1177/2156759X1001400202

Uwah, C., McMahon, H., & Furlow, C. (2008). School belonging, educational aspirations, and academic self-efficacy among African American male high school students: Implications for school counselors. *Professional School Counseling, 11*(5), 296–305. https://doi.org/10.5330/PSC.n.2010-11.296

Walker, B. J. (2010). The cultivation of student self-efficacy in reading and writing. *Reading & Writing Quarterly, 19*(2), 173–187. https://doi.org/10.1080/10573560308217

Wentzel, K. R. (1997). Student motivation in middle school: The role of perceived pedagogical caring. *Journal of Educational Psychology, 89*, 411–419. https://doi.org/10.1037/0022-0663.89.3.411

Wigfield, A., & Wentzel, K. R. (2007). Introduction to motivation at school: Interventions that work. *Educational Psychologist, 42*, 191–196. https://doi.org/10.1080/00461520701621038

Woolfolk Hoy, A. (2000). Educational psychology in teacher education. *Educational Psychologist, 35*(4), 257–270. https://doi.org/10.1207/S15326985EP3504_04

Yu, M. V. B., Johnson, H. E., Deutsch, N. L., & Varga, S. M. (2018). "She calls me by my last name": Exploring adolescent perceptions of positive teacher–student relationships. *Journal of Adolescent Research, 33,* 332–362. https://doi.org/10.1177/0743558416684958

Yurgelun-Todd, D. (2007). Emotional and cognitive changes during adolescence. *Current Opinion in Neurobiology, 17*(2), 251–257. https://doi.org/10.1016/j.conb.2007.03.009

Zeichner, K. M. (2017). *The struggle for the soul of teacher education.* Routledge. https://doi.org/10.4324/9781315098074

Zeichner, K. (2020). Preparing teachers as democratic professionals. *Action in Teacher Education, 42,* 38–48. https://doi.org/10.1080/01626620.2019.1700847

Zimmer-Gembeck, M. J., Rudolph, J., & Pariz, J. (2021). A cascade of rejection and appearance preoccupation: Adolescents' body dysmorphic symptoms and appearance rejection sensitivity over 4 years. *British Journal of Developmental Psychology.* https://doi.org/10.1111/bjdp.12377

CHAPTER 8

CONSIDERATIONS AND IMPORTANCE OF GENERATIONAL CHANGES FOR TEACHING

Elizabeth J. Pope
University of Arizona

Katrina A. Dotzler
University of Arizona

Heidi Legg Burross
University of Arizona

Paul A. Schutz
University of Arizona

Most, if not all of us, are familiar with the generation we belong to and the inevitable stereotypes that are associated with being a member of one generation (the "greatest generation") or another (millennials). Social scientists tend to group people into generations based on their cohort or birth year as a way of assessing how major cultural events impact the development of those who experienced those events (Doherty et al., 2015). Differences in the views, beliefs, and values based on the broader cultural context created by historical events (large and small) are often the focus of discussions among generations. These "back in my day" comparisons are a natural consequence of these generational comparisons. Generational changes serve as a constant reminder of the importance of environmental and cultural influences on human development.

While societies evolve and people change, some institutions have been somewhat slower to adapt, perhaps because of our continuous need to compare the present to romanticized versions of earlier times. One field where it is crucial to understand the current world in which young people exist is education. While it is tempting for educators to want to reproduce their experiences as students, doing so dismisses the prevailing cultural context that invariably influences the development of each successive generation. Meaningful and effective teaching practices that address the emergent concerns of students must take these social, historical, and generational shifts into consideration.

Educational psychology offers several theories that can help teachers and teacher educators understand generational changes to meet the needs of their students from one generation to the next. In doing so, the focus shifts from thinking about *how to teach* one generation to thinking about *how to understand and know* students not only as individuals, but as individuals living within a distinct historical and cultural context. For teacher educators, demonstrating and modeling exemplary practices relating to other generations can help their students learn to do the same once they are in their own classrooms.

Scholars have long debated the importance of nature (e.g., hereditary influences) and nurture (e.g., environmental influences including generational context) on human development. Over time, scholars have come to agree that both, as well as the transactions among them, are important to our overall developmental well-being. For example, if a child is not provided the adequate nutrition (i.e, nurture) needed to function as a biological organism (i.e., nature, physiological needs), not only will their physical well-being be compromised but also their psychological (e.g., autonomy, competency, and relatedness/belonging) needs may not be met (i.e., nurture). On the other hand, a child can have all the nutritious food they need, but if their psychological needs are not being met, their development and well-being may not be optimal.

Thus, although both are important, in this chapter we emphasize environmental influences—including generational changes involved in human development. To do so, we begin with a discussion of Bronfenbrenner's (1976) ecological systems theory (EST), which allows us to describe different levels of environmental influences as well as the importance of continual change over time. Next, we include a discussion of the basic needs articulated in self-determination theory ([SDT]; Deci & Ryan, 2000; Ryan & Deci, 2020). Our focus here is on optimal development which refers to removing barriers to opportunities and maximizing mental, social, emotional, and physical well-being. As such, we discuss the importance of meeting basic psychological needs that are important to optimal developmental outcomes.

In conjunction with EST and SDT, we also discuss the importance of teacher educators demonstrating and modeling approaches such as asset-based pedagogies (ABP) for teaching students from all backgrounds—but particularly Black, indigenous and people of color ([BIPOC]; López, 2017, 2019). ABP provides a framework to facilitate both students' and teachers' basic psychosocial needs, leading to developmental well-being within college and PreK–12 schooling contexts and ever-changing cultures and environments.

ECOLOGICAL SYSTEMS THEORY

Urie Bronfenbrenner's (1976) bioecological or EST examines the influence that people and institutions have on individual development, learning, and identity. For this reason, EST provides a logical lens for educators to view various environmental factors that contribute to generational change. It outlines the make-up of these changes as the individual grows and moves into new environments throughout their life span. Social scientists who study generational trends refer to these as life cycle, age, and period effects, all of which impact the developmental trajectory of individuals (Doherty et al., 2015). Opportunities and relationships throughout the life span shape how the individual interacts with these systems.

Bronfenbrenner's EST provides a rich framework for the many factors that influence development and learning and vary widely among individuals, shifting in influence as the larger cultural milieu continues to evolve. Although some of the basic structures tend to remain the same from generation to generation, the continual change as suggested by the chronosystem plays an important role in the adoption of generational and cultural norms, views, and values among individuals at any given time. For example, textbook analyses revealed increased attention to diverse cultural and ethnic representations, allowing more PreK–12 students to see examples like themselves in learning (Vitta, 2021). Therefore, it is imperative that teachers and teacher educators view learning and development of their students as inevitably bound to the cultural context of the present time. Self-determination theory is useful to closely examine how these cultural views and values influence individual students' motivation, learning, and development.

Ecological Systems

Picture looking down on a tree stump to help visualize the organization of the ecological systems (see Figure 8.1). The circle at the center of the stump is the *individual* or self, which could be a teacher educator, a preservice teacher, or an elementary school student for our example. Along with these individual factors are basic needs related to motivation and learning, such as a need for autonomy, competence, and relatedness. Self-determination theory posits that, as individuals, we all possess an inherent need for growth which can be fostered through activities and experiences that meet these basic needs (Deci & Ryan, 2000).

Immediately surrounding the individual center circle is the *microsystem* (Bronfenbrenner, 1976). This layer is made up of the individuals who directly influence individuals on a regular and reoccurring basis: household members including family, and peers, teachers, and friends. Their proximity to the individual emphasizes the regularity and power of these multidirectional influential relationships. Multidirectional influence involves not only the individual being affected by those entities, but also affecting them. For example, just as our friends shape our interests and mannerisms, they

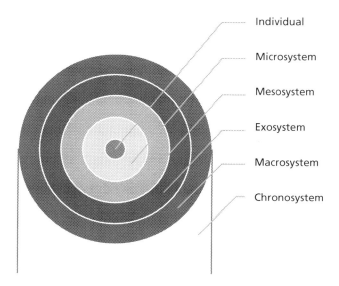

Figure 8.1 Bronfenbrenner's ecological systems.

tend to adopt ours. Helping preservice teachers picture their place in their future PreK–12 students' microsystems is an important way for them to begin to visualize their role and impact as a teacher on the development of their future students.

The layer outside the microsystem is the *mesosystem*, where interactions among other people that influence individuals take place (Bronfenbrenner, 1976). For a student in the PreK–12 system, everyday examples of the mesosystem include parent–teacher conferences, surprise party preparations, parents planning family vacations with grandparents, and so forth. Sometimes, PreK–12 students themselves may not be part of these interactions, but they are nonetheless influenced by what occurs in these situations. Helping preservice teachers identify various interactions in their own lives as well as those that might impact PreK–12 students is one way that teacher educators can illustrate the complexity of these influences for various individuals.

Immediately outside of the mesosystem lies the *exosystem* (Bronfenbrenner, 1976). This is populated by the institutions and individuals with whom students do not directly and regularly interact but are still affected by these factors. These can include factors such as mass media, governmental organizations, and politicians. Often the effects of the decisions and behaviors of those in the exosystem are filtered through the other systems for their indirect influences on individuals. It is often in the exosystem where we can most easily see changes that impact a generational cohort. Teacher educators can encourage their preservice teachers to think through how these decisions at the exosystem level may impact their roles as future educators as well as the experiences of their future students. For example, preservice teachers may develop awareness of how changes in federal school funding legislation can determine if PreK–12 students have access to after school care. However, most PreK–12 students are completely unaware of these big-picture political decisions, aside from perhaps overhearing adults grumbling about them or seeing snippets in news reports. These policies could determine parents' work schedules and opportunities for students and, thereby, have impacts on their lives.

The outermost ring of the metaphorical tree stump, encompassing the other systems, comprises the *macrosystem* (Bronfenbrenner, 1976). Lacking tangible entities, the macrosystem contains the values, norms, laws, traditions, and beliefs of individuals' cultural milieu. These macrosystem values permeate the other systems as they provide the frameworks for interactions and behaviors. Many of the elements contained in the macrosystem are the trends identified as major markers of various generations. Most individuals weave among groups regularly, from school or work to home to place of worship to friends' homes. The values of varied groups often differ, and individuals learn to navigate among these potentially treacherous differences through observation of and feedback from others (Bandura, 1976). For example, a PreK–12 student from a two-mother household may be confronted by a classmate at school (microsystem) claiming that this family structure violates the classmate's beliefs about what the general culture (macrosystem) dictates, as communicated through the classmate's home (mesosystem). Handling these types of clashes requires a level of sophistication that most elementary school students have yet to develop. Teaching preservice teachers to be able to guide PreK–12 students through the experience can help both preservice teachers and PreK–12 students better understand the diversity of viewpoints and backgrounds.

The *chronosystem* relates to how time influences the individual. For example, a student as an 8-year-old in 2022 is different than they would have been at the same age in 1992, or as a 25-year-old in any year. As generational studies and Bronfenbrenner suggest, the intersection of our age and era affects who we are and what makes up the other systems. Imagine the dendrochronology (study of tree rings) of an older individual's systems tree stump: crosscuts of lower/younger sections reveal different populations in the systems than those found in the higher/older years. Coworkers replace classmates. Friends are more geographically dispersed and have diverse interests. We might find that institutions never known (or existing!) in childhood are the workplaces in adulthood. For example, a child in school in the early 2000's might never imagine that "social media influencer" and the work associated with such a position would ever exist. Social media influencer refers to people who sample goods and services for online subscribers, usually with financial incentives from the companies behind these products (Martineau, 2019). A growing number of people now earn substantial incomes as product and lifestyle influencers on social media platforms such as YouTube.

Bronfenbrenner in Modern Context

When Bronfenbrenner proposed and refined his theory in the 1970s and 1980s, notions such as "Facebook official" relationships, eLearning, and instant or direct messages (IMs/DMs) were figments of science fiction. However, the theory remains relevant and can be applied in the modern context to help teacher educators and their students. Indisputably, today the internet and social media directly influence children as young as elementary age (even earlier in some cases) and should be considered within the ecological systems. Recently, researchers placed social media generally in individuals' microsystem (Cala & Soriano, 2014), which fits its definition of including regular and direct interpersonal interactions. A finer dissection of how individuals interact with and classify others linked on social media may provide greater distinctions.

One example of modernizing Bronfenbrenner's theory which could be applied in a teacher education setting is by asking preservice teachers to attempt to classify social media influencers (even the name begs for Bronfenbrenner's application). Because there tends to be an interactive component to social media influencer–viewer relationships through comments and online chats, "How should these be classified in levels of ecological systems? Are these personal microsystem interactions or broader exosystem influences, much like celebrities?" The answer is not simple and perhaps not the same for all influencer–viewer situations. In most situations, the viewer/fan/consumer is much more affected by the posted comments and behaviors of the influencer than vice versa. The fan's comments and reposts may not even be read by the influencer, so that multidirectional nature probably better fits an exosystem classification. Online communications and relationships add a level of complexity and influence on ecological systems that must be considered as important by educators. Discussions such as these in a teacher education classroom can help preservice teachers begin to examine the world in which their future students live and interact. This awareness of current context is key for educators at all levels to foster meaningful learning.

Working Across Generations

When thinking about current preservice teachers and the PreK–12 students they will be working with, it is useful to describe some recent macrosystem characteristics in the United States. According to the National Center for Education Statistics (National Center for Education Statistics, 2021), during the 2017–2018 school year, 79% of teachers in public schools identified as White (Spiegelman, 2020). In addition, in 2016, 76.6% teachers identified as female (Ingersoll et al., 2018). When compared to the racial/ethnic background of students enrolled in public schools in 2018, 47% of students identify as White, with 15% Black, 27% Hispanic, 5% Asian and 1% Indigenous students. These data show that the majority population of U.S. public schools is now comprised of racially minoritized students. In addition, the racial make-up of school shows a trend to increasing segregation. For example, in 2018, only 6% of White students were attending public schools where most of the students (i.e., 75%) were minoritized (National Center for Education Statistics, 2021). On the other hand, 59% of Black students and 60% of Hispanic students attend schools that are made up of over 75% minoritized students. Currently, school segregation is increasing, with the majority of students now identifying as BIPOC, and over 75% of the teachers are White female. Thus, potential cultural mismatches among teachers and their students are possible.

In addition to the changing demographics of students in PreK–12 classrooms, notable changes in the ecological systems have impacted the context where teachers and students of all ages interact. For example, regular use of social media blurs personal opinions with general reputable news sources, which can be evidence of the generational differences that might affect classifications in the theory (e.g., a social media figure in the microsystem for one person might be in the exosystem for their parents or college professors). Prior to the introduction of social media platforms such as the now-antiquated MySpace, or more recent platforms such as Facebook, TikTok, YouTube, and Instagram, news was accessed through televised and radio broadcast channels, as well as by subscriptions to print media. While viewers and readers could choose the media, most news came from rigorously researched sources that may have represented a more balanced view of events.

Many students now get information from social media, where readers have more options with less-than-rigorous journalistic standards (Shearer, 2021). Where information was historically "take what you get," we now have information that is self- and system-curated to fit our idiosyncratic interests, views, and biases. Teacher educators and teachers need to be aware of this shift in information literacy.

What it means to be media-savvy and a critical consumer of information has shifted across generations. Preservice teachers and their students now need to be carefully prepared to weed through voluminous and often inaccurate sources of information. Information from and about the microsystems and exosystems can appear in the same social media feeds on the same screen, making validation and sourcing an onerous but necessary task for all.

Educating preservice teachers to assist their future students to be diagnostic and critical when consuming information must be approached cautiously. Not only do teacher educators need to prepare preservice teachers to be critical consumers in arenas that barely existed, if at all, during the professors' own school days, they also need to negotiate interactions among generations in an ever-changing educational landscape much like the preservice teachers will need to do with their PreK–12 students. The chronosystem most directly speaks to generational differences. Each generation defines itself by how it differs from those that came before and after. Factors such as digital technology, fashion, parenting practices, music, politics, language/slang, and world events (e.g., COVID-19 pandemic) distinguish the identities of generational memberships. The bridging of generations—with younger students and potentially older parents and grandparents of students—requires educators at all levels to understand and respect generational differences.

At risk of aging herself and as a vibrant example of "back in my day" thinking, one of the authors of this chapter remembers looking at an undergraduate college classroom filled with young women who wore their hair long, straight, and blonde and who carried huge handbags to store their giant sunglasses. Had she not been familiar with heiress and reality television star Paris Hilton, she might have thought the students were emulating her own style. In another case, undergraduate students offered "Netflix and chill" for use in a classroom example. The professor initially took the example at face value and continued the lesson, but then stopped, faced the students, and proclaimed that she knew what it entailed—to be met with grins by undergraduates who thought they had snuck one past her. Staying up with popular trends and styles that students and preservice teachers follow can help college and future PreK–12 educators to incorporate student interests into their lessons. Students are more attentive and can learn more easily when content maps onto their experiences.

Exploring what students of the next generation(s) are "into" is only part of the educator's task. PreK–12 students are being raised by parents (and guardians) who are obviously members of an older generation, and some who may not often have or need opportunities to examine what "kids today" know or are doing. Preservice teachers must therefore consider the views and experiences of their partners in educating students: parents and guardians. Understanding microsystem and exosystem influences allows for better communication and understanding between classrooms and homes for parents, teachers, and students.

SELF-DETERMINATION THEORY

Much like Bronfenbrenner's theory, the tenants of SDT are thought to remain the same across generations and transcend cultural and societal differences (Reeve et al., 2004; Reeve et al., 2018). SDT is predicated on the belief that, as human beings, we are all naturally driven to achieve a sense of well-being through the satisfaction of three basic psychological needs: perceived autonomy, competence, and relatedness. Well-being is the optimal state for happiness and productivity and allows for healthy growth and development in individuals (Deci & Ryan, 2000; Ryan & Deci, 2020).

Autonomy

Autonomy is the perception that one is engaging in activities and behaviors one takes an interest in and places value on the activities. Naturally, an important piece of establishing a sense of autonomy is the development of one's intrinsic values and beliefs (Deci & Ryan 2000; Ryan & Deci, 2020). As Bronfenbrenner (1976) described, our individual values and beliefs are influenced by the various surrounding ecological systems. For example, a young person who grew up in the United States in the 1950s existed in a very different world than a young person growing up today. The beliefs and values endorsed by parental figures and teachers, as well as their expectations for young people, were quite different in the 1950s, as were more general cultural norms and changes in the post-World War II United States. It makes sense that children of that era internalized many of these prevalent beliefs and values as they grew to adulthood.

From an SDT perspective, the behaviors undertaken by an individual may be more autonomy-supporting the closer in line these are with one's internalized beliefs and values (Reeve et al., 2004). It is perhaps for this reason that some PreK–12 students may question why they need to learn "basic" skills like spelling or cursive handwriting, both of which have become increasingly less critical as computers and word processing programs (with spell-check) are in common use in classrooms. Many college students question the need to take general education courses that add time and financial cost to their degree, when they do not see the direct benefit in terms of developing expertise related to their major area of study or perceived future career. Students holding these beliefs may experience either a sense of amotivation (i.e., lack of motivation) or require external motives and rewards to engage in learning skills for which they do not see any utility or cultural value.

Such perspectives on the benefits of general education requirements mirror generational shifts. Debates about whether college students in the early part of this millennium (born after 1980) are better classified as "generation me" (Twenge, 2013) or "generation we" (Arnett, 2013) expose the importance and the challenge of examining these trends for teachers and teacher educators alike. Twenge (2009, 2012) has long argued that generational changes necessitate modifications to curriculum, methods, and approaches to learning and motivation. The more recent "digital natives" of Generation Z (who were born after 1995) not only expected more use of technology in classrooms (Cilliers, 2017; Mohr & Mohr, 2017), but have entered adulthood during the COVID-19 pandemic. What will PreK–12 classroom teachers from generations born before their students need to know to best reach and prepare their students? How can classroom teachers best prepare their students to navigate an increasingly complex body of knowledge or translate scientific expertise into meaningful learning experiences? (Hamby, 2015; Moura et al., 2016).

Rather than maintaining traditional "teacher-controlled" classrooms, teachers and teacher educators should strive to create autonomy-supportive classrooms that tap into students' beliefs, perspectives, and values. Increasing teacher awareness of how various system influences affect student behavior and development, of the diversity represented in their classroom, and using those funds of knowledge to advance knowledge through student-centered approaches can lead to successful learning, growth, and development for students (Reeve et al., 2004). Feelings of autonomy are achieved when individuals perceive the cause of their action to be internal; they are not doing something because they have been told to, but rather because they want to. Teacher educators can model and practice incorporating information into lesson plans that preservice teachers can then learn and present. In doing so, they are more likely to feel they have control over their education and can replicate this practice in their own PreK–12 classrooms. When autonomy needs are fulfilled, students of any age may experience more interest, enjoyment, and inherent satisfaction in learning (Deci & Ryan 2000; Ryan & Deci, 2020).

Competence

Competence is largely developed and practiced through engagement in autonomy-supporting behaviors. Competence is important to well-being as it provides a sense of satisfaction and growth for the individual. Like autonomy, the need for competence has evolved across generations. Whereas someone in the 1950s might expect to graduate and hold a career with focused expertise, modern-day careers often require global communications and abilities that span technology and emotional intelligences in addition to job-specific mastery. Learners experience and develop competence when they are provided with developmentally appropriate, challenging tasks that align with their own internal values and beliefs and when they have success at those activities (Reeve et al., 2018). The role of the teacher is then to select the appropriate level of challenge for the task, provide reasons why students would find the task useful (meaningful) given their individual goals and values, and provide support and feedback throughout as students gain mastery over the task. Reeve et al. (2018) describe this process as PreK–12 teachers engaging in "structure providing" instructional practices as opposed to controlling practices (e.g., "Do as I say, because I say") which thwart feelings of autonomy and competence.

Relatedness

Learners' sense of relatedness is also impacted by the various systems described by Bronfenbrenner's theory. Relatedness refers to having a sense of affiliation and belonging with others. With global technologies and communications, the importance of relatedness is now much different than our hypothetical 1950s individual experienced. The current increased potential for connecting to people across the world is mitigated by the more impersonal nature of interacting through electronic means—email, chat messages, and even videoconferencing often impede our ability to read subtle communication nuances like sarcasm and body language. Our 1950s individual had a narrower, but more intimate world of personal, live contact. Current larger social groupings coupled with greater opportunities for miscommunications change the relatedness landscape.

Most teachers and teacher educators understand the importance of establishing good rapport with their students to create a classroom environment that is conducive to learning. These relationships influence both individual development and classroom climate. When students of any age experience a sense of relatedness, especially in combination with autonomy-supportive behaviors of teachers, they are not only primed for learning, but they are also engaged in a healthy relational dynamic that transcends classroom life, affecting multiple members of students' microsystems. When in relationships with others, humans feel a greater sense of satisfaction and harmony when each person can give and receive autonomous support—as opposed to trying to exercise control over others (Reeve et al., 2018).

Teachers, teacher educators, and self-determination theorists recognize that teaching goes beyond encouraging students to do work or simply transferring knowledge to students. Rather, an important role for educators is to help students develop in the healthiest ways possible so that they can achieve fulfilling and productive experiences. For teachers to foster and maintain relationships with their students that support students' autonomy and satisfy their need for relatedness, teachers must know their students as individuals—and understand the people, relationships, and institutions that comprise the social and institutional systems influencing students' lives, and the values and beliefs that these systems endorse. This kind of holistic understanding of students enables teachers to create classroom environments where students' basic psychological needs are fully supported.

ASSET-BASED PEDAGOGIES

For BIPOC students, there is concern that teaching and learning occur within the context of a White cultural lens, alongside of classroom policies and procedures that reinforce White cultural standards (Alim & Paris, 2017; Ladson-Billings, 1995; Lee, 2017; López, 2017, 2019; Paris, 2019). Scholars such as Ladson-Billings, Lee, Paris, and others suggest that, rather than viewing BIPOC students as having deficits and "lacking" the beliefs, skills, and abilities that teachers may value, all students are best served when teachers recognize the strengths that students bring to the classroom. To mitigate the potential negative influence of deficit beliefs and approaches, these scholars have advocated for approaches such as ABP (López, 2017, 2019). ABPs encourage teachers, administrators, and other school personnel to focus on the personal and cultural strengths that every student possesses (López, 2017, 2019).

Among some of the ways the deficit ideology manifests itself in schools: Black students are underrepresented in gifted education programs in U.S. public schools up to 47% less than what would be expected if Black gifted students mirrored the percentage of Black students in these schools (Ford, 2017). For Hispanic students, the underrepresentation is as much as 37% below what would be expected based on the percentage of Hispanic students in schools (Ford, 2017). Regarding school discipline, a report from the National Women's Law Center (Patrick, 2017) reported that Black girls made up only 20% of girls enrolled but accounted for 54% of girls being suspended—in *preschool*.

Two important aspects of ABP can help teachers meet students' basic needs for autonomy, competency, and relatedness. First, *critical awareness* of one's own biases and the biases present in the larger societal systems (including schools; Alim & Paris, 2017; Ladson-Billings, 1995; Lee, 2017; López, 2017, 2019; Paris, 2019). Second, teachers and teacher educators need to develop their competencies for building on the personal and cultural knowledge that students bring to the classroom (Alim & Paris, 2017; Ladson-Billings, 1995; Lee, 2017; López, 2017, 2019; Paris, 2019). In other words, from an ABP perspective, the goal is to help preservice teachers develop an understanding of the social historical contextual experiences of BIPOC students' critical awareness, relatedness, and belonging. It is through that critical awareness that they can build on their students' prior cultural knowledge and incorporate that knowledge into their students' experiences in the classroom to build competency and autonomy.

CONCLUSION

We have described various transacting systems and their importance to understanding human development. In addition, we have discussed how changing demographics and trends within those systems may affect learners' efforts to meet their basic psychological needs for autonomy, competence, and relatedness. It is important to remember that, within college and PreK–12 schools, educators are the link among the various ecological systems.

Bronfenbrenner's EST provides a framework for identifying these various systems of influences on students' learning and development. Self-determination theory allows for closer examination of the impact of these systems on learners' successes at satisfying their basic needs and flourishing as they grow and develop. Asset based pedagogies help teachers and teacher educators leverage current cultural contexts to facilitate healthy development for all students. Taken together, these theoretical perspectives inform one another and can help teachers and teacher educators reframe generational differences in a way that is meaningful and impactful for students' development.

When working with preservice teachers it is necessary to emphasize that teaching at any grade level involves not only content and skills instruction, but also the ability to develop supportive relationships with students that help develop a sense of autonomy over their lives and competence for academic tasks. Bronfenbrenner's EST and Deci and Ryan's SDT are useful for preservice teachers and teacher educators to support students across generations as they mediate social historical influences and develop greater well-being in their students and themselves.

The utilization of ABP is another way that preservice teachers can appropriately and meaningfully respond to students' developmental needs. By using these pedagogical approaches preservice teachers can avoid adopting deficit perspectives that fail to recognize generational differences and demographic changes that impact the make-up of the student body in their PreK–12 classrooms. In combination, EST, SDT, and ABP all work together to enable preservice teachers to work across generations in an effective manner.

Teachers must know who their students are as individuals situated among layers of cultural and generational contexts. Knowing how the world in which students live impacts their learning and development will enable teachers to meet students' basic needs in the context of a culturally relevant, meaningful curriculum.

KEY CHAPTER TAKEAWAYS

- Examine personal biases and communication methods, especially as these relate to teaching students who are Black, indigenous, and people of color (BIPOC).
- Among the activities that help preservice teachers meet their own needs for autonomy, competence, and relatedness are engaging in autonomy-supportive practices such as problem based learning as opposed to more controlling teacher directed practices which tend to thwart feelings of autonomy, competence, and relatedness. In other words, develop students' autonomy, competence, and relatedness, by creating activities that provide them opportunities to engage their beliefs, skills and strategies.
- Among the strategies that preservice teachers can use to build on their students' personal and cultural ways of knowing include learning about their students' interests, families, and cultures, and incorporating the strengths that students bring into lesson planning and classroom activities (e.g., ABP).
- Teacher educators can invest in the social and historical influences and trends of different cultures and generations of preservice teachers and the students they will serve.

KEY WORDS

Asset-based pedagogies
Autonomy
Chronosystem
Competence
Ecological systems theory
Exosystem
Macrosystem
Microsystem
Nature vs. nurture
Relatedness
Self-determination theory
Social media

REFERENCES

Alim, H. S., & Paris, D. (2017). What is culturally sustaining pedagogy and why does it matter? In D. Paris & H. S. Alim (Eds.), *Culturally sustaining pedagogies: Teaching and learning for justice in a changing world* (pp. 1–21). Teachers College Press.

Arnett, J. (2013). The evidence for generation we and against generation me. *Emerging adulthood, 1*(1), 5–10. https://doi.org/10.1177/2167696812466842

Bandura, A. (1976). Self-reinforcement: Theoretical and methodological considerations. *Behaviorism, 4*(2), 135–155. http://www.jstor.org/stable/27758862

Bronfenbrenner, U. (1976). The experimental ecology of education. *Educational Researcher, 5*(9), 5–15. https://doi.org/10.2307/1174755

Cala, V. C., & Soriano, E. (2014). Health education from an ecological perspective. Adaptation of the Bronfenbrenner model from an experience with adolescents. *Procedia-Social and Behavioral Sciences, 132,* 49–57. https://doi.org/10.1016/j.sbspro.2014.04.277

Cilliers, E. J. (2017). The challenge of teaching generation Z. *PEOPLE: International Journal of Social Sciences, 3,* 188–198. https://doi.org/10.20319/pijss.2017.31.188198

Deci, R. M., & Ryan, E. L. (2000). Self-determination theory and facilitation of intrinsic motivation, social development, and well-being. *American Psychologist, 55,* 68–78. https://doi.org/10.1037//0003-066X.55.1.68

Doherty, C., Kiley, J., Tyson, A., Jameson, B. (2015). *The whys and hows of generations research.* Pew Research Center. https://www.pewresearch.org/politics/2015/09/03/the-whys-and-hows-of-generations-research/

Ford, D. Y. (2017). Desegregating gifted education for culturally different students: Recommendations for equitable recruitment and retention. In J. DeCuir-Gunby & P. A. Schutz (Eds.), *Race and ethnicity in the study of motivation in education* (pp. 183–198). Routledge.

Hamby, S. (2015). On scientific writing in the information era: Tailoring papers for internet searching and other 21st century realities. *Psychology of Violence, 5*(2), 103–111. https://www.ascd.org/el/articles/the-changing-face-of-teaching

Ingersoll, R., Merrill, L., & Stuckey, D. (2018). The changing face of teaching. *Educational Leadership, 75*(8), 44–49. https://eric.ed.gov/?id=EJ1178310

Ladson-Billings, G. (1995). Toward a theory of culturally relevant pedagogy. *American Educational Research Journal, 32*(3), 465–491. https://doi.org/10.3102/00028312032003465

Lee, C. D. (2017). An ecological framework for enacting culturally sustaining pedagogy. In D. Paris & H. S. Alim (Eds.), *Culturally sustaining pedagogies: Teaching and learning for justice in a changing world* (pp. 261–273). Teachers College Press.

López, F. A. (2017). Altering the trajectory of the self-fulfilling prophecy: Asset-based pedagogy and classroom dynamics. *Journal of Teacher Education, 68*(2), 193–212. https://doi.org/10.1177/0022487116685751

López, F. (2019). How educational settings inform Latino student identity and achievement. *Policy Insights from the Behavioral and Brain Sciences, 6*(2), 170–177. https://doi.org/10.1177/2372732219860859

Martineau, P. (2019, December 6). *The wired guide to influencers*. Wired. https://www.wired.com/story/what-is-an-influencer/

Mohr, K. A. J., & Mohr, E. S. (2017). Understanding Generation Z students to promote a contemporary learning environment. *Journal on Empowering Teaching Excellence, 1*(1), Article e9. https://doi.org/10.15142/T3M05T

Moura, M., Almeida, P., & Geerts, D. (2016). A video is worth a million words? Comparing a documentary with a scientific paper to communicate design research. *Procedia Computer Science, 100*, 747–754. https://doi.org/10.1016/j.procs.2016.09.220

National Center for Education Statistics. (2021). *Racial/ethnic enrollment in public schools*. IES NCES. https://nces.ed.gov/programs/coe/indicator/cge

Paris, D. (2019). Naming beyond the white settler colonial gaze in educational research. *International Journal of Qualitative Studies in Education, 32*(3), 217–224. https://doi.org/10.1080/09518398.2019.1576943

Patrick, K. (2017, July 19). *How many girls of color are really pushed out of school? It could be more than we thought* [Blog Post]. National Women's Law Center. https://nwlc.org/how-many-girls-of-color-are-really-pushed-out-of-school-it-could-be-more-than-we-thought/

Reeve, J., Ryan, R. M., & Deci, E. L. (2004). Self-determination theory: A dialectical framework for understanding sociocultural influences on student motivation. In. D. M. McInerny & S. Van Etten (Eds.), *Big theories revisited* (pp. 31–60). Information Age Publishing.

Reeve, J., Ryan, R. M., & Deci, E. L. (2018). Sociocultural influences on student motivation as viewed through the lens of self-determination theory. In. D. M. McInerny & S. Van Etten (Eds.), *Big theories revisited* 2 (pp. 15–40). Information Age Publishing.

Ryan, R. M., & Deci, E. L. (2020). Intrinsic and extrinsic motivation from a self-determination theory perspective: Definitions, theory, practices, and future directions. *Contemporary Educational Psychology, 61*, Article e101860. https://doi.org/10.1016/j.cedpsych.2020.101860

Shearer, E. (2021, January 12). *More than eight-in-ten Americans get news from digital devices.* Pew Research Center. https://www.pewresearch.org/fact-tank/2021/01/12/more-than-eight-in-ten-americans-get-news-from-digital-devices/

Spiegelman, M. (2020). *Race and ethnicity of public school teachers and their students* (Data Point NCES 2020-103). National Center for Education Statistics, Institute of Education Sciences, U.S. Department of Education. https://nces.ed.gov/pubs2020/2020103/index.asp

Twenge, J. (2009). Generational changes and their impact in the classroom: Teaching Generation Me. *Medical Education, 43*(5), 398–405. https://doi.org/10.1111/j.1365-2923.2009.03310.x

Twenge, J. (2012). Teaching generation me. *Teaching of Psychology, 40*(1), 66–69. https://doi.org/10.1177/0098628312465870

Twenge, J. (2013). Overwhelming evidence for generation me: A reply to Arnett. *Emerging Adulthood, 1*(1), 21–26. https://doi.org/10.1177/2167696812468112

Vitta, J. P. (2021). The functions and features of ELT textbooks and textbook analysis: A concise review. *RELC Journal*, 1–8. https://doi.org/10.1177/00336882211035826

CHAPTER 9

IT DOESN'T END AT 18

Insight Into Adult Human Development as an Instrumental Area for Preservice Teachers to Understand, Apply, and Teach

Abbie M. Bordewyk
University of Louisville

Allison Fowler
Spalding University

Kate E. Snyder
Bates College

The broad field of educational psychology has long neglected to regard adulthood with the same importance as childhood and adolescence in lifespan human development. Early researchers believed that most development happened prior to adulthood, and this belief shaped what would become a tradition of focusing upon early development often at the expense of investigating developmental processes in adults (Louw & Louw, 2020).

Teaching Human Development for Educators, pages 183–193
Copyright © 2024 by Information Age Publishing
www.infoagepub.com
All rights of reproduction in any form reserved.

Now, as teacher preparation programs face the monumental task of deciding what coursework will produce well-prepared, quality teachers when students graduate from their program, educational psychology courses have tended to be placed peripherally, often serving as a "gatekeeper" course to entering the teacher education program, implying the "real" teacher education begins with coursework following (Patrick et al., 2011).

Given the rapidly shifting demographics and structure of adult life (Arnett & Mitra, 2020), it would benefit both teacher educators, who primarily teach young adults, and preservice teachers, who will interface with other adults when they enter the workforce such as more senior colleagues and parents, to learn about adult human development beyond simply child and adolescent development. These preservice educators, often considered emerging adults themselves, may also be served by learning about this developmental period to better understand themselves (Baum & King, 2006). To provide more effective pedagogy and educational support, those who prepare teacher candidates should be well-versed in theory and literature that addresses the factors impacting their students' development. Examples include the role of societal and cultural systems throughout lifespan development (Bronfenbrenner & Evans, 2000; Pope et al., this volume).

Thus, this chapter expands upon the importance of teacher educators understanding adult development, as well as what is most important to know, alongside the importance of teaching this knowledge to preservice teachers and how it will better prepare them for careers in education. Our focus is twofold. First, we discuss what teacher educators need to know about adult development to effectively teach teacher candidates about human development. In this section, we focus on the continuing nature of development (physical, cognitive, and social) with an emphasis on emerging adulthood. We conclude this section with a brief overview of a useful tool for explaining this content, Bronfenbrenner's bioecological systems theory. Second, we explain why it is important for teacher candidates to understand adult development—to better understand themselves, to understand where their students are headed developmentally, to relate to their students' parents/caregivers, and to better relate to their senior colleagues who are likely to serve as professional role models and mentors to them.

ADULT DEVELOPMENT: ESSENTIAL KNOWLEDGE FOR THE TEACHER EDUCATOR

The characteristics of the many 18–22-year-old preservice teachers that fill teacher educators' classrooms continue to shift. These early years of adulthood have seen drastic changes as the median age of life events such as marriage and childbearing have been raised by several years, alongside the overall higher number of people receiving higher education and an overall increase in lifespan expectancy. Arnett (2000) noted that these sociological changes led to an alteration in the overall developmental arc of the late adolescent years and early twenties, leading him to develop the theory of *emerging adulthood*, a unique developmental window between (approximately) age 18 to 25 (Arnett 2000, 2007).

When considering essential knowledge of adult development, care should be taken not to teach an overly simplistic view of emerging adulthood as a strictly age-based, universal phenomenon. Despite widespread acceptance as a new theory with an entire new scholarly journal created to address the topic (*Emerging Adulthood*), this new proposed developmental period is not without substantial critique (Bynner, 2005; Côté, 2014; Syed, 2016). In fact, Côté (2014) went so far as to call it a "dangerous myth," cautioning that it is too easy to confuse a description of what young adults *actually* do with a prescription of what they *should* do. With these caveats in mind, we turn to a discussion of major facets of emerging adulthood as proposed by Arnett (2007): continued and intense exploration of personal identity, feelings of instability, a focus on the self, feeling "in-between," and feeling a sense of possibility.

Emerging Adulthood: Content and Caveats

Arnett (2000) identifies five key features of emerging adulthood. Emerging adults are seeking out new experiences and developing their sense of self (*identity exploration*). During this time, typical markers of adulthood like purchasing a home or settling into a career are delayed. Instead, emerging adults experience more turnover in their jobs and living situations (*instability*). With the decrease in other-centric obligations like marriage and child-rearing, emerging adults can prioritize their own interests and desires (*self-focus*). Not quite a teenager, but not quite an adult, emerging adults report feeling somewhere in the middle (*feeling in-between*). Despite their current feelings of instability, during emerging adulthood there is an increased sense of hope and possibilities about what is to come (*optimism about the future*).

It is particularly relevant for teacher educators to be aware of the identity development of emerging adults because the undergraduate experience in the United States is framed as not only essential for one's career path, but also an opportunity to broaden horizons and gain valuable and unique experiences (Smith & Wertleib, 2005). In other words, undergraduate education is a setting ripe for identity development. Students who are more flexible and open to exploration in late adolescence may experience stronger identity achievement later in their early/emerging adult years (Becht et al., 2021). Teacher educators can help foster identity achievement for teacher candidates through opportunities for curricular and self-exploration (e.g., variety in teaching experiences, exposure to a range of grade levels, diverse student populations).

Despite the increase in popularity and adoption of this "new" developmental stage of emerging adulthood, the idea is certainly not without criticism. Some researchers have reservations about the legitimacy of emerging adulthood as truly distinct from other developmental stages (Côté, 2014), and something that truly warrants designation as a "developmental stage" in its own right (Syed, 2016). Another major concern is the universality of the proposed developmental period (Hendry & Kloep, 2010). In other words, "Is emerging adulthood cross-culturally relevant?" or "Is it an experience of the middle- and upper-class Western young adults?"

Arnett (2007) has responded to some of the critiques of emerging adulthood, with some evidence that suggests his findings can be generalized across socioeconomic classes, and that the key features of emerging adulthood do appear in samples outside of the United States and Europe (Nelson & Chen, 2007). However, it is important for teacher educators to be mindful of the caveats, limitations, and critiques of emerging adulthood. In fact, grappling with this portion of adult development in the curriculum may be especially beneficial for teacher candidates in better understanding themselves and others.

Continued Development Beyond Adolescence

As emphasized by the very idea of emerging adulthood and regardless of critiques of it being a true developmental stage, it is critical for teacher educators to be aware that development does not "complete" at age 18 or after adolescence. Traditional treatment of cognitive stages in individual constructivism can often give this impression as students are left thinking that cognitive development is fully "done" after reaching formal operations, for example. Rather, development continues in its physical, cognitive, and social dimensions.

Even at the end of their undergraduate education, most college-aged students do not have a fully developed prefrontal cortex (Casey et al., 2000). This area of the brain plays a key role in many important self-regulatory and critical thinking processes including executive functioning, working memory, and inhibitory control. This means that although preservice teachers may be increasing in their self-reliance and adult responsibilities, they still require structure and scaffolding in their educational contexts to thrive.

In addition to the development of the frontal lobe, young adults are also developing their epistemic beliefs (i.e., theories of knowledge). College students often require guidance from their instructors to move beyond the belief that knowledge is certain (*dualism*) to the belief that knowledge is context dependent (*relativism*; Black & Allen, 2017). Instructors can encourage students to develop towards the latter epistemology through exercises in metacognitive awareness, as well as exposure to and critical analysis of multiple perspectives.

Most people reach physical maturation in early adulthood. The average undergraduate will have reached their full height, as well as their peak in muscle tone and visual acuity (Broderick & Blewitt, 2020). Although this is a generally healthy time of life, it is also a time marked by increase in substance abuse. Universities continue education efforts to inform undergraduate students of the risks and potential consequences associated with drug use, underaged drinking, and overconsumption of alcohol (Hennessy et al., 2019). Use of alcohol, particularly binge drinking, is associated with use of marijuana and e-cigarettes (Jackson et al., 2020; Roys et al., 2020). In addition to the negative physical outcomes of smoking and binge drinking, college students who engage in abuse of drugs and alcohol may also be more likely to suffer from poor mental health (Kenney et al., 2018).

Much of Arnett's description of emerging adulthood centers around the social development that takes place during this period. The instability and constantly changing nature of emerging adults' social functioning can show up in the classroom performance of undergraduate students as the fluctuation of jobs and housing impacts their schedules and time available to perform schoolwork (Silva et al., 2017). In regards to their relationships, even with lower rates of marriage and children, emerging adults still experience a shift in attachment figure from parents to friends and romantic partners (Dykas & Siskind, 2020). Stronger attachments to peers is associated with more positive social outcomes broadly (Holt et al., 2018).

Knowledge Beyond Young Adulthood: Middle and Late Adulthood

Instruction on adult development can address commonly held but inaccurate beliefs about adult development. Such instruction has been found to reduce negative attitudes towards aging populations and the aging process (Allan & Johnson, 2008). Having a more accurate and positive view of aging is important for preservice teachers as they enter a workplace with more senior colleagues and begin engaging with the caregivers of their students. Thus, to provide this important instruction, teacher educators should have accurate views and knowledge of middle adulthood and aging as well.

In preparing pre-teachers to work across a variety of diverse settings, teacher educators should engage in their own reflexive examination of held biases and misconceptions and intentionally make space for preservice teachers to do so as well. One such bias relating strongly to one's view of the importance of adult development is ageism, or negative stereotypes about individuals based on older age (Palmore, 2015). Examples of ageist beliefs include the notion that older adults are less able than their younger counterparts to work efficiently or adapt to change (Redman & Snape, 2002). Ageist beliefs about older teachers may contribute to ageist policies and/or experiences for older adults in the profession (Watts, 2014). This is the case even for policies with benign intentions (Angus & Reeve, 2006). Having an understanding of ageism, as well as further insight into one's own internalized ageism, is critical for teacher candidates, considering that internalization of ageist beliefs at young ages becomes harmful as individuals grow older (*stereotype embodiment*; Levy, 2009). Professional functioning can be negatively impacted by ageist beliefs and these beliefs have implications for preservice teacher's future professional practice.

IMPLICATIONS FOR PRESERVICE TEACHERS: FUTURE PROFESSIONAL PRACTICE

Having discussed key knowledge that teacher educators need to know when teaching adult development, we now turn to a discussion of how this content benefits teacher candidates. We see two primary benefits. First, teacher candidates will learn more about themselves and their current development; in other words, learning about adult development is learning about their own developing selves. Second, they will better understand and appreciate the complexity of development among their more senior colleagues and the caregivers (i.e., parents and other adults) of their future students. Whether for themselves or others, knowing that development is both ongoing and variable will help them in their daily practice.

Understanding Emerging Adulthood: Benefits for the Preservice Teacher

Because teacher candidates are learning about themselves through learning about adult development, it is a time ripe for identity formation and exploration of the self. Indeed, development of personal teacher identity is associated with social and personal identity development among teacher candidates (Friesen & Besley, 2013). Given the level of self-focus and identity exploration reported among emerging adults (Ritchie et al., 2013; Tagliabue et al., 2016) and the critical emphasis on self-reflection in teacher preparation programs (Baum & King, 2006), it may be especially beneficial for teacher educators to frame adult development curriculum as an opportunity for teacher candidates to self-reflect on their development.

Content Knowledge in Adult Development: Shaping Expectations, Perceptions, and Interpersonal Interactions

Instruction in adult development not only helps to combat biases, but also serves as foundational knowledge for teachers as they navigate professional relationships with their colleagues and the parents of their students. When developmental coursework ends with adolescence, teacher candidates miss out on information relevant to their future educational practice. For example, parenting and attachment styles may be covered in child development courses but could be missing important information and perspectives about those concepts as they pertain to adults specifically. Without this knowledge, teachers may not know that attachments continue developing throughout the lifespan and parents' engagement (or lack thereof) with the child (Fraley & Roisman, 2019).

Further, foundational understanding of development in middle adulthood could improve teacher's communication with and compassion for parents. For example, parents in midlife may be more likely to experience stressors that result from needing to simultaneously address concerns from several different areas of their lives (e.g., children, spouse, work). Parents in low socioeconomic status groups report their stressors to be more severe (Clay, 2003). Relatedly, there is a misconception among some educators that less parental involvement is a result of a lack of care. However, results of interventions aimed at improving equity for parents indicate that issues with parental involvement are often a result of systemic barriers for marginalized populations (Cranston et al., 2021; Keller et al., 2021).

Finally, teacher educators may find it especially helpful to know where their students are headed developmentally beyond adolescence, such as emphasized in a lifespan developmental approach. For example, given research on stereotype embodiment, teacher educators can be more mindful of avoiding child or young adult literature containing harmful ageist stereotypes, or consider discussions on ageism with older students. Understanding ageism will help teacher candidates screen for problematic ageist content in children's books, which remains alarmingly present among both classic and contemporary children's literature (Crawford, 2000; Henneberg, 2010). Self-reflection with their own beliefs about the aging process may also be beneficial. Promising tools have been developed, including validated measures to assess ageism among younger populations (Marchetti et al., 2022), that may be helpful in assisting teacher candidates in reflecting on their own knowledge and attitudes toward aging, especially if these views are likely to be transmitted to students.

CONCLUSION

Having content knowledge in adult development benefits teacher educators as they work to best prepare teacher candidates for the field of education. The benefits are comparable to a first-grade teacher benefitting from understanding early childhood development; knowing what your students are undergoing developmentally across domains allows one to be a more efficacious, attuned educator with realistic expectations (Gentrup et al., 2020). Knowing where teacher candidates may be at in all facets of their development allows for making the best use of classroom time and engagement, challenging them appropriately given their cognitive development, and being attuned to socioemotional and identity development that will certainly play a role in shaping their professional identities.

Finally, many young teacher candidates can also benefit from understanding adult development—particularly their own emerging adulthood. Such knowledge can enable self-understanding and more effective relationships with peers, mentors, and colleagues, as well as with the parents of their students.

KEY CHAPTER TAKEAWAYS

- Knowledge of adult development is essential for teachers and particularly for those preparing to become teachers.
- Many preservice teacher candidates are emerging adults—a developmental period that has several unique characteristics that influence their behaviors and attitudes, including feelings of being "in-between" adolescence and adulthood.
- Having an accurate and positive view of adult life and aging is important for preservice teachers as they enter the professional workplace where they interact with more senior colleagues and engage with parents and other caregivers of their students.

KEY WORDS

Adult development
Ageism
Emerging adulthood
Lifespan development
Middle adulthood

AUTHOR NOTE

Correspondence concerning this chapter should be addressed to Abbie Bordewyk, Department of Counseling and Human Development, University of Louisville, 1905 S 1st St, Louisville, KY 40208, United States. Email: amsell03@louisville.edu

REFERENCES

Allan, L. J., & Johnson, J. A. (2008). Undergraduate attitudes toward the elderly: The role of knowledge, contact and aging anxiety. *Educational Gerontology, 35*, 1–14.

Angus, J., & Reeve, P. (2006). Ageism: A threat to "aging well" in the 21st century. *Journal of Applied Gerontology, 25*, 137–152.

Arnett, J. J. (2007). Emerging adulthood: What is it, and what is it good for? *Child Development Perspectives, 1*, 68–73. https://doi.org/10.1111/j.1750-8606.2007.00016.x

Arnett, J. J., & Mitra, D. (2020). Are the features of emerging adulthood developmentally distinctive? A comparison of ages 18–60 in the United States. *Emerging Adulthood, 8*, 412–419.

Baum, A. C., & King, M. A. (2006). Creating a climate of self-awareness in early childhood teacher preparation programs. *Early Childhood Education Journal, 33*, 217–222. https://doi.org/10.1007/s10643-005-0050-2

Becht, A. I., Nelemans, S. A., Branje, S. J. T., Vollebergh, W. A. M., & Meeus, W. H. J. (2021). Daily identity dynamics in adolescence shaping identity in emerging adulthood: An 11-year longitudinal study on continuity in development. *Journal of Youth & Adolescence, 50*, 1616–1633. https://doi.org/10.1007/s10964-020-01370-3

Black, S., & Allen, J. D. (2017). Part 3: College student development. *The Reference Librarian, 58*, 214–228.

Broderick, P. C., & Blewitt, P. (2020). *The life span: Human development for helping professionals.* Pearson.

Bronfenbrenner, U., & Evans, G. W. (2000). Developmental science in the 21st century: Emerging questions, theoretical models, research designs and empirical findings. *Social Development, 9*, 115–125.

Bynner, J. (2005). Rethinking the youth phase of the life-course: The case for emerging adulthood? *Journal of Youth Studies, 8*, 367–384. https://doi.org/10.1080/13676260500431628

Casey, B. J., Giedd, J. N., & Thomas, K. M. (2000). Structural and functional brain development and its relation to cognitive development. *Biological Psychology, 54*, 241–257. https://doi.org/10.1016/S0301-0511(00)00058-2

Clay, R. A. (2003). Researchers replace midlife myths with facts. *Monitor on Psychology, 34*(4). https://www.apa.org/monitor/apr03/researchers

Côté, J. E. (2014). The dangerous myth of emerging adulthood: An evidence-based critique of a flawed developmental theory. *Applied Developmental Science, 18*, 177–188. https://doi.org/10.1080/10888691.2014.954451

Cranston, J., Labman, S., & Crook, S. (2021). Reframing parental involvement as social engagement: A study of recently arrived Arabic-speaking refugee parents' understandings of involvement in their children's education. *Canadian Journal of Education, 44*(2), 371–404. https://doi.org/10.53967/cje-rce.v44i2.4439

Crawford, P. A. (2000). Crossing boundaries: Addressing ageism through children's books. *Reading Horizons: A Journal of Literacy and Language Arts, 40*, 161–174. https://scholarworks.wmich.edu/reading_horizons/vol40/iss3/1

Dykas, M. J., & Siskind, D. G. (2020). Turning from parents: Psychological distancing and attachment-related changes in regret for immediate contact in emerging adulthood. *Emerging Adulthood, 8*(3), 195–208. https://doi.org/10.1177/2167696818799833

Fraley, R. C., & Roisman, G. I. (2019). The development of adult attachment styles: Four lessons. *Current Opinion in Psychology, 25*, 26–30. https://doi.org/10.1016/j.copsyc.2018.02.008

Friesen, M. D., & Besley, S. C. (2013). Teacher identity development in the first year of teacher education: A developmental and social psychological perspective. *Teaching and Teacher Education, 36*, 23–32. https://doi.org/10.1016/j.tate.2013.06.005

Gentrup, S., Lorenz, G., Kristen, C., & Kogan, I. (2020). Self-fulfilling prophecies in the classroom: Teacher expectations, teacher feedback and student achievement. *Learning and Instruction, 66*, 101–296.

Hendry, L. B., & Kloep, M. (2010). How universal is emerging adulthood? An empirical example. *Journal of Youth Studies, 13*, 169–179. https://doi.org/10.1080/13676260903295067

Henneberg, S. (2010). Moms do badly, but grandmas do worse: The nexus of sexism and ageism in children's classics. *Journal of Aging Studies, 24*, 125–134. https://doi.org/10.1016/J.JAGING.2008.10.003

Hennessy, E. A., Tanner-Smith, E. E., Mavridis, D., & Grant, S. P. (2019). Comparative effectiveness of brief alcohol interventions for college students: Results from a network meta-analysis. *Prevention Science, 20*, 715–740. https://doi.org/10.1007/s11121-018-0960-z

Holt, L. J., Mattanah, J. F., & Long, M. W. (2018). Change in parental and peer relationship quality during emerging adulthood: Implications for academic, social, and emotional functioning. *Journal of Social and Personal Relationships, 35*(5), 743–769. https://doi.org/10.1177/0265407517697856

Jackson, K. M., Sokolovsky, A. W., Gunn, R. L., & White, H. R. (2020). Consequences of alcohol and marijuana use among college students: Prevalence rates and attributions to substance-specific versus simultaneous use. *Psychology of Addictive Behaviors, 34*, 370–381. https://doi.org/10.1037/adb0000545

Keller, J. G., Miller, C., LasDulce, C., & Wohrle, R. G. (2021). Using a community-based participatory research model to encourage parental involvement in their children's schools. *Children & Schools, 43*, 149–158. https://doi.org/10.1093/cs/cdab015

Kenney, S. R., DiGuiseppi, G. T., Meisel, M. K., Balestrieri, S. G., & Barnett, N. P. (2018). Poor mental health, peer drinking norms, and alcohol risk in a social network of first-year college students. *Addictive Behaviors, 84*, 151–159. https://doi.org/10.1016/j.addbeh.2018.04.012

Levy, B. (2009). Stereotype embodiment: A psychosocial approach to aging. *Current Directions in Psychological Science, 18*(6), 332–336. https://doi.org/10.1111/j.1467-8721.2009.01662.x

Louw, D., & Louw, A. (2020). *Adult development and ageing.* UJ Press.

Marchetti, A., Lommi, M., Barbaranelli, C., Piredda, M., De Marinis, M. G., & Matarese, M. (2022). Development and initial validation of the Adolescents' Ageism Toward Older Adults Scale. *The Gerontologist, 62,* e150–e161. https://doi.org/10.1093/geront/gnab023

Nelson, L. J., & Chen, X. (2007). Emerging adulthood in China: The role of social and cultural factors. *Child Development Perspectives, 1,* 86–91.

Patrick, H., Anderman, L. H., Bruening, P. S., & Duffin, L. C. (2011). The role of educational psychology in teacher education: Three challenges for educational psychologists. *Educational Psychologist, 46,* 71–83. https://doi.org/10.1080/00461520.2011.538648

Redman, T., & Snape, E. (2002). Ageism in teaching: Stereotypical beliefs and discriminatory attitudes towards the over-50s. *Work, Employment and Society, 16,* 355–371.

Ritchie, R. A., Meca, A., Madrazo, V. L., Schwartz, S. J., Hardy, S. A., Zamboanga, B. L., Weisskirch, R. S., Kim, S. Y., Whitbourne, S. K., Ham, L. S., & Lee, R. M. (2013). Identity dimensions and related processes in emerging adulthood: Helpful or harmful? *Journal of Clinical Psychology, 69,* 415–432. https://doi.org/10.1002/jclp.21960

Roys, M. R., Peltier, M. R., Stewart, S. A., Waters, A. F., Waldo, K. M., & Copeland, A. L. (2020). The association between problematic alcohol use, risk perceptions, and e-cigarette use. *The American Journal of Drug and Alcohol Abuse, 46*(2), 224–231. https://doi.org/10.1080/00952990.2019.1654486

Silva, M. R., Kleinert, W. L., Sheppard, A. V., Cantrell, K. A., Freeman-Coppadge, D. J., Tsoy, E., Roberts, T., & Pearrow, M. (2017). The relationship between food security, housing stability, and school performance among college students in an urban university. *Journal of College Student Retention: Research, Theory & Practice, 19*(3), 284–299. https://doi.org/10.1177/1521025115621918

Smith, J. S., & Wertlieb, E. C. (2005). Do first-year college students' expectations align with their first-year experiences? *NASPA Journal, 42*(2), 153–174. https://doi.org/10.2202/1949-6605.1470

Syed, M. (2016). Emerging adulthood: Developmental stage, theory, or nonsense? In J. J. Arnett (Ed.), *The Oxford Handbook of Emerging Adulthood* (pp. 11–25). Oxford University Press.

Tagliabue, S., Crocetti, E., & Lanz, M. (2016). Emerging adulthood features and criteria for adulthood: Variable-and person-centered approaches. *Journal of Youth Studies, 19,* 374–388.

Watts, N. (2014). Grumpy old teachers? An insight into the life experiences of veteran teachers. In M-P. Moreau (Ed.), *Inequalities in the teaching profession: A global perspective* (pp. 87–100). Palgrave Macmillan.

ABOUT THE CONTRIBUTORS

Ann Allred, MAT, is an eighth grade English teacher at Williamsburg Middle School in Arlington, Virginia. She received her master's in middle level education with concentrations in English and math from James Madison University in 2021. She completed her bachelor's degree in interdisciplinary liberal studies in 2020. Her research interests include supporting gifted learners in the classroom and developing character through literature.

Carly Offidani-Bertrand, PhD, is a professor in the human development department at California State University who takes a sociological perspective to understanding the relationships between health and inequality among marginalized populations—particularly BIPOC communities and people facing legal stigma. Dr. Offidani-Bertrand is currently leading an NSF funded project examining how discrimination shapes pathways towards entrepreneurship among BIPOC communities. She also continues to publish and theorize about the role of sociopolitical narratives in shaping meaning-making processes of marginalized individuals, and the way these narratives shape coping strategies that impact their physical and mental health. Dr. Offidani-Bertrand received her PhD in comparative human development from the University of Chicago.

Elias Blinkoff is a PhD candidate in developmental psychology at Temple University. His research explores how principles from the science of learning connect to educational policy and practice. He currently studies how these principles apply in the classroom, from kindergarten to higher education. Mr. Blinkoff is particularly interested in evaluating different methods of implementing this science of learning-based approach in collaboration with educators, students, and communities.

Abbie M. Bordewyk, MEd, is a doctoral candidate in counseling psychology at the University of Louisville. She has taught over 10 sections of a human development course designed for the teacher preparation program, which all undergraduate preservice teachers take before admittance to the education program. Clinically, Bordewyk provides psychotherapy and assessment services to undergraduate and graduate college students. More specifically, she specializes in working with current or former student-athletes. Bordewyk's research interests include the role of religion and spirituality in mental health, the impact of religious practices on development in childhood and adolescence, and the aspects of identity salience that lead to psychological well-being in collegiate student-athletes.

Rebecca West Burns is the Bill Herrold endowed professor and director of clinical practice and educational partnerships for the College of Education and Human Services at the University of North Florida. Her community-engaged scholarship is situated within clinically based teacher education where she studies supervision, school–university partnerships, and teacher leadership. She has received national recognition for her exemplary school–university collaboration and her impact on urban education. Her most recent books include *(Re)Designing Programs: A Vision for Equity-Centered, Clinically Based Teacher Preparation* (Information Age Publishing, 2021), and the second edition of Carl Glickman's best-selling ASCD (2020) book, *Leadership for Learning: How to Bring Out the BEST in Every Teacher.*

Heidi Legg Burross, PhD, is a professor of practice in educational psychology at the University of Arizona. Her teaching and research interests vary and include examining indicators of success and student well-being for underserved populations, adult learning and development, and graduate student preparation for academic professions. Dr. Burross has also recently been working in assessment development and evaluation for law schools.

Russell N. Carney, PhD, is professor emeritus at Missouri State University, having spent nearly 30 years in the psychology department there. At MSU, he taught primarily courses related to educational psychology, child development, and tests and measurements. Prior to that, he spent 10 years working in the public schools—first as a math teacher, and later, as a school psychologist. Dr. Carney has published 30 articles in refereed journals, including *Contemporary Educational Psychology, Journal of Educational Psychology, Applied Cognitive Psychology, Teaching of Psychology, Journal of Experimental Education, Early Childhood Education Journal, Educational Psychology Review,* and *American Educational Research Journal*. He has also published 15 test reviews over the years in Buros *Mental Measurements Yearbook* series. For his contributions, he received Buros "Distinguished Reviewer Award" in 2017. Dr. Carney has been a long-time member of AERA and APA and is a fellow in the Psychonomic Society.

Katrina Dotzler is a second year educational psychology PhD student at the University of Arizona. Her research interests include the implications of modern technology for teaching techniques and course format, specifically within career and technical education. As a research assistant, she is contributing to her advisor's NSF-RAPID project pertaining to student experiences related to COVID-19 at Hispanic serving institutions.

Kerrijo Ellis, MEd, is a doctoral student in curriculum and instruction with a specialization in educational psychology at the University of South Florida. Through her research, she aims to use transformative learning theory and related instructional practices to promote and nurture culturally responsive preservice teachers and teacher educators. Her research interests also include teacher identity, ethnic–racial identity development, and service learning/cultural immersion programs and their impact on preservice teachers' future practice. Kerrijo strives to cultivate educators who are culturally responsive and holistic in their educational practice.

Carlton J. Fong, PhD, is an assistant professor in the graduate program in developmental education and the Department of Curriculum and Instruction at Texas State University. Dr. Fong received his doctorate in educational psychology with an emphasis on human development. As a scholar-activist at the intersection of educational psychology and higher education, Dr. Fong uses a sociocultural lens to study motivational and affective factors influencing postsecondary student engagement, achievement, and persistence. Specifically, he examines the motivation factors associated with feedback and the psychosocial development of community college students. His research has been published in *Review of Educational Research, Educational Psychology Review, Journal of Educational Psychology, Contemporary Educational Psychology, Journal of College Student Development,* and *Journal of Diversity in Higher Education.*

Allison Fowler, PhD, is an assistant professor and undergraduate program director in the School of Professional Psychology at Spalding University. She earned her doctorate from the University of Louisville in Educational Psychology, Measurement, and Evaluation. Dr. Fowler's lab (DREAM TEAM) involves collaboration with both graduate and undergraduate students in research related to achievement motivation and educational psychology broadly. She also serves as the research coordinator for the Rowen

Specialty Clinic for Women, a sub-clinic of Spalding's Center for Behavioral Health. Dr. Fowler teaches coursework in developmental psychology, statistics, and research methods.

Richard Garries is an undergraduate student at Virginia Commonwealth University and is earning his bachelor's degree in art education and painting. He earned his associate's degree from Thomas Nelson Community College. His research centers on motivation and communication for students in underrepresented communities and low-income families. Focusing on this, he aims to help students find the desire to improve their skills and better understand the ideas present in their artwork, in spite of their socioeconomic status and inequitable conditions.

Hailey Gibbs, PhD, is a senior policy analyst on the early childhood policy team at the Center for American Progress in Washington, DC. She received her PhD in human development from the University of Maryland College Park. Her prior academic research interests included preschool children's understanding of misinformation and selective trust, their question-asking, and their understanding of the relation between evidence and knowledge-building. More specifically, she examined the characteristics of informants, including evidentiary behaviors and question-asking abilities, that appealed to young children as indicators of reliability. In her postdoctoral work with Dr. Kathy Hirsh-Pasek, Dr. Gibbs examined the ways in which children's educational experiences could be extended into their everyday environments, with particular interest in how playful learning can support the development of critical thinking skills. In her policy work, Dr. Gibbs examines the broader conditions under which young children develop and learn, and the policies and practices that best support family and child well-being at community, state, and national levels.

Roberta Michnick Golinkoff, PhD, is Unidel H. Rodney Sharp Professor of Education at the University of Delaware. Having published dozens of peer-reviewed articles and book chapters, Golinkoff is passionate about transforming formal and informal education to align with the science of learning and development. Many accolades acknowledge her research and dissemination efforts. Indeed, 5 of her 16 books were written for the public and practitioners. Her research, funded by federal agencies and the LEGO Foundation, is known globally. With the Jacobs Foundation, she is co-founder of the Learning Sciences Exchange, a fellowship program inviting professionals in diverse fields to leave their silos and work together for society's benefit. Her project, Playful Learning Landscapes, embeds physical installations into communities to promote child well-being and a new family of language screeners (Quick Interactive Language Screener [QUILS]) identifies children with language issues. Both are prime examples of translational science. Her sixteenth book, *Becoming Brilliant: What Science Tells Us About Raising Successful Children* (APA LifeTools, 2016), reached the New York Times bestseller list, and its follow up, *Making Schools Work: Bringing the Science of Learning to Joyful Classroom Practice* (Teachers College Press, 2022), offers a framework for transforming education. She was recently named to the National Academy of Education.

Dana L. Haraway, PhD, is a professor in the College of Education at James Madison University. She received her doctorate in administration and supervision from the University of Virginia. She earned additional graduate degrees in school psychology and community agency counseling, and her bachelor's in special education. She has over 10 years of experience working in the public schools as a teacher, a school psychologist, and an administrator. Her research interests include educational psychology and responsive classrooms, restorative practices, teacher preparation, assessment, and mentoring.

Keshia L. Harris, PhD, is a developmental psychologist who specializes in mixed methods research on colorism, mental health, and cross-cultural education studies among African descent and Latin American descent adolescents. As a research associate at the Renée Crown Wellness Institute of the University of Colorado Boulder, Dr. Harris leads a new program centered on mindfulness, movement, and racial healing for Black high school girls in Boulder County. Her most recent peer-reviewed publications include "Positive Racial Identity of Black Brazilian and Colombian Adolescents Amidst Systems of Educational Oppression" (*Journal of Research on Adolescence*, 2021), and "Silence Is Not an Option: Oral History of Race in Youth Development Through the Words of Esteemed Black Scholars" (*Journal of Youth Development*, 2021). Dr. Harris is a Spelman alumna, a graduate of Columbia University, and holds a PhD in comparative human development from the University of Chicago.

Sarah Kiefer, PhD, is professor of educational psychology in the College of Education at the University of South Florida. Her research focuses on supporting adolescent learners by examining the interplay between social and academic factors at school, including academic and social motivation, peer relationships, and teacher–student relationships. She conducts longitudinal school-based research using quantitative, qualitative, and mixed-method designs to understand students' motivational experiences with peers and teachers, and how schools are responsive learning environments. Dr. Kiefer has published over 30 peer-reviewed articles in premier journals, including *Developmental Psychology*, the *Journal of Educational Psychology*, and the *Journal of Applied Developmental Psychology*. She is a consulting editor for *Child Development* and an editorial board member for the *Journal of Applied*

Developmental Psychology, Journal of Experimental Education, and *School Psychology Review.* Dr. Kiefer served as a grant review panel for the Institute of Educational Sciences. She is a co-PI on an intervention study funded by IES titled, "Efficacy of a Selective Intervention to Improve Middle School Students' Subjective Well-Being." Dr. Kiefer is the former vice president of the American Educational Research Association's Division E, Counseling and Human Development. Her goal is to serve as an advocate for supporting the development of today's youth through engaging in school-based research, guiding prospective and current educators to strive for excellence in teaching, and collaborating with educational professionals on a local, national, and international level.

Alison C. Koenka, PhD, is an assistant professor at the University of Oklahoma. Prior to transitioning to OU, she was an assistant professor at Virginia Commonwealth University. She earned a bachelor's degree in honors psychology at McGill University, a PhD in developmental psychology at Duke University, and received postdoctoral training in educational psychology at The Ohio State University. Dr. Koenka's research program explores students' motivation in science, technology, engineering, and mathematics (STEM) domains across secondary school and higher education. In doing so, she pursues two intersecting lines of inquiry: (a) the motivational consequences of academic feedback and (b) the motivational experiences of youth from understudied and/or minoritized populations. Her work aims to foster more equitable motivational experiences and outcomes for these youth.

Lisa Looney, PhD, is an associate professor in the Department of Child Development at California State University, San Bernardino. She received her PhD in human development with an emphasis in educational psychology from the University of Maryland, College Park. Dr. Looney's research includes examining development and behavior within educational contexts, with a focus on motivational constructs as they relate to teachers and students. While much of her research has focused on development, motivation, and self-processes (e.g., self-efficacy, self-worth) of teachers in PK–12 settings, her areas of inquiry have also expanded to include examination of these constructs with faculty at institutions of higher education and with parents.

Andréa C. Minkoff, PhD, is an assistant professor in the child and adolescent development master's program in the LaFetra College of Education at the University of La Verne. At the University of La Verne, Dr. Minkoff teaches graduate level courses on educational psychology, human development, methods of research, infant and toddler development, studies in attachment, and graduate seminar. Her scholarly interests focus on children's developing understandings of race, gender, language, and belonging, identity and intergroup relations in schools, and preparing critically conscious early childhood educators. Dr. Minkoff earned her PhD from the Graduate School of Education and Information Studies at the University of California, Los Angeles. Prior to that, she earned her MAT in liberal studies preliminary multiple subject credential, and a BA in psychology from Occidental College.

Korinthia D. Nicolai is a doctoral student at Virginia Commonwealth University and is earning her doctorate in educational psychology. She earned her associate's degree from Northern Virginia Community College and her bachelor's degree in psychology from James Madison University. Her research interests lie at the intersection of motivation, belonging, and race/racism and their dynamic interplay. In conducting this work, her primary goal is centering historically marginalized students' experiences and voices and fostering equity.

Kathy Hirsh-Pasek is the Lefkowitz Faculty Fellow in Psychology at Temple University and a Senior Fellow at the Brookings Institution. Her research examines the development of early language and literacy, the role of play in learning, and learning and technology. She is the author of 14 books and hundreds of publications, has won numerous awards in her field, and was inducted into the National Academy of Education. Vested in translating science for lay and professional audiences, her *Becoming Brilliant: What Science Tells Us About Raising Successful Children* (APA LifeTools), released in 2016, was on the New York Times Best Seller List in Education.

Elizabeth Pope, PhD, is an associate professor of practice in the Department of Educational Psychology at the University of Arizona. She earned her PhD in educational psychology from the University of Arizona and her bachelor's degree in elementary education from The University of South Florida. Her research focuses on various aspects of social-emotional development and well-being including the role of teacher–student relationships, understanding student experiences of failure, and exploring how students and teachers cope with stress and trauma associated with COVID-19. She works with undergraduate and graduate students teaching childhood and adolescent development, psychological measurements in education, motivation in learning and development, and other introductory educational psychology courses—both in-person and using innovative and interactive eLearning formats online.

Raven Robinson, PhD, is an assistant professor of teacher education—foundations and clinical practice at the University of North Florida. She earned her PhD in curriculum & instruction, with a concentration in elementary education and cognate in educational psychology, from the University of South Florida. Dr. Robinson's research investigates teacher education, equity, and motivation with an intersectional focus on teacher candidates' and inservice teachers' beliefs and practices. She began her career as an elementary classroom teacher in urban, Title I and Renaissance schools, and has experience teaching students across various grade levels and diverse backgrounds. As a teacher educator, Dr. Robinson honors teaching as a complex, theoretically-informed process for emancipatory action to establish and maintain culturally responsive and sustaining beliefs and practices to improve student outcomes. She has presented at regional, national, and international conferences, with publications in peer-reviewed academic journals and book series. Dr. Robinson teaches elementary education teacher candidates across their clinical experiences, as well as introductory educational psychology, centered on K–16 student success. She also serves as a methodologist and graduate-level course designer/instructor for ProjectInTERSECT Program—a multi-year SEED grant—to provide local, elementary classroom teachers with evidence-based professional development for equitably integrating STEM+C practices while earning advanced credentials from the University of North Florida.

Paul Schutz's research interests include emotions in education, teacher identity development, race and ethnicity in educational contexts, and research methods and methodologies. He is a past president of the American Psychological Associations Division 15: Educational Psychology, a former coeditor of the *Educational Researcher: Research News and Comments*, and a coeditor of the upcoming *Handbook of Educational Psychology, Volume 4* (Routledge, 2024). Recent publications include *Teachers' Goals, Beliefs, Emotions, and Identity Development* (Routledge, 2020); "Why Talk About Qualitative and Mixed Methods in Educational Psychology? Introduction to Special Issue" (*Education Psychologist*, 2020); and "Joint Displays for Mixed Methods Research in Psychology" (*Methods in Psychology*, 2021).

M Cecil Smith, PhD, is dean of the School of Education at Southern Illinois University Carbondale. He is the editor or coeditor of seven books on adult literacy, adult learning and development, adult and continuing education, and teaching educational psychology, and he recently concluded editorship of the journal, *New Horizons in Adult Education and Human Resource Development*. He has published more than 60 peer-reviewed articles in a range of journals within adult education, literacy, educational technology, and educational psychology. Prior to his appointment at Southern Illinois, he was associate dean for research and graduate education in the College of Education and Human Services at West Virginia University. While a faculty member at Northern Illinois University, he taught courses in adolescent development, adult development, and lifespan development to hundreds of aspiring and in-service teachers over 25 years.

Kate E. Snyder earned her MA and PhD in developmental psychology from Duke University. She is on the faculty at Bates College in the Department of Psychology. In her research program, she focuses on understanding the role of achievement motivation in the development of academic underachievement, particularly among academically gifted students. Her research has been published in *Gifted Child Quarterly, Journal of Educational Psychology, Educational Psychologist,* and many other outlets. In 2017, she received the Early Scholar Award from the National Association of Gifted Children. She teaches coursework in developmental and educational psychology.

Gabriel Velez, PhD, is an assistant professor and developmental psychologist in the Department of Educational Policy and Leadership in the College of Education at Marquette University. He also serves as the faculty director of the Black and Latino/a Ecosystem and Support Transition (BLEST) Hub at Marquette, and the chair of the Faculty Research Team for the Center for Peacemaking. Dr. Velez studies identity development in adolescents, particularly in relation to civic development, human rights, and peace, including young people's understandings and responses to peace education and restorative practices in their schools. He was recently awarded a Spencer Foundation Small Research grant to study Black and Latino/a students perceptions and meaning making of school-based restorative justice, and is coeditor of *Restorative Justice: Promoting Peace & Well-being* coming out later this year. Dr. Velez received a BA in history and literature from Harvard University, and an MA and PhD from the University of Chicago in comparative human development.

Gabriela Wilson is an adjunct faculty in the child and adolescent development master's program in the LaFetra College of Education at the University of La Verne. She received her master's in child and adolescent development from the University of La Verne where she now teaches educational psychology and human development for graduate students. Her research interests include human development and improving the educational practice. Specifically, she is interested in the developmental trajectories of children and adolescents and how these trajectories impact the teaching experience from the educator's standpoint. She is also interested in examining educational structures that directly affect children's and adolescents' academic, social, and motivational development.

SUBJECT INDEX

6 Cs model, 25–31

A

Accreditation, 97–98
Achievement goal theory, 121, 122
Adolescence, 139, 148, 151
Adult development, 184–185
Adulthood, 184–188
African American students, 56
Asset-based pedagogies (ABP), 176–177
Assignments, 76, 77, 83. 84, 85, 88, 89
    and personal relevance, 125–126
    and scaffolding, 124–125
    and student choice, 123–124
Association for Middle Level Education
    (AMLE), 97, 98, 101, 107

B

Behavioral standards, 58, 59
    and zero tolerance, 59
Belonging, 116, 119, 126–128
Biases, 54, 55, 58, 50, 61, 74, 76, 172, 177,
    188, 189

C

Case study, 78–79, 98–105
Class discussions, 100, 101, 102
    and guest scholars, 129–130
    and students' sense of belonging, 116,
        119, 126–128
Common Core State Standards, 34
Components of teaching, 142–145
Conceptual change, 73–75, 81, 88–89
Content and pedagogical experts, 140, 145
COVID-19 pandemic, 64–65
Creative innovation, 16, 26, 30, 32
Critical race theory, 116
Critical thinking, 16, 21, 22, 26, 29–30, 32, 33
Culturally responsive pedagogy, 75, 81, 87,
    98, 100, 104, 106, 107

D

Deficit perspective, 140, 146
Developmental systems experts, 146, 147,
    149, 152, 153
Developmental theory, 72–80
Dominant norms, 149

E

Ecological systems theory, 167–170
Educational psychology, 96–98
Engagement, 16, 19–20, 23–25, 27, 30–31, 34
Emerging adulthood, 184–190
Examinations, 122–123

F

Funds of knowledge, 120, 128

H

Human development, 12, 13, 17, 34, 36

I

Identity/Identities, 48, 49, 50, 51, 52, 53, 54, 55, 56, 58, 61, 63, 65, 139, 141, 145, 148, 150
    Students', 128–129
    Teachers', 75–76
Inclusion, 116–119, 123, 124, 129, 130
Inquiry
    Collaborative, 72, 80–90
    Practitioner, 84
Intersectionality, 141–142, 144–145, 149

L

Learning
    Active, 17–19
    Engaged, 19–20
    Iterative process of, 23–24
    Joyful, 24–25
    Meaningful, 20–22
    Science of, 13, 14, 15, 16, 25, 30, 33, 34, 35, 36
    Socially interactive, 22–23
Lesson plan, 79–80

M

Middle schools, 97–101
Motivation, 24, 116, 121–128, 138, 140, 142–143, 146–148, 151

P

Partnerships
    PK–12 schools, 85–87
    and teacher leader academy, 85
Phenomenological Variant of Ecological Systems Theory (PVEST), 48, 49, 51, 52, 53, 54, 55–65
Positionality, 52, 54, 56, 58
Preservice teachers, 96, 97, 98, 99, 101, 102, 104, 105, 107, 184, 186, 187, 188, 190

R

Race-focused research, 116
Reflective blog, 77–78

S

Scaffolding, 19, 20, 124–125
School Reform Initiative (SRI) protocols, 83
Schools to Watch (STW) program, 101
Secondary level educators, 149–151
Self-determination theory, 173–176
Signature assignments, 72, 76, 77–80, 89
Simulations, 80, 82, 89
Social cognitive theory, 116
Social media, 170–172
Stereotype threat, 116–117, 121–123
Student development, 73–74
Student discussions
    with small groups, 82–84
Systems theories, 139, 143, 146, 147, 149, 152, 153, 154

T

Teacher education, 13–15, 21, 24, 27, 33–35, 97–98
   and research, 72, 74, 76, 77, 80, 88, 89
Teacher–student relationship, 148, 151, 153

Testing, 53, 61

W

World of Words (WOW), 20

Printed in the United States
by Baker & Taylor Publisher Services